Gardening
step by step

About this book

This fully illustrated guide to gardening gives complete information on how to create and maintain your perfect garden even if only limited time and money are available. Step by step instructions cover every aspect of gardening, from planning and designing the garden, soil analysis, gardening equipment, flowering plants, trees, shrubs and climbers, to vegetables and fruit, special-purpose gardens, pests and diseases and the gardener's calendar.

In this edition the final three pages are reserved as a diary for your own month by month notes about your garden.

Gardening
step by step

David Carr

First published in hardcover in 1978

This edition published in 1984 by
Octopus Books Limited
59 Grosvenor Street

London W1

© 1978 Hennerwood Publications Limited

ISBN 0 7064 2063 2

Printed in Hong Kong

Contents

The start of a good garden

Both the first-time gardener and the experienced gardener confronted with a new garden are full of bright hopes and grand ideas. Realizing them is another matter, but great expectations certainly form the base of many fine creations. Inevitably, one person's idea of what makes a good garden will differ from another's and the best treatment for a plot will also have to take into account regional differences in soil, climate and plant needs.

A garden is shaped by practical limitations and personal taste, but most garden designers are agreed on three requirements: function, appearance, and harmony.

A functional garden should serve its purpose and meet the needs of its owner.

Appearance depends on neatness, effective use of colour, and a design which provides points of interest in keeping with their surroundings.

Harmony is achieved when the garden is planned in relation to the house and its surroundings. Although an attractive setting makes designing easier, gardens of great merit are found in differing environments, both in the city and in the countryside. Charm and excellence do not depend only on size or situation.

Do not be tempted to flatten everything in sight in your new garden and start from scratch. Apart from making a lot of unnecessary work for yourself, it is almost certain that the existing garden will have at least ·one good feature worth preserving; perhaps a fine old tree or an unusual rose bush. Problem features can be minimised by drawing attention away from them or by disguising them altogether.

The selection and care of appropriate plants can be undertaken confidently once the principles of plant requirements are grasped.

Assessing the site

You will need a considerable amount of information about the site and its surroundings before assessing ideas for the design and development of your garden. All gardens are limited to some extent by four considerations: personal preference, natural features of the site, climatic influence and drainage.

Personal preference

There are as many roles for a garden as there are gardeners, and only you know what you want from your piece of land. Most people aim for a garden that beautifies the space around or behind the house. This cosmetic role may be specific in certain instances, such as the disguise of blank walls, manhole covers or ugly buildings. Sometimes areas are set aside for growing food and these need particular care. When, for example, you are choosing a spot with sufficient light for Brussels sprouts, bear in mind that you are unlikely to want serried ranks of them in full view of the house. Similarly, flowers grown for cutting (or, in more ambitious years, for exhibition) will not best serve the overall design of the garden if they are too conspicuous.

For many people the best reward for an hour's gardening is another hour spent idling: a garden is its owner's play space, and the most important features of the leisure area are privacy and comfort. Young children will need a safe corner in sight of the house, perhaps with a little flower-bed of their own. The main problem with modern gardens is a lack of size which makes it difficult to set aside areas for special use, but fortunately there are such space-saving devices as trough gardens, movable tubs, and climbing plants, which will clothe generous expanses of wall or fence in return for their modest ground space.

The first-time gardener may not know enough about plants to know what he likes! In this case, colour is as good a starting point as any, until experience of differences in foliage and form leads to a more sophisticated choice. The table on page 60 offers basic information for choosing subjects for your flower garden.

'Instant' gardens need immediate and sometimes heavy expenditure and many people prefer to develop a garden gradually, thus lowering initial costs and spreading expenditure over a longer period. Any unfinished area can be put down to grass until it is developed.

RIGHT A small garden provides an attractive and practical outdoor room. The hard path is functional, and the planting provides a variety of colour and form.

8

Features of the site

Your garden will have an area, shape and natural qualities of its own such as the rise and fall of the land, any rocks or water, and the vegetation. Size is crucial as it affects the choice of what can be fitted in, since all plants need room to breathe. As small areas are used intensively, hard-wearing walking surfaces, although more expensive to lay than grass, should be used in confined spaces, especially for year-round purposes. On plots of regular shape, such as squares or rectangles, and particularly on small sites, designs tend to be more formal or regimented than on plots of irregular outline or large area, but with care and judgement in the beginning, the small garden need not lack character.

Changes in ground level can add interest; gentle slopes can be mown or planted, or, if funds permit, they can be stepped or terraced to make an attractive feature. Large differences in level can be treated with retaining walls, or formed into banks covered with colourful or interesting plants, which is an economical solution. Slopes steeper than one in three are best left as they are and not cultivated as heavy rain is likely to cause soil erosion.

The kind of soil in your garden can restrict the choice of plants; it would not be wise, for example, to plant rhododendrons on shallow chalk soils (see page 26, plants for particular soil types). Clay soils can cause flooding in wet weather because the rainwater is unable to drain away quickly.

If you have an intriguing view or such features as rocks and water or fine trees, highlight them in your design. Shelter, screening and divisions are important elements in any garden, to create privacy, protection from strong winds or sun, to hide eyesores or to protect children and pets from danger. Look around your garden and see where divisions are needed before choosing new materials and plants, remembering the significance of texture, colour and outline in plants, buildings and fencing structures.

Climate

The climate of the region in which you live will influence the successful growing of plants in your garden. For gardening purposes there are three broad categories of climate in Britain: arctic-alpine, oceanic, and continental.

Scotland and northern England, with harder winters and shorter growing seasons, have the *arctic-alpine* type of climate, except some of the Western

ABOVE A rock garden on a gentle slope.
RIGHT A retaining wall planted with *Alyssum saxatile* and *Phlox subulata*.
BELOW Ways of dealing with changes in level.

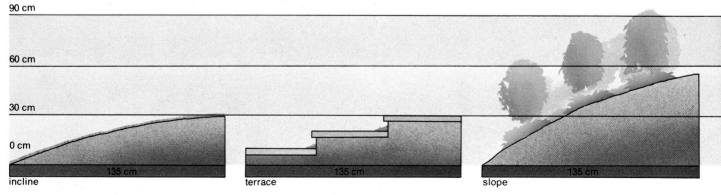

90 cm

60 cm

30 cm

0 cm

135 cm   135 cm   135 cm

incline   terrace   slope

10

Isles, parts of Dumfriesshire, and coastal areas of Cumbria. The upland areas of central England and northern Wales also fall into this category.

The south-west and lowland coastal areas of western England and Wales have milder winters, more humid weather and higher rainfall than south and eastern England. The former are in the *oceanic* region and the latter falls within the *continental* category, having hotter, drier summers than the rest of Britain.

The map reveals a pattern of decreasing average temperatures from south-west England to north-east Scotland. This is due to the warm Gulf Stream air being progressively cooled as it moves in a north-easterly direction. High ground in Wales, northern

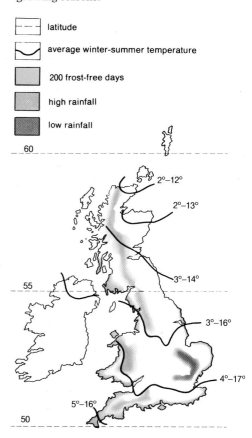

BELOW The general variations in climate between different regions affect the growing seasons.

- - - latitude

‿ average winter-summer temperature

200 frost-free days

high rainfall

low rainfall

60

2°–12°
2°–13°
3°–14°

55

3°–16°

4°–17°

5°–16°

50

retaining wall
135 cm

England and Scotland distorts, but does not alter, the general trend.

The influence of land and water, particularly on temperature, is very marked. The west coast is comparatively warm and moist, due to the influence of the Atlantic, and has fewer days of frost. The east coast, influenced by the continent, is generally drier and cooler. Inland areas of south-eastern and central England are hotter in summer and cooler in winter. Sites on high ground are not only cooler and wetter, but experience fogs and mists more frequently.

Towns and cities, with their roads,

paving, roofing and rapid surface drainage, are drier and warmer than the surrounding area by a few degrees; they encourage earlier flowering, but also tend to be draughtier. Gardens sheltered from north and east winds and south-facing can be an average of several degrees warmer than other less favoured sites, and their plants can crop weeks earlier even in the same street.

Coastal districts are usually noted for breezes; wind coming in off the sea meets no physical obstruction to reduce the air flow, and seashore buildings and vegetation take the full force. There is also the constant air flow between sea and land caused by their different temperatures. In summer, for example, on sunny days, the land is hotter; warm air rises, drawing in cooler air off the sea. At night this process is reversed, unless stronger regional air currents are at work.

Different kinds of plants, through selection and adaptation, have their own requirements for warmth, light and shade, water and humidity and this accounts for the variation in vegetation not only between regions and districts, but also within the same garden.

Temperature Small variations of warmth have a big effect on growth: the difference between the north of Scotland and southern England is an annual average temperature of about 5.5°C (10°F) at sea level. The effect of altitude is a drop of about 0.5°C (1°F) for each 90m (300ft) rise. For hardy plants, growth virtually ceases below 5°C (41°F) and their growing season is restricted to the period when the temperature is above that point. Plants shaded by buildings or trees can be 5.5°C (10°F) or more cooler than those in sunny situations even within the same garden.

Light and shade Sunlight affects plants in many ways. During the winter months the rays of the sun are weaker because they strike the ground at a lower angle. South-facing slopes are warmer than north-facing ground because the rays hit the slopes more directly. Some crops flower in the spring or autumn, others flower during the summer, triggered off by the mechanism within plants which responds to the number of hours of daylight or darkness to which they are subjected. This is one of the reasons why some varieties of vegetables, such as soya beans, Australian varieties of cauliflowers, and some lettuces, cannot be grown satisfactorily out of their natural season. The same is true of some flowers, so it is necessary to choose varieties with care. The number of daylight hours in Scotland is up to two hours less in mid-winter and two hours more in mid-summer than in southern England. The big difference between plants growing on east or west

ABOVE A sunny day in winter. Shadows are longer and weaker than in summer.
BELOW Seasonal intensity of shade from the midday sun. The difference is caused by the height of the sun and the angle of its rays.

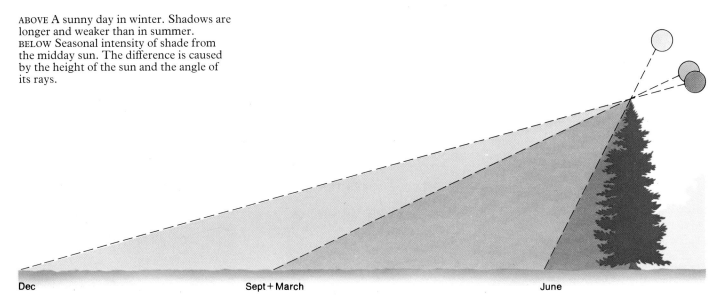

Dec   Sept + March   June

walls compared to a south aspect can be attributed to fewer hours of direct sunlight – they get about half the number. In 1977, a clematis plant growing on south and east-facing walls flowered 17 days earlier on the south-facing wall than on the one facing east.

Plants grown in full sunlight are stocky and sturdy, unlike their spindly counterparts on shaded sites.

Wind and shelter Plants protected by windbreaks can be several degrees warmer than others which are less sheltered. The lopsided windswept specimens seen in most coastal districts are examples of retarded growth on the windward side. More normal development occurs on the leeward side.

Rainfall and humidity Clouds, humid conditions, rain, and expanses of water such as the sea, exert a moderating influence, causing the weather to be less hot in summer and less cold in winter. The higher rainfall and humid conditions in western districts favour the growth of ferns, plums and black-currants, and the drier south-east is better for dessert apples. Damp humid conditions tend to encourage certain diseases; potato blight is an example.

ABOVE A garden in August with strong shadows. Plants should be positioned according to their preferences for light and shade.
RIGHT The effect of exposure and prevailing winds on a tamarisk in a seaside garden.

Understanding the soil

Sound soil management is essential to the success of any gardening venture, but first the nature of the soil has to be understood.

Soil has to be improved, modified or manipulated so that the best conditions for plant life can be created. Good conditions offer anchorage and support, sufficient food and warmth, adequate moisture and oxygen, and room for plants to develop.

The critical soil factors for effective gardening are: land drainage and porosity (the rate at which water drains through soil), and moisture retention, available plant foods, acidity and chalk content and warmth. Each type of soil has its own characteristics and is more suited to some kinds of plants than others, and garden soil can be measured sufficiently accurately with inexpensive do-it-yourself kits.

The composition of fertile soil

Fertile soil is easily worked, friable, and crumbly in texture. The fine crumbly surface layer of such soil is known as a good tilth. It is dark in colour, well-drained and yet retains moisture for growth. It contains reserves of plant food, and is warm enough to support sturdy balanced plant growth. Close examination of a handful of good soil will show that it is composed of moist crumbs or particles of solid matter, pieces of old root fibre, possibly a few small pebbles, a worm or two, and perhaps a quick-moving shiny-brown centipede. Fertile soil, far from being an inert lump of dirt, is literally teeming with life. In addition to the plants that can be seen growing on the land, and the worms and centipedes inhabiting it, there are more lowly forms of plant and animal life invisible to the naked eye. Bacteria form the largest part of the soil population, amounting to many millions in a mere handful of healthy soil.

ABOVE RIGHT The composition of good garden soil showing relative amounts of solids, air and water.
RIGHT Healthy garden soil viewed through a magnifying glass might look like this.

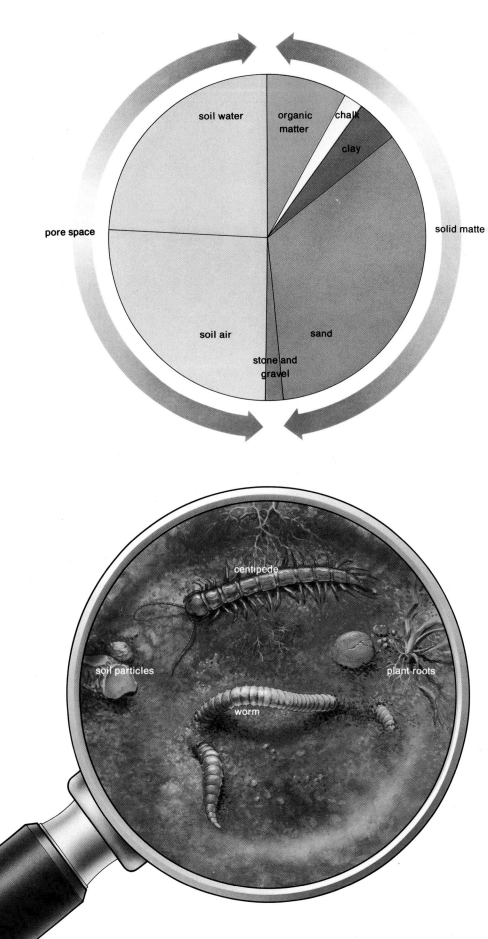

14

Clay soil from the Weald of Kent shows the general greyish colour and rusty mottled characteristic of waterlogged subsoils.

Deep, loamy soil, retentive of moisture and nutrients, on fertile 'brick earth'. The even brown colour indicates good subsoil drainage.

Sandy soil over Bagshot sands is loose and dry. In its natural state it lacks lime and plant nutrients.

There is a narrow margin between fertile and poor soils. By upsetting one factor – by overliming, or working a waterlogged soil, for example – yields can be considerably reduced for a year or more. Given care and attention, however, the land can be kept in good condition and improved upon without difficulty.

Pore Space

The spaces between the crumbs of soil are collectively called pore space. In a fertile soil about half the total volume consists of pore space, which is occupied in turn by water vapour, air, and water. The balance between water and air is crucial to plants. If the pore space is filled with water, roots will suffocate, while if it is full of air, plants die for lack of water. In a fertile soil, water is present around each particle as a thin film of moisture containing dissolved fertilizer and mineral salts. Air spaces separate each particle except during and immediately after rain or irrigation. When surplus rain or other water is drained away, fresh air and oxygen is sucked into the pore space. Clay soils have too much soil water, and sands and gravels have too little, for gardening purposes.

This shallow dry soil on the chalk of the Berkshire Downs still has a dark colour from the humus content built up under old grassland.

This heavy, fertile loam has little depth over the hard but brittle Cotswold limestone.

15

Soil solids

These can conveniently be considered under two headings: mineral, and organic matter.

Mineral matter For practical purposes, the mineral part of soil consists of: clay, sand, chalk, and plant nutrients. Fertile land contains all these materials in varying amounts, but within fairly narrow limits.

Clay is composed of very fine particles of matter which, even in small quantities can affect the soil properties. Clay soils can hold far more water and dissolved plant foods than sand, and are slow to drain. They are sticky when wet, and set rock hard when dry. Their management requires cultivation to be carried out only when the moisture content falls between these two extremes. Liming greatly improves its texture and clay also benefits from the addition of sand and manure.

Sand consists of comparatively coarse grains, and is free-draining, but low in plant nutrients. Sand helps to balance some of the undesirable effects of clay. Both *chalk and limestone* are neutral or alkaline and form a major constituent of soils in chalk and limestone districts. These materials can occur in soil as fine grains or coarse lumps.

Plant nutrients are chemicals in relatively small quantities in soil, either as solids or dissolved in water. The main elements needed for plant nutrition and which are supplied by fertilizer applications, are nitrogen, phosphorus and potassium, together with iron, magnesium and manganese. Substances such as sulphur, zinc and copper fall into the group known as trace elements, so-called because they are only required in minute amounts.

Organic matter Living and dead organisms and animal and plant remains come under this general heading.

The living material consists primarily of plants and roots, bacteria, and lower forms of life. The dead and decomposing remains are mainly manure and plant residues which perform the vital role of maintaining soils in good physical condition, assisting natural drainage, and releasing bacteria which break down harmful compounds in the soil. In certain parts of the country, such as the moss lands of Lancashire and the peat fens of Norfolk and Lincolnshire, land consisting predominantly of peat and other vegetable matter has been made highly fertile through the use of adequate liming, drainage and fertilizers.

Well-decayed organic matter is a rich dark brown colour and is called *humus*. It is a sweet-smelling and most valuable constituent of healthy soils.

Flora and fauna

No healthy, productive soil would be complete without beneficial bacteria and simple forms of animals and insect life. Bacteria break down organic matter, and assist in the weathering of soil particles which releases necessary nutrients, and they purify the soil and soil air by breaking down complex compounds and rendering them harmless. They also fix nitrogen from the atmosphere for the benefit of plants.

Although they can be a nuisance on lawns, earthworms perform a useful service in aerating the soil and assisting drainage. They aid the formation of humus by drawing fallen leaves underground into their burrows, and enrich the soil with their 'casts' or excreta.

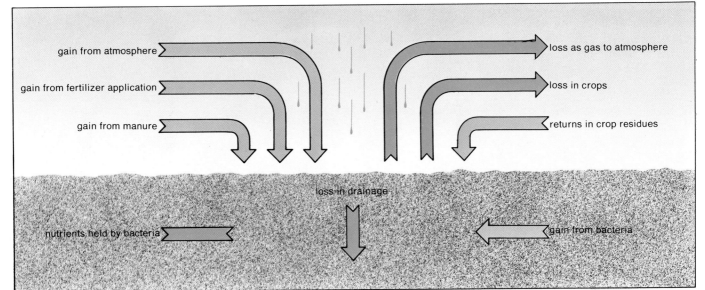

Recognizing soil types

Soils vary greatly, even within a field or garden. Successful cultivation and treatment depends on recognition of types of soil. There are many ways of classifying land, such as being heavy or light to work, and early or late depending on when it produces crops, but for practical purposes a system based on texture and composition is quite adequate.

Texture system

There are seven main types of soil: clay soils, heavy loams, medium loams, sandy loams, sandy soils, chalk and limestone soils, and peat soils. Any of these may be acid, neutral or alkaline in reaction, except chalk and limestone soils, which are usually alkaline. Each soil type behaves differently, and plants respond by showing preferences for one soil or another.

Soil type can be identified simply and with some certainty by safe chemical and physical tests, and by observation.

Chemical tests These are used to determine two sets of soil factors rather than identify soil type. Firstly they show the soil reaction or the pH value – how acid or alkaline the land is; and secondly the plant food levels (nitrogen, phosphate and potash) in a soil.

These tests can either be carried out professionally or at home. Most modern do-it-yourself kits (available from garden centres and hardware stores) are well tried and sufficiently accurate for the amateur gardener. To carry out your own tests, dig up one or more small soil samples from your garden and remove any stones or large lumps. Put some of the soil sample in a glass test tube and pour in the chemical reagent supplied in the kit. After corking the tube, shake up the soil and chemical together and allow the mixture to settle. Compare the colour of the solution against the supplier's colour chart to discover the pH, or acidity of your soil. Some charts also indicate

how much lime is needed to correct any imbalance.

The degree of acidity or alkalinity which plants can tolerate comfortably is quite narrow. The degree of acidity or alkalinity is measured on a scale in which pH 7 is neutral; numbers below 7 indicate acidity and those above 7,

alkalinity. For many subjects a pH level of 6 to 7 is about the limit.

Plant nutrient levels can be discovered by using other do-it-yourself kits, or by using specially treated tapers which, when dipped in a solution of soil and chemical, change colour and are read off a chart in a similar manner.

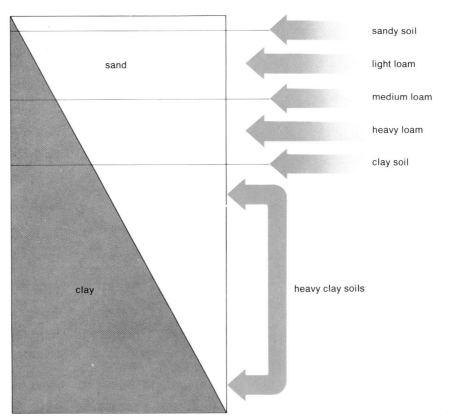

sandy soil
light loam
medium loam
heavy loam
clay soil
heavy clay soils

soil composition: sand and clay balance

ABOVE LEFT Humus in soil.
LEFT Ways in which soil gains and loses nutrients.
ABOVE RIGHT Soil composition: the effect of varying the proportions of sand and clay on the physical properties of soil.
RIGHT Soil testing with a simple kit.

Step-by-step making compost

Burn twigs, tree prunings and wood which would take a very long time to rot down. Scatter the ash over the ground afterwards.

For a large quantity of compost, cover the pile with a plastic sheet and weight it down at the corners.

Three suitable compost makers are the box bin with a detachable front (left above); a wire frame with a plastic liner, perforated to let air through (left centre); and a plastic dustbin, also perforated (left below). A covering such as a plastic lid stops rain getting in, keeps the compost warm, and helps it rot more quickly.

Building up a compost heap in layers.

5-7.5 cm (2-3 inch) layer of roughage such as pea and bean haulm.

10 cm (4 inch) layer of soft vegetable waste such as kitchen vegetable trimmings, lawn mowings.

5 cm (2 inch) layer of manure or a light sprinkling of sulphate of ammonia – 130g/m² (4 oz per sq yd).

Soft vegetable waste.

130g/m² (4 oz per sq yd) sprinkling of ground limestone.

Soft vegetable waste.

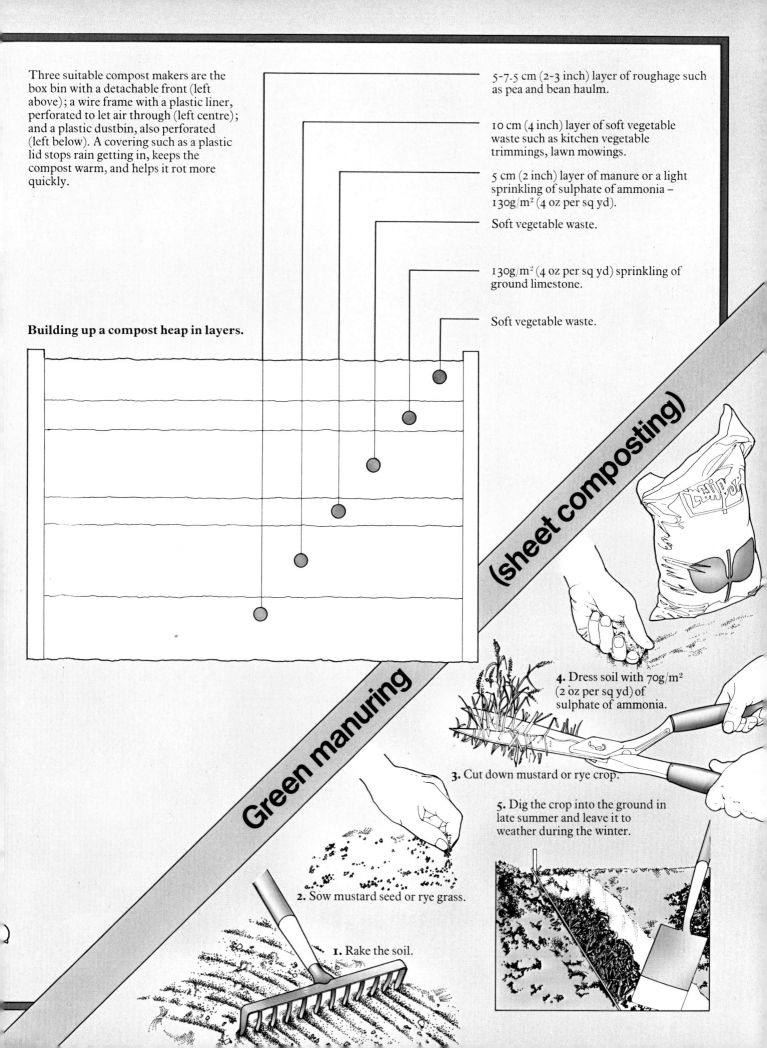

(sheet composting)

4. Dress soil with 70g/m² (2 oz per sq yd) of sulphate of ammonia.

3. Cut down mustard or rye crop.

5. Dig the crop into the ground in late summer and leave it to weather during the winter.

Green manuring

2. Sow mustard seed or rye grass.

1. Rake the soil.

Physical tests A trial dig of a hole to a spade's depth or more, will reveal a fair amount of information about a piece of ground.

Under wet conditions, clay soils will have puddles of water on the surface and be greasy to the touch. Clay will stick tenaciously to your spade and boots when digging. A sandy soil will be well drained and gritty in texture; feet and spade are easily cleaned, and the hole dug with comparative ease. Loams lie between the two extremes.

Under dry summer conditions clay soils become cracked, hard to cultivate, and lumpy. Conversely, sandy soil is easy to dig and is dry and dusty. If a bucket of water is thrown into the excavated hole, clay will not drain readily, but the water in sand will disappear rapidly. The loams will be intermediate in their response.

Digging chalk soils will reveal the tell-tale whitish subsoil of chalk or limestone, and whitish coloured lumps in the soil. Peat soils are usually dark, spongy and fibrous.

Observation Many plants are highly selective and, according to their presence or absence, you will be able to form a good idea of soil and climatic conditions. The following are a few well-established associations of plants and soils which can be seen in the wild and in cultivated areas.

Acid soils: heathers (calluna), rhododendrons, camellias, pine, Japanese maple, sheeps fescue (a fine-leaved type of grass), Scots pines and birches.
Wet soils: caltha (marsh marigold), forget-me-not, mimulus, astilbe, creeping buttercups, elders and willows.
Clay soils: similar to wet soils.
Medium loams: support vigorous mixed vegetation, roses, meadowsweet, brambles, bluebells, flowering thorns and hostas.
Sandy light soils: gorse, brooms, poppies, corydalis, tamarisk, helianthemum, geraniums.
Chalk soils: box and yew trees, viburnums, dogwoods, clematis and spindles, carnation, gypsophila and clovers in grass.

RIGHT Within an hour of heavy rain, clay soils (left) are noticeably slow to drain, sandy soils (right) drain quickly and evenly.

Soil type	Appearance	Physical qualities	Chemical status
Clay soil	Soil lies under water in wet weather. Sedges, rushes, buttercup, alder, willow in evidence.	Very slow to drain. Adhesive, greasy if wet or hard and lumpy when dry.	Naturally rich in plant food. Frequently neutral.
Heavy loam	Intermediate between clay and medium loam		
Medium loam	Strong-growing roses, shrubs and grasses.	Drains moderately quickly. Worked fairly readily.	Usually well supplied with plant food.
Light loam	Intermediate between medium and sandy soil		
Sandy soil	Light coloured soil. Gorse, broom and Scots pine. Heather in acid sands.	Quick draining. Easily worked in most conditions. Gritty to the touch.	Low level in nutrients. Often very acid. Needs regular feeding.
Chalk or Limestone soil	White or whitish subsoil. Dogwood, viburnum and clematis flourish.	Chalk is pasty when moist. Limestone is gritty to the touch.	Low in organic matter. Alkaline.
Peaty soil	Dark fibrous soil. Alder and willow trees often present.	Spongy and fibrous.	Low in phosphates. Often acid.
Stony soil	Often light-coloured. Many stones on surface. Sparse vegetation. Mountain ash present.	Shallow soils with large proportion of rock and stone	Low nutrient content. Needs regular and heavy feeding.
Acid soil	Heath grasses, heather, rhododendrons and fine-leaved fescue grasses abound.	Variable.	Variable.

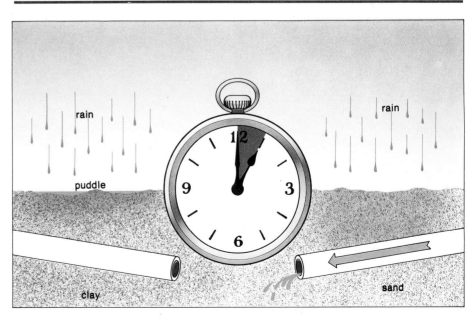

Manures, fertilizers and lime

If it is to produce good crops, the soil must have its reserves of various materials, such as humus, plant foods and lime, replenished at regular intervals. The organic matter is continuously being broken down, and without annual applications of fresh bulky manure, the crumb structure and the efficiency of aeration and drainage will rapidly deteriorate. Farmyard manure, compost and similar materials also supply certain foods, in addition to those gained from fertilizers.

Lime, which is continually being removed by crops and washed away by rain, is needed to neutralize the products of decay and to correct the pH of the soil. In conjunction with organic matter it creates and maintains land in good condition and by altering the structure of the soil, improves its drainage.

Manures

Improved soil conditions enable plant roots to forage more deeply for food and water, and the organic matter, when carefully used as a mulch or surface dressing, reduces moisture loss by acting like a sponge, and also provides trace elements and plant food. Dressings of manure are worked into the soil, usually in autumn and winter, or used as a surface dressing in spring and summer around fruit trees and bushes, roses and shrubs, to conserve soil moisture.

Types of manure There are two fairly distinct groups of manure: those which break down readily to release plant food; and those such as peat which are much slower to decompose, providing little by way of plant nutrients. The first group includes farmyard manure, composted straw or garden waste material, spent mushroom compost, and seaweed. Peat, pulverized tree bark, leaf mould, and spent hops belong in the second group.

Fertilizers

The new gardener may feel bewildered by the choice of currently available fertilizers. Very many materials are available, and there is often little to choose between the proprietary brands.

Some fertilizers are supplied as a base dressing *before* planting and others are supplied as a top dressing given while plants are growing. Base and top dressings usually provide the main plant requirements of nitrogen, phosphate and potash. They can be bought ready for use or mixed at home. Many gardeners use their own mixtures.

Base fertilizers are mostly available as ordinary or high potash types. The ordinary grades contain equal proportions of nitrogen, phosphate and potash, and are used for general feeding. The high-potash type are designed for fruit and flower crops and contain twice the amount of potash.

Top dressings can be applied dry or as a liquid feed. The many proprietary brands are sold as three grades: *high nitrogen*, used for celery and cucumbers; *ordinary grade*, for bringing on young plants; and *high potash*, for fruit and flowers, especially for exhibition purposes. The manufacturers' instructions should be followed carefully.

Lime

Lime is the common name for calcium, which is required by plants, beneficial bacteria and soil. In addition to helping to feed plants and bacteria, calcium in the soil under the action of manure, frost and wind, helps the soil to break up and become easier to cultivate. Lime is best applied during the winter months, some weeks after manure has been dug in, and two or three weeks before fertilizer dressings are applied. Unfortunately, calcium reacts with nitrogen in manures or fertilizers if they are applied at the same time, and causes a loss of nitrogen.

21

Popular fertilizers

Name	Analysis per cent			Fertilizer type
	N	P	K	
Bone meal	4	21	—	Base
Hoof and horn	13–14	—	—	Base
Potassium nitrate	15	—	45	Top
Nitro-chalk	15.5	—	—	Top
Sulphate of ammonia	21	—	—	Base and top
Sulphate of potash	—	—	48–50	Base and top
Superphosphate	—	16–18	—	Base and top

Home-made mixtures

Base fertilizer (1)

Hoof and horn–2 parts by weight
Superphosphate–2 parts by weight
Sulphate of potash–1 part by weight

Analysis per cent
5.6 N, 7.2 P, 10 K

Base fertilizer (2)

Superphosphate–2 parts by weight
Sulphate of ammonia–1 part by weight
Sulphate of potash–1 part by weight

Analysis per cent
5.2 N, 9 P, 12.5 K

Liquid feed

Potassium nitrate–1 part by weight

Sulphate of ammonia–1 part by weight

Analysis per cent
diluted to 28g/18 litres (1oz per 4 gal)
17.5 N, 22.5 K

N = nitrogen, P = phosphorus, K = potassium

Soil acidity can be corrected by applying ground limestone or hydrated lime, according to the findings of a soil test (see p. 17). When hydrated lime is used, as distinct from ground limestone, 25 per cent less material is needed to produce the same effect.

Feeding your plants

Soils can be tested for acidity and for the major plant foods (see page 17), and this is important for basic crop nutrition. Nitrogen, phosphates and potash exert the greatest influence on plant growth, and with a little practice it is not too difficult to diagnose any imbalance during the growing season.

Nitrogen

Is necessary for growth of leaf and stem; too much causes dark, luxuriant, soft growth at the expense of fruiting. Nitrogen deficiency results in poor growth, pale small leaves and small but high-coloured fruits.

High nitrogen levels, warm wet weather and rich heavy soils, all encourage strong leafy growth at the expense of flower and some fruits. Such conditions are well suited to growing celery, and members of the cabbage family. Plums, blackcurrants and cooking apples will also thrive.

BELOW Mulching with compost.
ABOVE RIGHT Preparing the soil for planting by digging in manure.
BELOW RIGHT The variation between the lengths of growing season in north and south England.

Phosphate

(Its main chemical element is phosphorus) is required for root and seed development and early maturity. A deficiency results in poor, stunted growth. Phosphate is very rarely found in excess in soil since it is not particularly soluble.

Potash

(Its main chemical element is potassium) is vital to the efficient manufacture of starch in the leaves and the functioning of the chlorophyll complex, and to harden up soft growth caused by heavy nitrogen dressings. An excess can cause magnesium or iron deficiency, resulting in yellowing of the leaves and stunting. A deficiency causes the leaf margins to turn reddish-brown.

High potash levels in the soil, dry sunny conditions, and light well-drained soil, will tend to produce hard growth, early flowering and fruitfulness.

Dessert apples, fruits, flowers and seed crops are encouraged by these factors.

Plant preferences

Vegetables, generally speaking, need generous applications of manure, and heavy balanced dressings of nitrogen, phosphate and potash, see chapter 7.

Fruits need adequate manure but the main nutrient emphasis is on fairly high dressings of phosphate and potash, see chapter 8.

Flowers require phosphates and potash, with low nitrogen levels to promote flowering, see chapter 5.

The feeding programme

Always spread manures or fertilizers evenly over the surface to be treated.
Autumn and winter: dig well-rotted manure into vacant ground and apply base dressings (slow-acting fertilizers) before planting new trees, shrubs and plants.

Lightly dig in manure around trees and shrubs, and apply a balanced top-dressing of fertilizer.

Spring and summer: apply fertilizer top-dressing to fruit bushes and roses, followed by a mulch to conserve moisture in summer. Liquid feeding with dissolved fertilizer can be carried out where growth is slow, but never feed plants that are dry; water them first.

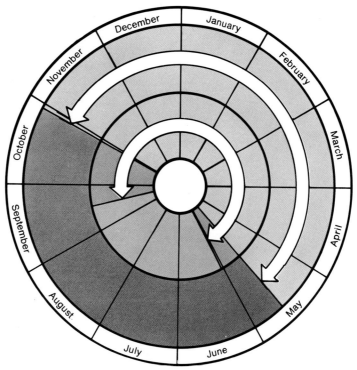

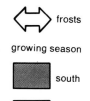
frosts

growing season

south

north

variation

Improving the soil

There are many soil-improving techniques, each beneficial in itself but providing the greatest impact when used in combination.

Cultivation Clay and other heavy soils can be improved simply by digging, but it is better to throw up the soil into ridges 60cm (2ft) wide in autumn, and allow frost, rain and wind to weather it and break up the lumps. A similar effect is achieved by digging trenches 60cm (2ft) wide to a spade's depth, and letting frost, rain and wind weather the ridges on each side of the trenches.

Forking

In spring when the land is dry enough to work, *lightly* fork over and level the land carefully to reap the benefit of winter weathering, especially on heavy soils.

Burning and ballasting

Burning is more suited to country districts, without smokeless zones. A layer of clay soil is placed over a slow-burning bonfire with air holes at the base and top. The granular burnt soil and the bonfire ash are afterwards scattered over the ground.

In ballasting, material such as clean sand or fine gravel is added to heavy soils to open them up. Over a few years they can be considerably improved by this process.

Sanding and marling

Occasionally, as in certain areas of Yorkshire, Kent, Hampshire, and Middlesex, the top soil rests on subsoil of a different nature. When a shallow layer of clay soil overlies a sand and gravel subsoil, if some of the sand or gravel is dug out, scattered over the heavy soil and mixed in, a considerable improvement can be made. Likewise, if a light sandy soil rests on clay, small

ABOVE A slow-burning bonfire covered with clay.
BELOW Ridging (left) and trenching (right) in winter.

quantities of the clay can be dug out and worked in a little at a time. This method has been practised for decades with some success, and is best carried out over a period of two of three years. Apart from the fact that clay or marl has to be weathered and is best worked in gradually, the energy and exertion involved in digging and cultivating is considerable.

Soil darkening

Soot improves the soil by darkening it, thereby helping it to keep warm since dark surfaces absorb heat while light surfaces reflect it, and provides small amounts of nitrogen and potash. Black or dark soil can be as much as $1°C (2°F)$ warmer than adjacent light-coloured soil under similar conditions. Where it can still be obtained household soot is an excellent soil conditioner, but avoid industrial substitutes. Soot is best allowed to weather for two or three months before coming into contact with plants. It can be spread over the land in winter to mellow, or weathered and worked in with the base fertilizer at about a spadeful per square metre (approximately $1\frac{1}{10}$ sq yd) before planting.

Green manuring

This consists of cultivating the land with a manure crop and making a seedbed for mustard seed or rye grass, which when part-grown is dug in. A scattering of sulphate of ammonia at the rate of $70g/m^2$ (2oz per sq yd) is applied to the part-grown manure crop just before the crop is dug in. This practice helps to overcome deficiencies in soil organic matter.

Drainage

All plants need some amount of air and water to grow and develop, but too much water or a prolonged build-up of cold air can be harmful. Even those soils which are naturally well-drained have produced better crops and suffered less from drought after improved drainage.

Land is made infertile by poor drainage or water-logging – a condition in which all the spaces between the soil particles are filled with water. Suffocation and death of plant roots are the direct consequence of stagnant water. The longer-term effects are an accumulation of soluble salts and products of decay. These harmful substances would be washed away by underground drains.

Wet soils are notoriously slow to warm up in spring, and also encourage the growth of weeds, such as sedges, rushes, thistles and docks. Such land is difficult to work, as crops can only use the soil layer above the water level.

Sandy soils, which feel gritty to the touch, drain more easily than clay, which resembles putty in texture.

When making a new garden or improving an established site, it is wise to check the drainage and this can be done by making a test dig. During the winter, dig out a hole 60cm (2ft) deep and cover it (with a dustbin lid for example) to prevent rain falling in. Inspect the hole daily, replacing the cover each time. If after 48 hours following heavy rain, less than 45cm (18in) of soil shows above the water table or water level, then attention to drainage is needed, especially if trees are to be planted.

Surplus moisture in gardens is usually best drained away by means of a soakaway or underground pipes or channels. Occasionally an existing drainage system becomes blocked through tree roots or ground subsidence, so it is advisable to check from time to time.

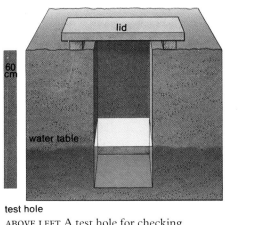

test hole

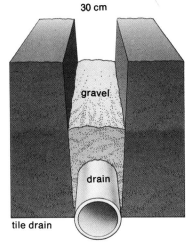

30 cm

gravel

drain

tile drain

ABOVE LEFT A test hole for checking drainage.
ABOVE RIGHT A land drain surrounded by gravel.

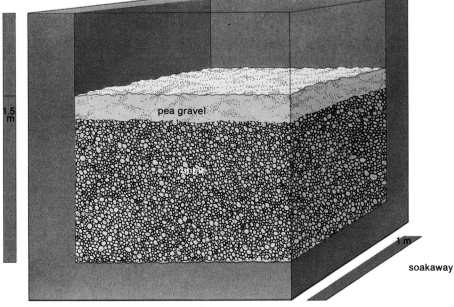

ground level

pea gravel

rubble

1 m

soakaway

Land drains These are usually 10cm (4in) diameter porous pipes, laid near the bottom of trenches, surrounded in gravel and connected to a soakaway, main drain or ditch at the lowest point of the site. The pipes should have a rise or fall of not less than 2.5cm (1in) in a 2.5m (8ft 4in) run. The correct depth of trenches varies from about 75cm (2ft 6in) on clay soils to 105cm (3ft 6in) on sandy soils. The distance between pipe runs on heavy soils is 1.5m (5ft), and up to 4.5m (15ft) on lighter land.

Air drainage Wind frost can cause much damage but spring frosts on clear calm nights, when fruit trees are in full blossom, can be devastating. Under these conditions cold air, being heavier than warm air, settles in layers, filling up valleys and hollows known as frost pockets. Freezing air rolls down from higher ground and any obstruction across the current of the cold heavy wind causes the freezing air to build up like water behind a dam. Openings in a hedge or wall will allow the cold air to flow to lower ground. In gardens which are completely surrounded by walls or hedges, the layer of cold air builds up and cannot escape unless openings leading to lower land are made.

Screens and windbreaks vary in their effectiveness according to their permeability, that is, how well they filter and deflect the wind. Solid barriers like walls are less effective than trees, shrubs or hedges, which filter the air currents and protect a rather wider strip on the lee of the wind.

The soakaway This method of drainage is suitable for small gardens (less than 6 × 9m (20 × 30ft) without a good outlet for water and is therefore particularly useful for town gardens. It consists of excavating a pit 1.5m (5ft) deep by 1m (3ft 4in) square, keeping the top soil and subsoil separate. (For those who are not used to digging, it is unwise to attempt too much at once.) Fill the soakaway, which should be sited in the lowest part of the plot, two-thirds deep with clean broken bricks and rubble, covered with a 10cm (4in) layer of pea gravel (an aggregate of pea-sized bits of gravel), and finally cover with topsoil. If there is not enough topsoil, you will have to buy good quality soil: subsoil is not suitable as it hinders drainage.

ABOVE LEFT A soakaway – the best method of drainage for the small garden.
BELOW Freezing air rolls down from higher ground and obstructions will cause the freezing air to build up in frost pockets.

cold air flowing downhill

frost pocket

Plants for Different Soils

Note: The majority of cultivated plants will grow and thrive on neutral soils, which are neither acid nor alkaline.

In a similar manner soils which are medium loams, neither stiff clays nor sands, can be used without difficulty for most crops.

The following lists of plants are designed to meet the more difficult situations where special soil conditions exist.

Key to tables

Site requirements S = Sunny   Sh = Shade

Season and Nature of Interest

Y = All year   W = Winter   Sp = Spring
Su = Summer   A = Autumn   St = Stem
L = Leaves   Fl = Flowers   Fr = Fruits/berries

TOP Mountain ash
BOTTOM Laburnum

26

	Site Requirement	Season/Nature of interest
Trees suitable for Acid, Neutral or Chalk Soils		
Betula pendula Birch	S or Sh	Y/St Su/L
Cercis siliquastrum Judas tree	S	Sp, Su/Fl
Crataegus oxycantha Thorn	S	Sp/Fl A/Fr
Ilex aquifolium Holly	S or Sh	Y/L A,W/Fr
Laburnum anagyroides Laburnum	S	Sp, Su/Fl
Robinia pseudoacacia False Acacia	S	Su/L, Fl
Sorbus aria Whitebeam	S	Sp,A/L,Fl A/Fr, L
Sorbus aucuparia Mountain Ash	S	Sp/Fl A/Fr
Trees suitable for Heavy Soils		
Acer negundo variegatum Variegated Box Elder	S	Su, A/L
Betula pendula Birch	S or Sh	Y/St Su/L
Crataegus oxycantha Thorn	S	Sp/Fl A/Fr
Ilex aquifolium Holly	S or Sh	Y/L A,W/Fr
Laburnum anagyroides Laburnum	S	Sp, Su/Fl
Malus baccata Siberian Crab	S	Sp/Fl A/Fr
Prunus cerasifera atropurpurea Purple-leaf Plum	S or Sh	Sp/Fl Su-A/L
Prunus serrulata various Flowering Cherries	S	Sp/Fl A/L
Sorbus aria Whitebeam	S	Sp, A/Fl, L A/Fr, L
Trees for Sands and Gravels		
Acer griseum Paperback Maple	S	Y/St A/L
Betula pendula Birch	S or Sh	Y/St Su/L
Crataegus oxycantha Thorn	S	Sp/Fl A/Fr
Ilex aquifolium Holly	S or Sh	Y/L A/Fr
Juniperus Juniper	S or Sh	Y/L
Pinus mugo Mountain Pine	S	Y/L
Shrubs requiring Acid Soils		
Andromeda polifolia Andromeda	S or Sh	Y/L Sp, Su/Fl
Azalea various Swamp Pink	S or Sh	Sp, Su/Fl

	Site Requirement	Season/Nature of interest
Calluna vulgaris Scotch heather	S	Y/L Su, A/Fl
Camellia japonica various Camellia	Sh	Sp/Fl
Erica various Heath or heather	S	Y/L W, Sp, Su/Fl
Hamamelis mollis Chinese Witch Hazel	S	W/Fl
Rhododendron various Rhododendron	S or Sh	W, Sp, Su/Fl
Shrubs for Chalk Soils		
Aucuba japonica Spotted Laurel	S or Sh	Y/L A, W/Fr
Berberis various Barberry	S	Y/L Sp, Su/Fl A/Fr
Buddleia davidii Butterfly Bush	S	Su, A/Fl
Buxus sempervirens Box	S or Sh	Y/L
Euonymus fortuner variegata Creeping Evergreen Spindle	S or Sh	Y/L
Forsythia suspensa Golden Bell	S	Sp/Fl
Hypericum various St John's Wort	S or Sh	Su, A,/Fl A/Fr
Mahonia aquifolium Oregon Grape	S or Sh	Y/L Sp/Fl
Olearia various New Zealand Daisy Bush	S	Y/L Su/Fl
Philadelphus coronarius Mock Orange	S	Su/Fl
Rosa various Rose	S	Su, A/Fl A/Fr
Rosmarinus officinalis Rosemary	S	Y/L Sp/Fl
Spartium junceum Spanish Broom	S	Su, A/Fl
Symphoricarpos various Snowberry	S or Sh	A, W,/Fr
Syringa vulgaris Lilac	S	Sp, Su/Fl
Vinca various Periwinkle	S or Sh	Y/L Sp, Su/Fl
Weigela floribunda	S	Su/Fl
Shrubs for Heavy or Clay Soils		
Aucuba japonica Spotted Laurel	S or Sh	Y/L A, W,/Fr
Berberis various Barberry	S	Y/L Sp, Su,/Fl A/Fr
Chaenomeles speciosa various Flowering Quince	S	Sp, Su/Fl
Cornus various Dogwood	S or Sh	Y/St
Corylus maxima purpurea Hazel	S or Sh	Su/L

	Site Requirement	Season/Nature of interest
Cotoneaster various Cotoneaster	S or Sh	A, W,/Fr
Forsythia suspensa Golden Bell	S	Sp/Fl
Hamamelis mollis Chinese Witch Hazel	S	W/Fl
Hypericum various St John's Wort	S or Sh	Su,A/Fl A/Fr
Mahonia various Oregon Grape	S or Sh	Y/L Sp/Fl
Philadelphus coronarius Mock Orange	S	Su/Fl
Pyracantha atalantioides Firethorn	S or Sh	A, W/Fr
Ribes sanguineum Flowering currant	S or Sh	Sp/Fl
Rosa various Rose	S	Su, A/Fl A/Fr
Skimmia japonica Skimmia	S or Sh	Y/L Sp/F W/Fr
Symphoricarpos albus Snowberry	S or Sh	A, W/Fr
Viburnum opulus various Guelda Rose	S	Su/F A/L A,W/Fr
Shrubs for Peaty Soils		
Andromeda polifolia Andromeda	S or Sh	Y/L Sp, Su/Fl
Azalea various Swamp Pink	S or Sh	Sp, Su,/Fl
Calluna vulgaris Scotch Heather	S	Y/L Su, A,/Fl
Cornus various Dogwood	S or Sh	Y/St
Daphne mezereum Mezereon	S or Sh	Sp/Fl
Eucryphia glutinosa Eucryphia	S	Su/Fl A/L
Magnolia soulangeana Magnolia	S	Sp, Su/Fl
Pernettya mucronata Pernettya	S or Sh	Y/L Sp/Fl A, W,/Fr
Pieris floribunda Pieris	S or Sh	Sp/L, Fl
Rhododendron various Rhododendron	S or Sh	W, Sp, Su,/Fl
Shrubs for Sandy Soils		
Berberis various Barberry	S	Y/L Sp, Su,/Fl A/Fr
Calluna vulgaris Scotch Heather	S	Y/L Su, A/Fl
Cistus cyprius Rock Rose	S	Su/Fl
Cytisus scoparius Broom	S	Su/Fl
Erica various Heather or Heaths	S	Y/L W, Sp, Su/Fl

TOP Mahonia
BOTTOM Magnolia

28

TOP Azalea
BOTTOM Snapdragon

	Site Requirement	Season/Nature of interest
Genista tinctoria Dyer's Greenwood	S	Su/Fl
Helianthemum alpestre Sun Rose	S	Su/Fl
Juniperus various Juniper	S or Sh	Y/L
Lavandula spica Lavender	S	Y/L Su/Fl
Rosmarinus officinalis Rosemary	S	Y/L Sp/Fl
Spartium junceum Spanish Broom	S	Su, A/Fl

The majority of herbaceous perennials and bedding plants prefer neutral soil conditions, but the following will thrive in chalk soils

Herbaceous Perennials for Chalk Soils

	Site Requirement	Season/Nature of interest
Achillea various Yarrow	S	Su/Fl
Brunnera macrophylla Anchusa	S or Sh	Sp, Su/Fl
Centranthus ruber Valerian	S	Su/Fl
Convallaria majalis Lily-of-the-Valley	S or Sh	Sp/Fl
Doronicum caucasicum Leopard's Bane	S	Sp/Fl
Erigeron hybridus Fleabane	S	Sp, Su/Fl
Geranium endressii Pink Cranesbill	S	Su/Fl
Gypsophila paniculata Gypsophila	S	Su/Fl
Iris various Iris	S	Su/Fl
Lavatera Mallow	S	Su/Fl
Tulip Tulip	S	Sp/Fl

Annuals and Bedding Plants for Chalk Soils

	Site Requirement	Season/Nature of interest
Antirrhinum majus Snapdragon	S	Su/Fl
Arabis arendsii Wall cress	S	Sp, Su,/Fl
Aubrieta deltoidea Purple Rock-cress	S	Sp, Su/Fl
Bellis perennis Double Daisy	S or Sh	Sp, Su/Fl
Campanula various Bell flower	S	Su, A/Fl
Centaurea cyanus Cornflower	S	Su/Fl
Cheiranthus various Wallflower	S	Sp/Fl
Delphinium consolida Larkspur	S	Su/Fl
Viola wittrockiana Pansy	S	Sp, Su, A/Fl

29

Getting equipped

The buying of new tools merits careful forethought. The tool or appliance should be necessary and efficient, of well-tried design, reasonably priced and safe to operate (moving parts should be covered by guards), economical to maintain and easy to handle. One of the hallmarks of good design is simplicity – the greater the complexity, the greater the chance of breakdown. Assessing the construction, safety, economy, and ease of handling is very much a matter of comparing similar models.

Before buying tools and equipment, especially motorized appliances which deteriorate rapidly if left in the open, make sure that there is somewhere safe, dry and convenient to store them. Some tools may be used very infrequently, and it is better to hire these rather than spend a lot of money on items which will be on the toolshed rack far more frequently than in the gardener's hands.

Essential tools

The selection of tools you *need*, rather than those you would *like*, depends on your particular garden. Some implements are used for specific purposes, while others can have a variety of uses. The spade, for example, can be used for planting trees as well as preparing the ground for potatoes or other vegetables.

Identifying the appliances you need

There are four broad categories of necessary equipment: general purpose; flowers, vegetables and soft fruits; trees, shrubs and climbers; and lawns and hedges.

General-purpose items are used in most gardens and are the first priority. They include a spade, a digging fork, a good pocket knife, and a watering can with a rose. A medium-sized garden will need a sieve and wheelbarrow.

The growing of flowers, vegetables and soft fruits requires tools for working the soil and killing weeds, simple pruning, sowing and planting, spraying and watering. The most useful tools are an iron rake, one or more hoes, a cultivator, a trowel, a small handfork, a pair of secateurs, a sprayer, a measuring rod, a dibber, and a bucket.

A medium-sized plot will need a hosepipe and fittings. In wet districts, two short lengths of planking, 1.5m (5ft) long × 15cm (6in) wide, can be invaluable to work from and avoid churning up wet soil.

Trees, shrubs and climbers require extra pruning tools in addition to the foregoing items, and where there are fruit trees, spraying equipment will be required. Necessary items for this group include: steps or ladders, a pruning saw, a long-arm pruner, and a sprayer with lance for tall subjects.

Tools for lawns and hedges are fairly specialized and are mainly for cutting and trimming, but also include items to aerate and scarify turf. The basic requirements for the care of lawns and hedges are a wire rake, a pair of shears, a lawn mower, a pair of edging shears, a spade, a fork, a watering can, a wheelbarrow, a sprayer, a bucket and hosepipe. A sprinkler is useful in dry districts.

Equipment which is used less frequently – power cultivators or lawn aerators for instance, can usually be hired, as can smaller hand tools such as a pickaxe.

Choice of equipment

The most expensive gardening appliance is not always the best. When comparing makes, note the construction and materials as well as the design. Watch out for potential weak spots which can result in broken metal parts, handles coming adrift, or bent and unusable pieces. Poorly finished products will give you splinters and blisters, which are not only unpleasant, but make it difficult to carry on gardening. A useful test of sound metal in spades, forks, rakes and cultivators is to hold them off the ground by the handle and give the metal section a sharp tap with a coin; good metal produces a resonant ringing tone. The working parts of shears, saws, knives and pruning tools are generally best made from high quality carbon steel.

Stainless steel spades, trowels and forks, though more expensive, are easier to keep clean. The methods of fixing handles vary, but the socket or solid join is the most reliable. In the intermediate price range, the tang and ferrule method used for rakes, trowels,

ABOVE Common garden tools with various joins between blade and handle:
1 Socket (solid)
2 and 3 Ferrule and tang
4 Pressed steel split ring
5 Rivets and straps

and small hand forks, is satisfactory. The pressed-steel tool can be reasonably satisfactory, but be wary of those with thin metal which may bend, and badly fitting handles secured by nails or small screws that can work loose. Strong, well-made handles can be constructed from wood, tubular metal or plastic. Wood and plastic tend to be warmer to the touch in winter and cooler in strong sunlight.

Sprayers, sprinklers, watering cans and other tools made of rust and corrosion resistant materials are preferable, if design and construction are satisfactory.

Basic equipment

To keep garden tools working efficiently and to prolong their useful life and reduce rust and corrosion to a minimum, it is important to clean them after use, and, in the case of cutting implements, to keep them suitably sharpened.

Before putting tools away, clean them and wipe the metal parts with an oily rag (a rag dipped in sump oil, for example). Replace badly worn moving parts as soon as possible before they wear out or break. In the interests of safety, equipment should never be left lying around.

When using any tools or equipment which require strenuous effort (such as spades, forks and saws) for the first time, do not attempt more than half an hour at a stretch.

Spade

There is little difference between a squared or rounded blade, but the tread or flange can cause heavy soil to stick, making for unsatisfactory work. The choice of an O- or T-shaped handle is a matter of taste. Try it out for comfort before buying. The socket, or solid join, of shaft and blade is more reliable than the rivet and strap.

For deep digging, the blade should enter the ground almost vertically, putting weight on the foot to force the spade down. A trench in front of you is necessary for incorporating manure and double digging. A spade can do the work of many tools.

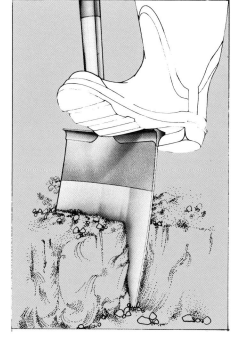

LEFT Garden spade with a squared blade and flange.

ABOVE The cyclical action of digging. Use the weight of the body to push the spade into the ground, lever the soil forward before lifting it, and turn the soil over as it is dropped in place.

General purpose border fork (left) and broad-pronged digging fork (right). Use the fork for lifting plants before transplanting (top).

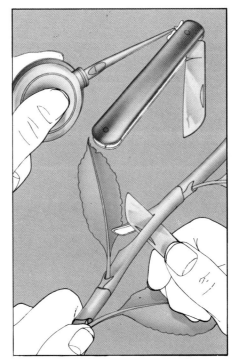

Oiling a pocket-knife (above) and cutting a shoot (below).

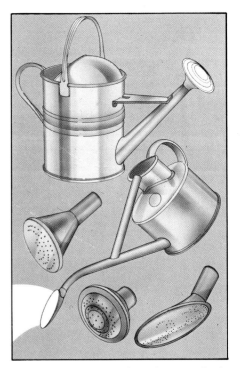

Watering cans and rose attachments. Oval-shaped roses provide a wider and more gentle distribution of water.

Garden fork

This tool is made in various patterns, but usually has four prongs, made of stainless or forged steel, which are of three types: rounded, squared, or flattened. The choice of handle, the method of securing the stem to prongs, and materials employed, are much the same as for spades.

Manure or compost handling; the pricking of fertilizers into the soil surface; breaking up, loosening and shattering lumps of earth; spiking or aerating turf; and gathering up tree and hedge prunings, are just a few uses of the fork. The broad-pronged version is not often seen, and apart from its use on heavier soils and for digging and lifting potatoes, it does not merit first priority status. Forks with narrow round or square prongs, however, are second only to the spade in importance.

Safety note A fork should be treated with great care. If you leave it in the garden even while you answer the telephone or have a cup of tea, make sure the prongs are pushed firmly into the ground. After use, store the fork out of reach of small children.

Pocket knife

A general purpose type which fits comfortably in the hand and has a good quality straight steel blade is the most useful knife to start with. A blunt knife is obviously useless, and straight blades are easier to sharpen than curved ones. A folding model is preferable to a fixed blade type as it can be carried about with safety.

In addition to cutting flowers, and string or twine, and trimming herbaceous or semi-hardwood shoots, a sharp knife is excellent for paring away saw wounds when pruning. When cutting any hard piece of wood, make the stroke of the blade away from and not towards you.

Keep the knife clean and sharp. An oilstone is excellent for sharpening blades.

Safety note Handle knives carefully; exercise caution when closing and opening blades, and make sure the cutting edge is protected when the knife is closed.

Watering can

Commonly available capacities are 4.5 and 9 litres (1 and 2 gal). Plastic cans are cheaper and lighter to carry than the japanned metal ones. A coarse oval and a fine round rose are useful, preferably made of brass that does not corrode.

When watering small seedlings and young plants it is better to use a rose, as a strong stream of water can knock the seedlings out of place in the drills. Avoid watering plants in strong sun unless shading can be placed over them for an hour or so. The water may evaporate quickly in the heat and dry out the tender roots.

Safety Note Always wash the can and roses immediately after applying any chemicals with mild detergent, and rinse thoroughly. Never use a can which has contained hormone weed killer for any other purpose.

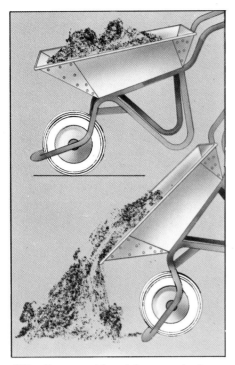

Wheelbarrow with weight over wheel.

Rakes: always push rake teeth into the soil when laying a rake down to avoid being hit by the upswinging handle.

Using draw hoe to make a V-shaped drill and for chopping weeds (above and right). 3-prong cultivator to loosen soil (below left). Dutch hoe push-pull action to kill weeds (below right).

Wheelbarrow

The user should be able to handle the wheelbarrow easily and without strain under most conditions.

Wooden barrows may look very nice, but they are heavy to handle, fairly costly, difficult to clean, and can rot. They are also less easy to sterilize for use when handling potting composts.

Metal barrows are made in different sizes, thicknesses and lengths.

The home gardener is not usually concerned with intensive use, so a well-designed and well-made lightweight galvanized barrow will serve most purposes. Where leaves have to be transported, extendable sections to increase the barrow capacity are handy.

Balance is important for easy use. The barrow body should be placed well over the wheel—thus ensuring that the weight is carried by the wheel and not the user. Wheels have pneumatic tyres or thin rubber rims. Pneumatic tyres are more suitable for models which will be used regularly over soil, rubber rims are more suitable for hard surfaces, such as paths. Wheel hubs with ball bearings are the easiest to manage.

Keep the barrow clean, and the hub well oiled or greased. With pneumatic models avoid running over broken glass or nails.

Iron rake

A 10- or 12-tooth steel head is a convenient size. A tang and ferrule connection is more satisfactory than a split socket and screw, and a 1.35m (4ft 6in) handle or shank is a convenient size.

The main functions of this tool are to create a fine tilth, that is, to reduce the surface soil to a fine crumbly consistency by pushing and pulling the teeth in comb fashion through the earth, to prepare seedbeds, rake up stones and rubbish, and level the topsoil.

Safety note Hang up the rake in the shed or storage area after use. When the rake is laid on the ground, place the head teeth down, to prevent anyone stepping or falling on the teeth or being knocked by an upswinging handle. A painful blow from the rake can black an eye or break a tooth.

Hoe

There are two basic types; the push or Dutch hoe, and the draw hoe. The former has a flat blade, which is used almost parallel with the ground. The draw hoe blade is at right angles to the handle. There are several variations of each type. Carbon steel heads are stronger, but more expensive than pressed steel. The carbon-steel hoes are constructed and fixed as the rakes are, whereas pressed steel ones usually have split ring fittings.

The Dutch hoe is used with a pushing action, to sever weeds and loosen the soil crust; walk backwards as you use it. The draw hoe is used with a chopping motion, with the operator moving forwards.

The draw hoe is also used to earth up, that is, to draw soil round plant stems, and to make shallow drills for seed sowing. It is more suitable for use on heavy soils than the Dutch hoe. Take similar safety precautions for the hoe as for the rake.

Cultivator

This consists of 3- or 5-prong tines, and is excellent for scarifying (breaking up) surface soil and weed killing.

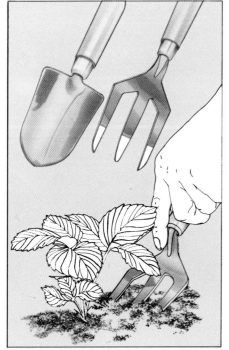

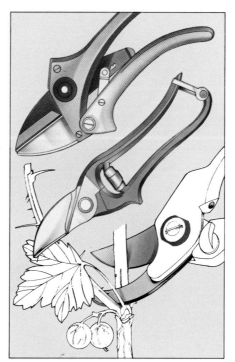

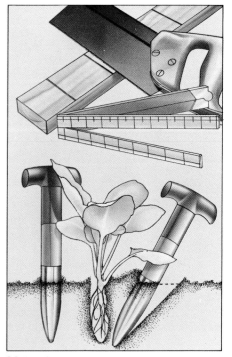

Trowel and handfork. The handfork can be used with a twisting action to loosen hard soil.

Anvil (top) and double-action (below) secateurs.

Measuring rod (above) marked off with saw cuts Dibber (below) makes a hole for the plant and firms the soil around its roots.

Trowel

Where bedding plants and vegetables are grown in any numbers, a good trowel is indispensable. A carbon-steel scoop is preferable to pressed steel, giving harder wear but the stainless-steel type, although more expensive, is the most satisfactory as it is the easiest to use and keep clean.

The trowel is used for digging holes in which the roots of small subjects can be spread out when planting, and for covering the roots with fine soil and firming lightly.

Handfork

A short-handled, carbon-steel, three- or four-pronged fork, with a tanged, fixed handle, gives good service. Stainless-steel models are longer lasting and easier to clean, but they are more expensive.

Use the handfork to loosen the soil crust in confined spaces with delving and loosening action, which comes with practice.

Safety note Keep all forks away from very young children.

Secateurs

There are many variations of the two main types, the double cut and the anvil. The anvil is less elegant, but reliable and reasonably priced. Choose a size that suits your hand, and a model with a safety catch. The more expensive doublecut models, when sharp and in mint condition, tend to be favoured by exhibitors, but are not essential for general purposes.

Keep the blades sharp and the moving parts well oiled, and do not use secateurs for cutting any plant material more than 15mm ($\frac{3}{4}$in) thick. Avoid using a twisting action when severing tough pieces. Never use secateurs for cutting wire, metal or twine.

Safety note Avoid leaving secateurs where they can cause injury. Ensure that the cutting faces are closed and the safety catch is on when not in use.

Measuring rod and dibber

Although you can buy both these items, they can be easily made at home. For a measuring rod, use a 2m (6ft 6in) wood lath, suitably marked for measuring by shallow saw cuts at 15cm (6in) intervals. A dibber can be made from a 20cm long × 2.5cm diameter (8in × 1in) dowel, rounded at one end.

Use a measuring rod when planting to achieve the correct distance between plants. Use the dibber to plant small subjects such as small cabbage plants, and to sow large seeds such as broad beans. Make a hole with the dibber to the correct depth, and firm the soil round plant roots or seeds after planting.

Bucket and neatly stored hose-pipe with adjustable nozzle.

Portable steps, firmly placed on level ground.

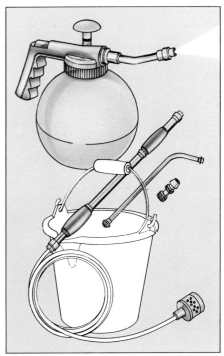

Pneumatic hand spray (above) and double-action sprayer with parts (below).

Bucket and hose pipe

For cheapness, ease and convenience, those made of plastic will serve their purposes well. A 9 litre (2 gal) bucket is a handy size. An 18m (60ft) length hose pipe is adequate for most small gardens, but up to twice that length may be needed for medium size plots, especially if they are long and narrow.

Keep buckets and pipes clean and store away from frost and strong sunlight when not in use.

Safety note Do not leave coils or stretches of hose-pipe lying about after use as they are easy to trip over.

Steps and ladders

Aluminium or alloy types are lightweight and easy to carry. All steps and ladders need to be kept in a good state of repair; wooden models deteriorate more quickly. You will need a ladder or steps for trimming tall hedges, tying climbing plants to their supports, and pruning trees. Put them away after use since as well as needing protection from the weather, steps left outside the house make life easy for burglars.

Safety note Never use broken or faulty steps or ladders, not even for one small job, and always make sure that they are firmly placed on level ground.

Sprayer

There are models of varying shape and size to suit most purposes. They usually work by compression or suction. The former type pumps air into an air-sealed canister, which forces the spray out when a valve is released. The suction types depend on the continuous action of a pump to deliver the spray. The main advantage of compression sprayers is that spraying can be continued without having to pump at the same time. The chief points to look for are construction from rust- or corrosion-resistant materials such as plastic or brass, adjustable nozzles for coarse or fine spraying, convenient size, and cost. If an extension lance can be fitted it will serve for spraying fruit trees.

Read the maker's instructions carefully before use.

Safety note Wash hands, sprayer and other items thoroughly after spraying. Use gloves and goggles if poisonous substances have to be used, but avoid poisons wherever possible. Keep people and pets away when spraying with poison. Store spray material, correctly labelled, in cool conditions, out of reach of pets and children and preferably under lock and key. Always follow manufacturer's instructions.

35

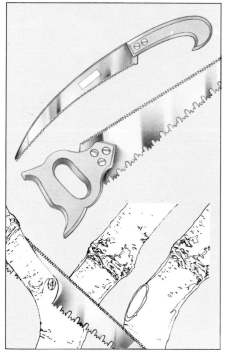

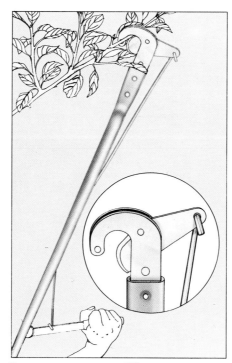

Grecian saw (top) and ordinary coarse-cut pruning saw (centre).
Lopping a branch, making an undercut first (below).

Long-arm pruner, blade action (above), handle operation (below).

Broad wire rake (above) for scarifying lawns, and fantail (below) for smaller areas.

Pruning saw
There are several types available: single- and double-edged, straight and curved, fixed and folding-bladed. The double-edged type with a rigid blade is best. The setting of the teeth should ensure that the saw groove is cleared with each stroke. A good blade will give a resonant ringing tone when slightly bent and released quickly. This tool is used to remove unwanted or surplus wood of 15mm ($\frac{3}{4}$in) thickness and over. To reduce the chance of splitting, undercut larger limbs to one-third of their diameter before overcutting. Examine branches for wire or nails before sawing, or the blade and teeth may be damaged. Clean and oil blades after use and ensure the teeth are sharp.

Safety note Before and during saw-work, make sure the area below is clear of people and pets. High (6m (20ft) plus) or heavy tree work is best left to the expert.

Long-arm pruner
These are made in various lengths; avoid those that are too heavy. The blades should be of good carbon steel, clean and sharp and have a smooth action.

Safety note Avoid balancing on the top of step ladders with these pruners. Keep the blade in the shut position when not in use.

Wire rakes
Wire or fan-tail rakes with 8 to 20 teeth are similar in most other respects to the iron rake and are needed for good lawn care.

Wire rakes are excellent for combing vigorously through turf to remove old dead grass, scattering worm casts, gathering up leaves and twigs, and for aeration.

Safety note Always hang up wire rakes when not in use. When placing them on the ground, make sure the teeth are face down, as you would with an iron rake.

Hand shears, notched (top), straight (centre). Long handled edging shears (below).

Rotary lawn mower (top left) and view of underside showing the propellor-like cutting blade.

Side wheel cylinder mower (top right) and parts (below) from left to right: grassbox, front roller, cylinder, rear roller.

Shears – grass, hedge and edging

There are many models to choose from, so select one which is the right weight and balance for you. Shears should have a non-slip adjustable locking nut; buffers, to prevent fingers from being knocked together; hollow-ground, forged steel blades (nicked in the case of hedge shears); and securely fixed handles.

Grass cutting with shears is fairly straightforward, but hedge cutting can present problems. Use your measuring stick as a guide to ensure level cutting of the top and sides. Take care not to cut wire or the blades may be blunted and damaged. Use the nicked part to cut heavier hedge shoots.

Safety note Avoid leaving shears where they may fall and cause injury. After cleaning and oiling, place them safely away after use.

Lawn mower

There are two main classes of domestic mowers, the cylinder or reel, and the rotary cutters.

The first group, which can be manually or power-driven, are used on lawns which are kept well mown. There are side-wheel models, which are usually cheaper but cannot cut close to lawn edges, and rear-roller mowers, which not only cut close to the edges, but also roll the lawn and collect the mowings in a grass box. A cylinder width of 30 to 35cm (12 to 14in) is adequate for most gardens. Electric models are quieter than the petrol-engined types.

Rotary cutters usually have petrol motors and are of the wheeled or the hover type. The hover model is very useful for cutting grass on steep slopes.

Before mowing, remove all hard objects from the lawn. Adjust the machine according to the maker's instructions and check that there are no loose nuts and bolts, and that the mower is in good working order. After mowing, clean and dry the machine, and oil all moving parts as advised by the manufacturer.

Safety note *Never* adjust a power mower while the engine is running even if you think the machine may have broken down. The cutter blades and other moving parts should have the necessary guards or covers on during use. Take care when oiling, mending and cleaning lawn mowers as the blades can spin.

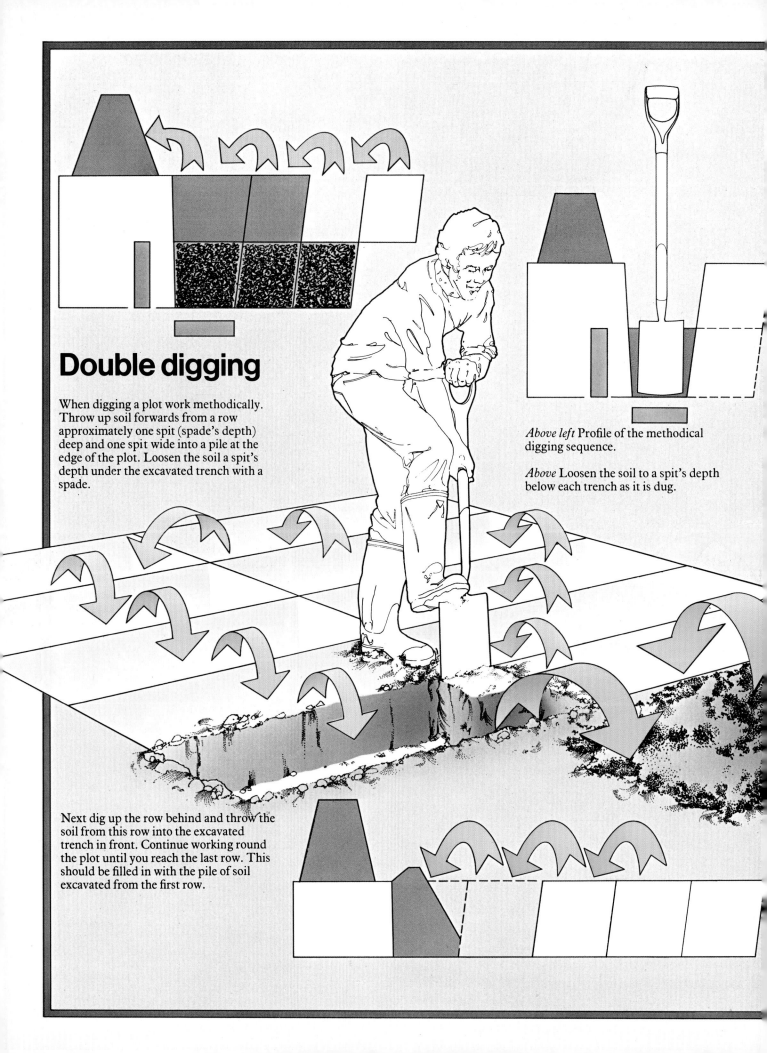

Double digging

When digging a plot work methodically. Throw up soil forwards from a row approximately one spit (spade's depth) deep and one spit wide into a pile at the edge of the plot. Loosen the soil a spit's depth under the excavated trench with a spade.

Above left Profile of the methodical digging sequence.

Above Loosen the soil to a spit's depth below each trench as it is dug.

Next dig up the row behind and throw the soil from this row into the excavated trench in front. Continue working round the plot until you reach the last row. This should be filled in with the pile of soil excavated from the first row.

Step-by-step digging

1. T-handled spade with a rounded blade. A rounded blade can be easier than a square blade on heavy soils.

2. A spade with a square blade and an O-shaped handle.

3. and 4. Border spades with rounded and splayed blades.

5. Digging fork with a socket fitting.

6. Digging fork with a strap fitting.

7. and 8. Border forks with parallel prongs and splayed prongs. The choice between them is a matter of personal preference.

Far left As the soil is thrown into the next trench, it may not always fill the trench exactly. Level the plot once all the digging is completed.

Left If the spade is not inserted vertically, the trench dug will not be a full spit's depth.

Right When digging ridges, expose as large a surface area as possible for wind and frost to have maximum effect in winter.

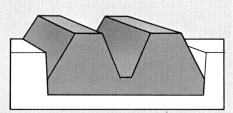

Planning and planting

Designing a garden

Garden design is based on certain fundamental principles and these should be considered before planning your first layout and work programme. As most modern gardens share an area of 160 to 320m² (200 to 400 sq yd) with a house and garage they will generally have to satisfy several requirements. When preparing the plan, write these down. As the scheme develops, fill in against each item alternative ways of dealing with it, and then decide on the best set of solutions for your site.

The *appearance* of the garden must please the eye; before rushing off to order trees and plant up flower beds, have a good look at your garden from all angles and aim to blend all its features into an harmonious whole. This is difficult to achieve and will inevitably take several seasons.

Paths, walls or hedges laid in straight lines that criss-cross and break up the plot will make a small garden appear smaller still. A curved line is more graceful and leads the eye more slowly to the focal point of the plot, giving an illusion of increased size. Meandering paths can provide a pleasanter walk – especially if flanked with fragrant and eye-catching planting schemes – than those that follow a straight line.

Path edges should either be well defined and kept clear of weeds or bordered with ground cover plants such as candytuft, to conceal the meeting of paving stone or path, and lawn or flower bed. For paths, walls and sheds choose building materials in keeping with the house and the region as a whole, using local stone where possible. Buildings and planting schemes should be related to each other. For example, it would be a mistake to surround a detached bungalow with trees that will eventually dwarf it and provide excessive shade. At the other end of the scale, a very low planting scheme with little colour will throw into unflattering relief a house that stands alone. Flowers, shrubs and small trees of different heights soften an outline and present a more restful view.

The second consideration is *cost*. It is essential from the start to plan your garden so that you can afford to maintain it, or you run the risk of being

forced to give up in despair after a couple of years and let nature take over. Give priority in the first year to work on any paths, drives and boundaries, as these give the garden a basic framework on which you can elaborate in succeeding years. Similarly, plants which will be permanent and take some time to reach maturity – such as hedges and decorative or fruiting trees – should be ordered and planted as soon as possible, otherwise more complicated schemes (or the laying of a lawn) will have to be disturbed to provide for them.

In the first year, buy only the basic tools and equipment for the necessary work. A spade for digging, a fork for lifting and turning, a rake and hoe. Make a measuring rod and use string and sticks for laying out individual plots. Choose the right tools for your height and strength; if you find gardening tiresome because you have the wrong implements, you will spend less time on the plot and the design will suffer. Leave the buying of major and specialized equipment such as lawn-

mowers and pruning shears until you have a lawn to mow and trees to train.

Any garden can be given an instant face-lift with the provision of colourful bedding plants – that is, annuals or perennials bought as young plants from a nursery and used for temporary display. However, this is a very expensive way of beautifying your garden and many bedding plants put in soil that has been neglected for some time die for lack of nourishment or from soil-borne diseases.

In subsequent years you will be able to cut the cost of bedding plants by growing your own from seed, and by propagating from established plants (see page 64). You will also find that most gardeners are only too happy to give cuttings and offsets to a fellow enthusiast. Weed and disease-free offerings are a splendid way of stocking up the garden, and it is likely that what thrives on your neighbour's soil will do equally well on yours.

A site which is being developed over a period of time does not have to look like a battlefield; any area which is to be

LEFT A carefully planned and immaculately maintained garden. The lawn and hard paths share a formal geometric look while the bedding plants have been chosen with particular attention to colour, shape and height.

BELOW An informal front garden in June.

BOTTOM A garden planted with heathers and conifers rather than bedding plants for year round interest.

BELOW A narrow town garden with effective use of a raised flower bed and climbing plants to cover the boundary wall.

left undeveloped can be seeded down to grass and mown, and the turf can be lifted and used again when the area is finally laid out. There will inevitably be a period, after the essential clearing and cleaning of the site has been completed, when the garden looks comparatively bare, but this is a useful time to observe the nature of the plot; to learn how light and shade strike it, what kind of soil you have to work, how heavy rain affects the land, and so on.

The last but most crucial question in the design is the *choice of plants*. This is a matter of personal taste, but for lasting satisfactory results the plants should also suit your site and soil. Avoid planting too closely or using over-vigorous trees or plants in confined spaces, as their demands on your time can be considerable. Plants of naturally tidy habit, such as heathers and dwarf conifers, need much less attention than roses, for example, but they grow more slowly. For detailed advice on choosing the right plants for different soils and sites, see chapter 3, and for trees and shrubs chapter 6.

The model garden before transformation. This garden, abandoned for years, is about the worst state in which a small garden might be tackled by the amateur gardener. Very little of the existing site can be left as it is. The fence and shed are both in need of such extensive repair that they are probably better replaced. The boggy patch on the left indicates extremely poor drainage so a soakaway must be built. Fortunately, there may be some unpolluted rubble amongst the pile in the foreground which can be used for the soakaway. The rest must be cleared away. The attractive old birch tree at the far end of the garden (the south-west corner) will cast a lot of shade in summer, so careful thought must be given to how the shade area can be put to good use.

The first task is to make a plan of the existing garden, and a plan of this garden appears on page 44.

Making a plan

The first stage of the programme is to prepare a plan of your garden. However limited your artistic skills, it is worth making a scale drawing of the site. How much detail you include will depend on whether the aim is to improve an existing garden or to start from scratch. To make a plan you will need a tape measure, compass, spirit level, a ball of string, some wooden pegs, six 1.5m (5ft) canes, a 2m (6ft 8in) straight edge to check levels and for measuring, pencils, squared paper, a pen and a centimetre rule, and a flat surface to draw on.

Measure the length and width of the plot, noting any irregularities of outline. Where the aim is to improve an existing garden, you will need to note the size and position of existing beds and their present occupants. Reproduce all these outlines on graph paper. A suitable scale is 1:25 (4cm to represent one metre).

When starting from scratch it is essential to show the whole area including all buildings, boundaries, doorways and entrances, paths and any drives. Indicate proposed and existing features, compass bearings, and the position of trees, shrubs, and water courses. Details of drains, levels, prevailing wind, shaded areas, sunny spots, and any outstanding views should also be recorded on the plan. Use the pegs, straight edge and spirit level to obtain the levels, using the house as the main reference point. Stand the pegs firmly in the soil, so that the straight edge is exactly level (check with the spirit level) when resting on the pegs. Deal with any changes in level as described on page 10.

Ink in all details on the squared paper. If you have drawn up a list of the garden's functions use it in conjunction with the plan to arrive at a finished design. Make sketches of your proposals on tracing paper and place them over the site plan, trying out the various alternatives one by one. When you have decided upon a design, you can then make out a timetable for putting it into practice.

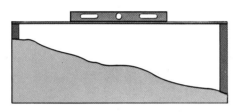

ABOVE Finding the level. Use the house as the main reference point.

BELOW A plan of the dilapidated model garden, see page 42.

BELOW RIGHT A plan of the proposed garden, see completed garden on page 48.

FAR RIGHT An alternative plan, adapted to accommodate a vegetable plot (brown area).

Key

1 Nepeta
2 Daphne
3 Forsythia
4 Potentilla
5 Pyracantha
6 Viburnum
7 Group of rose bushes (hybrid tea)
8 Rosa
9 Skimmia
10 Berberis
11 Aucuba
12 Buxus
13 Berberis
14 Elaeagnus
15 Symphoricarpos
16 Rhododendron
17-20 Dwarf conifers
21 Tubs of flowers
22 Hydrangea
23 Climbing roses
24 Clematis
25 Erica

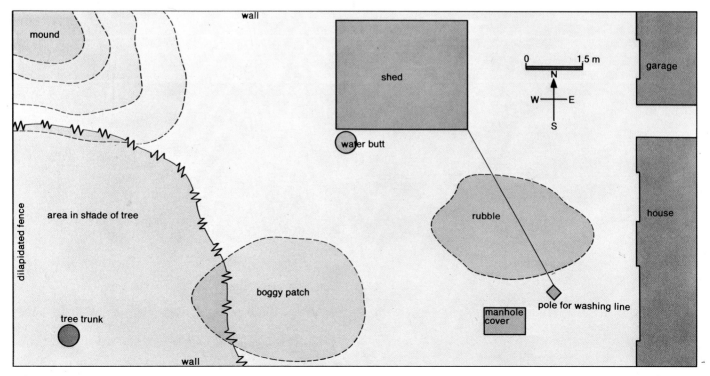

The model garden

Shown here is the site plan of the imaginary garden drawn on page 42, which includes most of the worst problems you are likely to encounter in a badly neglected site. The plot has been remodelled to provide a family garden. The pile of builder's rubble and washing line in full view of the back window are replaced with a spacious paved area brought to life with tubs of flowers (one of them hiding the manhole cover), climbing roses against trelliswork, and a clematis against the back wall of the house. The trellis provides a screen for the laundry area, still in easy reach of the house but in a corner where the proximity of the garage would make planting tricky.

The dilapidated fence at the west end of the plan has been replaced with a wall of patterned blocks, which provides a solid boundary but allows air and light to filter through.

The tumbledown shed is dismantled and a solid new one put up on the unpromising boggy patch, made firmer and well-drained by the rubble now buried beneath it. The new shed is centrally placed to serve the whole garden and is easily reached from the patio by stepping stones set into the lawn slightly lower than the level of the grass to facilitate mowing.

In the south-west corner of the garden an old birch tree casts a deep shadow, but provides an attractive view from the house. Little will grow under its branches but as it is distant from the house this a good spot for the composting area, hidden behind the shed. In the north-west corner, the mound is kept and planted with heathers.

In the new garden, the curving lawn is bordered by four main planting schemes. The most ambitious and demanding of these, the herbaceous border, is fully described in chapter 5. The other three are composed of shrubs and conifers which, after planting, require minimum attention and provide year-round colour and cover. Though energy and thought are needed to plan and plant such a garden, maintenance in subsequent seasons is confined to the lawn, a little pruning and training, and care of the herbaceous border.

The introduction of fruit and vegetables inevitably means more time working in the garden, but many people feel that home-grown produce is worth the effort. To prepare this particular site for vegetables, generous manuring would be necessary since the soil will have lost much nourishment over the years of neglect. The far end of the plot would be used for vegetables, and the south-facing part of the herbaceous border for fruit—cordon apples and pears or fan-trained blackberries against the wall and trellis, and black or red currant and gooseberry bushes in front.

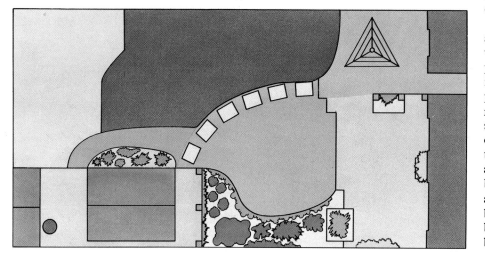

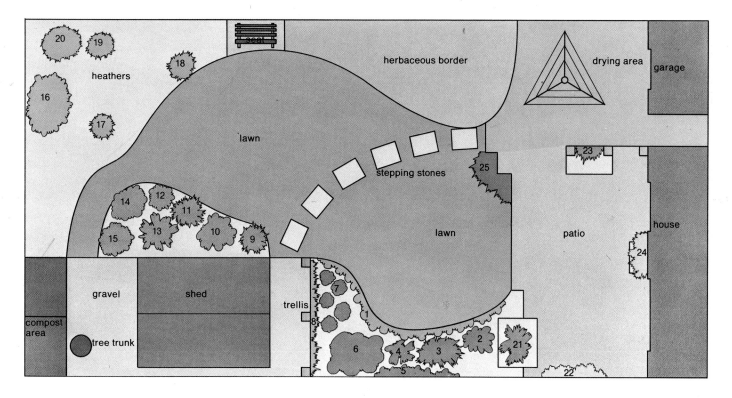

Programme of tasks

The work needed to turn a neglected site into a plot that deserves the name of garden can be covered in twelve steps. As there will be items on the timetable that do not apply to your site, it is certain that three or four hours a week devoted to gardening could bring your dream garden closer to reality within a year.

1. *Clearing the site.* The best time to start the basic groundwork is in early spring. Aim to remove all rubbish and to clear and dig out perennial weeds by the end of April. Difficult weeds can be cleared with a hormone weedkiller. Take care that no chemicals contaminate water and ponds and keep them away from children or pets.

2. *Excavate for, and lay paths and drives.* These jobs are much easier to do during the summer months. You may decide to have them laid professionally but it is still useful to understand the basic requirements.

The stability of a drive or path, particularly in winter, depends on a sufficient depth of hard dry foundation, covered with a waterproof capping. A serviceable drive to carry the average car might consist of a 15cm (6in) depth of 7.5cm (3in) hardcore covered with a 5cm (2in) layer of 18mm ($\frac{3}{4}$in) gravel and topped with a 10cm (4in) layer of concrete mixed in the proportion 1 part concrete:2 parts sand:4 parts washed gravel. For paths use the same materials, but at half the depth of the above. As an alternative, a 5cm (2in) layer of black or coloured tarmacadam could be substituted for concrete for paths, but would be laid on top of the concrete for drives. Surfaces should not be completely level, but slope from one side to the other or be raised in the centre. The fall should be 1:60, so that, for example, a 90cm (3ft) wide path would have a fall of 1.5cm ($\frac{5}{8}$in) from one side to the other, and if it were to be raised in the centre would have a .75cm ($\frac{5}{16}$ inch) fall from centre to edge.

3. *Lay drains*. Another major task probably requiring professional help, it is also best carried out in summer.

4. *Build sheds and walls, gates and fences*. Do as much as you can of this basic work in the first summer. When establishing boundaries, bear in mind that trees and hedges may grow to block drains, shed their leaves, and exclude light. To avoid contention go for hedges whose growth can be restricted, or fences or walls.

Badly built walls are dangerous. The foundations for a low wall should be at least twice as wide and the same depth as the thickness of the wall. Free-standing solid walls over 1.2m (4ft) high should be at least 22.5cm (9in) thick. Walls over 1.2m (4ft) high and

more than 3.6m (12ft) long should be professionally built.

Fence construction falls into the following categories: timber, steel, ironwork, wire mesh, plastic, and concrete.

Treat *timber* with a non-poisonous preservative, or the life of the fencing may be as little as three years. With care, timber can last at least 12–15 years. Concrete posts assist considerably in cutting maintenance costs. Heavy-gauge steel or iron railing, when regularly painted, can last indefinitely, but is very expensive.

Wire netting, though not exactly beautiful, is cheaper than many forms of fencing, but soon corrodes in coastal areas or in towns, unless protected with plastic coating.

Plastic mesh netting is one of the cheapest but also one of the most vulnerable barriers, as it is easily cut with a knife.

Concrete fencing is expensive but permanent, heavy and durable and requires no maintenance.

With all forms of fencing, strong supports are essential: common spacings are at 1.8m, 2.4m and 2.7m (6, 8 and 9ft), based on weight, type and height. Solid fencing, 1.8m (6ft) high is usually adequate for privacy. Corner and end posts require extra support to stop them being pulled in or over.

5. *Digging, levelling, manuring and liming*. These tasks need to be carried out in the autumn, before the ground becomes too wet or frozen to work, and to allow the winter to weather the soil in preparation for planting. Digging, manuring and liming are covered in chapter 2.

Changes of level can be achieved in various ways. Gardens on different levels offer wide scope for imaginative planting and provide architectural interest with varying widths and shapes. Steps can be used to link two areas of different levels (ramps should be no steeper than one-in-three). Lawns steeper than one-in-four will be difficult to mow.

Grassed or planted banks should be constructed carefully: where the ground level is being raised, keep back the topsoil to spread on the surface after levelling. Consolidate the earth as work proceeds, in layers no deeper than 15cm (6in) and make sure that the slope is no steeper than one-in-two. A rock garden is an excellent and decorative way to highlight variations in land form.

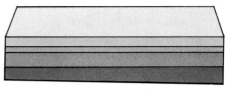
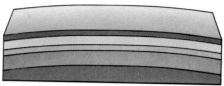

Laying a drive: surface sloping from one side to the other (top), and raised in the centre (bottom).

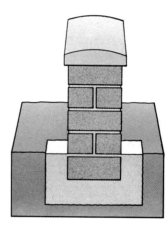

Foundations for a solid wall should be the same depth and twice as wide as the thickness of the wall.

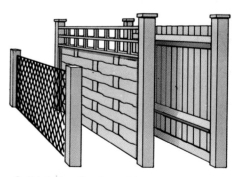

Solid timber fencing with strong supports.

LEFT The model garden in the making. The site has been cleared, paths and patio laid, a new wall erected and a soakaway built (under the foundations for the new shed where the boggy patch was). The soil has been dug and manured, and the flower borders pegged out.

6. *Ordering plants and materials* (this will vary from year to year). Most seedsmen issue catalogues towards the end of the year, and it is a good idea to place your order as soon as possible to be sure of getting the varieties you want.

7. *Planting and staking trees* is described in chapter 6. Obtain and fix stakes and prepare the planting hole in advance to receive trees straight from the nursery.

8. *Planting hedges and shrubs.* It is a good idea to plant hedges and shrubs in your first year. They take several seasons to establish themselves and fill their allotted space, so the sooner you can get them going the better.

9. *Laying lawns and turfing* is best carried out in the autumn on a site well prepared the previous spring. If you are carrying out major clearance and building work, leave the lawn until your second year.

10. *Preparing for flowers, fruit and vegetables*. Site preparation for these specialized groups of plants is described in the relevant chapters, and can be started in the first autumn for sowing and planting the following year. For fruit bushes and particularly for trees which will occupy ground for long periods of time, soil preparation must be thorough. For the vegetable plot, follow a crop rotation plan from the start and prepare each site accordingly (see chapter 7).

11. *Sowing annuals, biennials and perennials from seed*. Early in the second spring, start sowing seed for summer and autumn bedding schemes.

12 *Prepare a maintenance plan* for the year, tailoring the monthly plan in chapter 11 to your needs.

The model garden completed. Care has been given to plant out in such a way that when the plants are established and grow bigger they will not overcrowd each other. This is why the new garden has a rather 'bare' look.

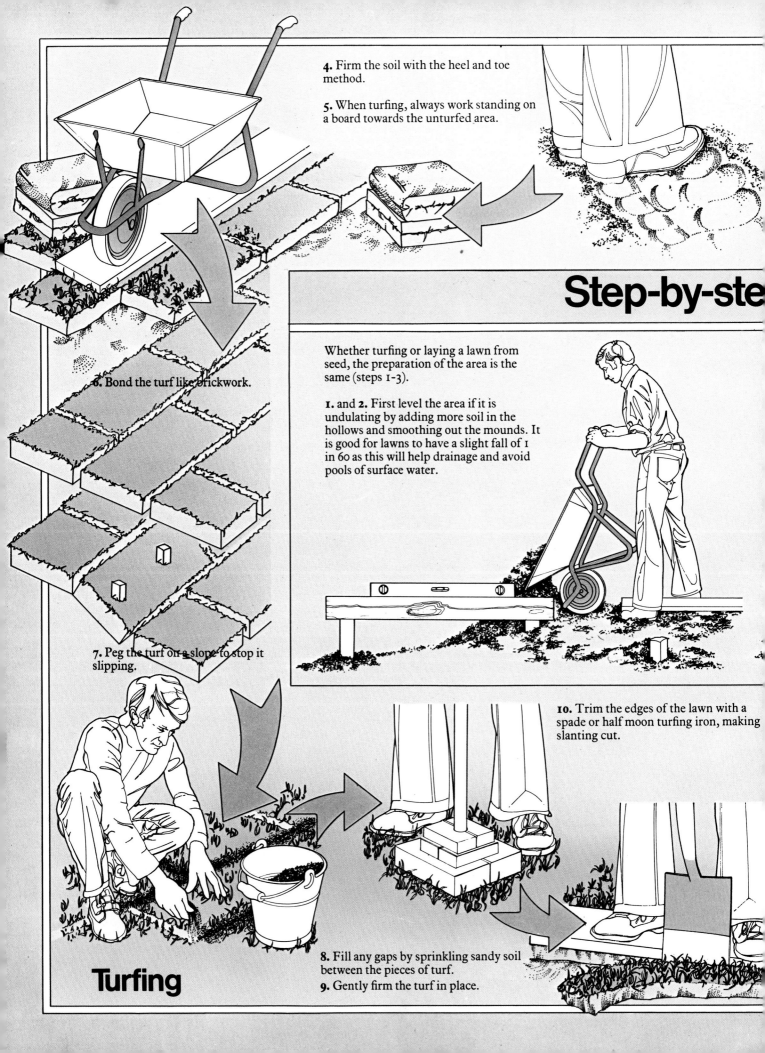

4. Firm the soil with the heel and toe method.

5. When turfing, always work standing on a board towards the unturfed area.

6. Bond the turf like brickwork.

Step-by-ste

Whether turfing or laying a lawn from seed, the preparation of the area is the same (steps 1-3).

1. and **2.** First level the area if it is undulating by adding more soil in the hollows and smoothing out the mounds. It is good for lawns to have a slight fall of 1 in 60 as this will help drainage and avoid pools of surface water.

7. Peg the turf on a slope to stop it slipping.

10. Trim the edges of the lawn with a spade or half moon turfing iron, making slanting cut.

8. Fill any gaps by sprinkling sandy soil between the pieces of turf.
9. Gently firm the turf in place.

Turfing

4. Firm the soil with the heel and toe method.
Mark the area for sowing into sections for correct seeding – 30-45 g/m² ($1-1\frac{1}{2}$ oz per sq yd).

aying a lawn

3. Rake over the ground to a fine tilth, removing stones and adding a general fertilizer if necessary. Do not let the area dry out.

5. Rake in the seeds and keep the area well watered, using a sprinkler attachment, as heavy watering would dislodge the seedlings.

Roll the lawn with a light roller after turfing or six weeks after sowing when the grass will be approximately 3 cm ($1\frac{1}{4}$ inches) high.

Sowing

chamaecyparis
philadelphus
cytisus

Quick-growing shrubs and hedging plants

Key

Sh = Use as shrub
H = Hedging
E = Evergreen
T = Suitable for towns
S = Suitable for coast
A = Acid
N = Neutral
C = Chalk
Size – single measure is space to leave between hedging plants
All measurements are average and approximate at ultimate size

Name		Soil	Site	Size m or cm ht × wth	Size ft or in ht × wth	Season and nature of interest
Carpinus betulus Hornbeam	H	N C	Open	60cm	24in	Spring to autumn foliage, dry leaves in winter
Chamaecyparis lawsoniana Lawsons Cypress	H E	A N C	Sun	45cm	18in	All year round foliage blue green and gold
Cotoneaster simonsii Cotoneaster	Sh H	A N C	Sun or Shade	45cm 2·4 × 1·8	18in 8 × 6	Autumn scarlet berries
Crataegus oxycantha Thorn or Quick	H	A N C	Open T	30cm	12in	Spring summer foliage and white flowers
Cupressocyparis leylandii Leyland Cypress	H E	N C	Sun S	90cm	36in	All year round foliage green and yellow
Cytisus scoparious Common Broom	Sh	N	Sun Open	2·4 × 2·1	8 × 7	Spring, whitish flowers
Elaeagnus ebbingei False Oleaster	Sh E	A N C	Open	3·6 × 2·4	12 × 8	All year round foliage grey green with silver undersides
Escallonia macrantha Chilean Gum Box	Sh H E	A N	Sun Mild	45cm 2·4 × 1·8	18in 8 × 6	All year round foliage, red flowers summer and autumn

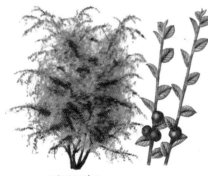

cotoneaster

ribes

spartium

elaeagnus   escallonia   forsythia

Name		Soil	Site	Size m or cm ht × wth	Size ft or in ht × wth	Season and nature of interest
Forsythia intermedia Hanging Golden Bell	Sh	A N C	T Open	2·4 × 1·8	8 × 6	Spring, yellow flowers
Ligustrum ovalifolium Privet	H	A N C	T Open	30cm	12in	Spring and summer foliage
Lonicera nitida Hedge Honeysuckle	H E	A N C	S Sun Mild	30cm	12in	All year round green foliage
Olearia haastii Daisy Bush	Sh H E	A N C	Sun or shade S	45cm 1·8 × 1·2	18in 6 × 4	All year round foliage Summer, scented white flowers
Philadelphus 'Sybille' Mock Orange	Sh	A N C	Open	2·4 × 1·5	8 × 5	Summer, scented, purple stained flowers
Potentilla friedrichsenii Shrubby Cinquefoil	Sh	A N C	Sun Open	1·2 × 0·9	4 × 3	Summer yellow flowers
Ribes sanguineum Flowering Currant	Sh	A N C	Sun or Shade	2·4 × 1·5	8 × 5	Spring, reddish pink flowers
Rosa various Rose	Sh H	A N	Sun	45cm 2·4 × 1·2	18in 8 × 4	Summer, autumn flowers, various colours, red hips
Spartium junceum Spanish Broom	Sh	A N C	Sun T and S	2·4 × 1·8	8 × 6	Summer yellow flowers
Symphoricarpus orbiculatus Snowberry	Sh	A N C	Sun or shade T	1·8 × 1·5	6 × 5	Summer, whitish flowers followed by pinkish-purple fruits in autumn
Tamarix tetrandra Tamarisk	Sh H	A N	Open S	45cm 3·0 × 2·4	18in 10 × 8	Spring, bright pink flowers
Weigela florida Diervilla	Sh	A N C	T Sun	2·4 × 1·8	8 × 6	Summer, red, crimson or pink flowers

symphoricarpos

tamarix

weigela

The flower garden

Flowers have various roles to play, whether it is to cover eyesores or provide material for the imaginative flower arranger. The key to success in a flower garden is the health and care of well-chosen plants, and although many modern aids for cultivating plants save time and trouble, they are no substitute for good garden practice and common sense.

The basic needs of plants are simple enough: a well-prepared soil and site; careful sowing and planting at the right time; adequate warmth, food and moisture; attention to training during the growing season, and pest, weed and disease control.

The guidelines set out in the following pages apply to flower growing in any size of garden both front and back and to containers.

The different flower types
Plants are recognized as belonging to various groups. This convention, once understood and applied, provides clues to plant behaviour and cultivation. The three main classifications of flowering plants are annuals, biennials and perennials.

Annuals are raised from seed, grow, set seed and die, all within one year.

Biennials need two growing seasons to complete their life process. They flower in the second season, then die.

Perennials flower for at least two years.

Hardiness rating
Many garden plants have been introduced into this country from warmer climates and are grouped according to their ability to survive here.

Hardy plants, which can be annuals, biennials or perennials, are those that can be grown outdoors and survive winters in most years. Half-hardy plants, which also include annuals, biennials and perennials, either require some protection to come through the winter unharmed, or require a longer summer growing season than our climate affords.

Planting categories
Summer bedding plants such as geraniums or antirrhinums are sown or planted out in late spring for a summer or autumn display.

Spring bedding plants like tulips and wallflowers are usually set out in flower beds in autumn to provide colour and interest in spring.

Herbaceous plants do not develop woody stems. An herbaceous border can consist of annuals, biennials or perennials. When shrubs are present it is called a mixed or shrub border.

Other groupings include classification by scent, colour and flowering season.

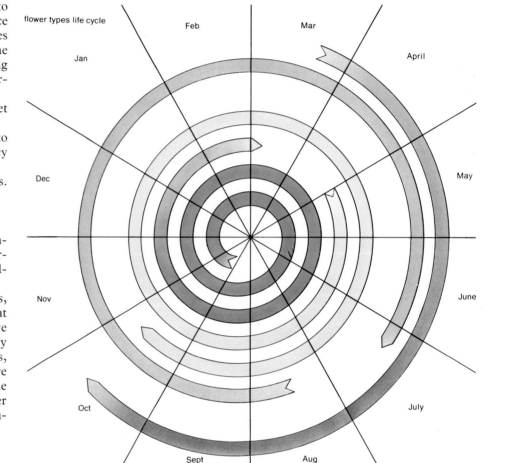

flower types life cycle

Jan / Feb / Mar / April / May / June / July / Aug / Sept / Oct / Nov / Dec

perennials ■ biennials □ autumn-sown annuals ■ spring-sown annuals ■

Practical classifications for flowers
Hardy annuals can be successfully sown, grown and flowered outside without protection. Examples include calendula, clarkia, cornflower and larkspur.

Half-hardy annuals are usually sown in a greenhouse or frame for planting outside when the weather is warmer. Lobelia, petunia and salvia are examples of this group.

Hardy biennials can be sown outside in May or June, overwinter outdoors and flower 12-15 months after sowing.

Canterbury Bell, forget-me-not and Brompton stocks are members of this class. Double daisy, Sweet William, and wallflowers are best treated as biennials, although they are really perennials since their flowers in later years are poor in quality and quantity.

Half-hardy biennials are treated as for hardy biennials, but sown and overwintered indoors. Freesia is an example. This type of plant is not widely used outdoors and for this reason half-hardy biennials do not feature on the table on page 60.

Hardy perennials are plants which for

practical considerations are planted from seed or division, flower for between one and five years according to type, and are then lifted, divided and replanted. Examples include golden rod, iris, and peony.

Half-hardy perennials are an important class of plants which are overwintered under cover or raised in greenhouses for outside planting. Begonia, dahlia, fuchsia and geraniums are members of this category.

Choosing the right flowers for your garden

A selection of plants which are well suited to your climate, soil, site and taste, will lay a sound foundation for your garden. The choice of a subject because of its colour or scent alone without due regard to the needs of the plant, can be disappointing and expensive. A visit to some local gardens, especially those where plants are labelled, can provide a fair amount of useful information. Make a note of those plants which flourish and you will learn something about the local soil and climate and the varieties likely to grow well, their habit, colour and flowering season. Observe your own garden at different times of the day and of the year, noting the sunny areas and the shaded or draughty spots, as well as the direction of the prevailing wind. While you may have limited control over climate, soil and site, in your choice of plants you can greatly influence the success of your garden.

Use this simple checklist to choose suitable flowering and other plants.

Site conditions
Sunny or shaded situation
Aspect – does it face N.S.E. or W.?
Exposed to wind or sheltered

Soil considerations
Acid or alkaline
Heavy or light
Fertile or poor

Plant habit
Height, spread and shape
Colour and flowering season
Expensive to buy or to maintain
Requires staking

Soil preparation

Most of the common flowering herbaceous plants, (which can include annuals, biennials and perennials), will grow and bloom satisfactorily on a wide range of soils. To get the soil into perfect condition, dig the ground to a spade's depth – 30cm (12in) – during autumn, and incorporate organic matter as you work, leaving the soil undisturbed until spring to be weathered by wind and frost. The organic matter can be in the form of well-rotted manure applied at the rate of 2.25kg/m² (5lb per sq yd) or as a 2.5cm (1in) layer of peat or pulverized bark. If you need the land for autumn planting, the soil should be prepared in summer and firmed before sowing or planting. Before setting out seeds or plants, the degree of soil acidity (the pH level) may need adjusting. Chalk-loving plants such as gypsophila or pinks will tolerate neutral soil, with a pH level of 7, but slightly above that figure is better. Additional lime is best applied two to three weeks before planting, at a rate based on the results of your soil test. Before planting or sowing, lightly fork in a proprietary base fertilizer dressing at the rate of 100 – 140g/m² (3-4oz per sq yd) which has an analysis of parts: nitrogen 5%, phosphate 5%, and potash 10%.

Spongy soil must be lightly firmed and raked again before plants or seeds are set out.

Before seeds are sown in their flowering positions, the beds need to be worked into a fine tilth to a depth of 7.5–10cm (3-4in).

FAR LEFT The relative life expectancy of annuals, biennials and perennials.

BELOW A glorious herbaceous border.

Laying out a mixed flower border

The size, shape and levels of a mixed flower border will be largely influenced by the existing site. Depth and breadth of the bed should be taken into account as much as the proposed colour schemes and season of interest, and the height and character of the plants should relate to each other and their surroundings.

A simple plan for a border in front of a hedge could have tall plants placed at the back and shorter subjects to the fore. With large borders it is better to set plants in groups rather than individually, or a spotty effect can be created. Tall spiky plants like delphiniums and verbascum contrast well with round-headed flowers like achillea and phlox, or with plants such as helenium that form a mounded clump.

The duration and times of the flowering season are quite important: borders close to the house need subjects that provide year-round colour although a traditional herbaceous border usually has a short but splendid season in summer. Small evergreen shrubs introduced in a mixed border provide a useful framework and give year-round interest.

Strong hues of red or yellow contrast well against shades of green and blue. White and cream blend harmoniously with most flower colours. Bronze, orange and pinks create a warm effect, compared with the coolness of blues and lavenders. Grey foliage blends or contrasts with red, cerise, pink and white shades.

Planting

Plant lifted plants in autumn or spring, and container grown subjects anytime except when in flower, or when ground is frozen or waterlogged. When the border has been dug, manured, limed and fertilized, the next stage is to measure out the planting positions with short sticks pushed into the ground. Measuring carefully saves future time and temper. Start planting at the back or at one end, and, working methodically, check soil level and plant positions occasionally, making sure plants are firm.

ABOVE Contrasting spiky heads of lupin (left) and foxglove (centre) with yarrow (back right) and phlox (front right).

BELOW Contrasting foliage of gladioli and phlox (back, left to right) and bergenia and hosta (front, left to right).

BELOW Marking out the border with sand and string.

RIGHT BELOW The completed mixed border (key right). This is the planting scheme used in the model garden.

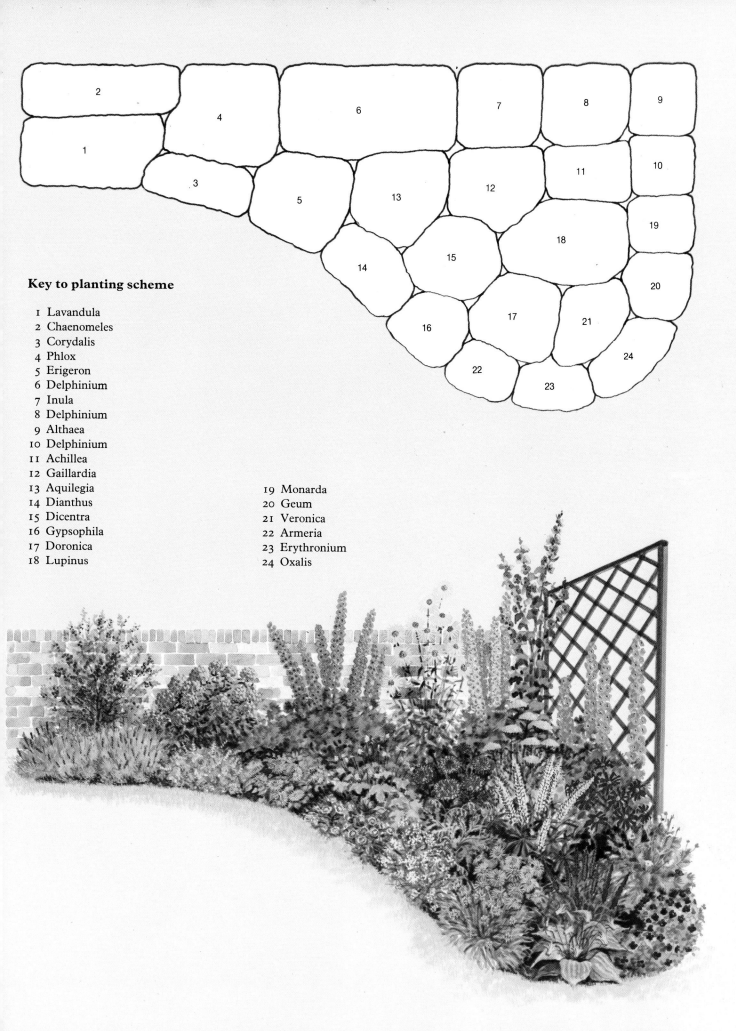

Key to planting scheme

1 Lavandula
2 Chaenomeles
3 Corydalis
4 Phlox
5 Erigeron
6 Delphinium
7 Inula
8 Delphinium
9 Althaea
10 Delphinium
11 Achillea
12 Gaillardia
13 Aquilegia
14 Dianthus
15 Dicentra
16 Gypsophila
17 Doronica
18 Lupinus

19 Monarda
20 Geum
21 Veronica
22 Armeria
23 Erythronium
24 Oxalis

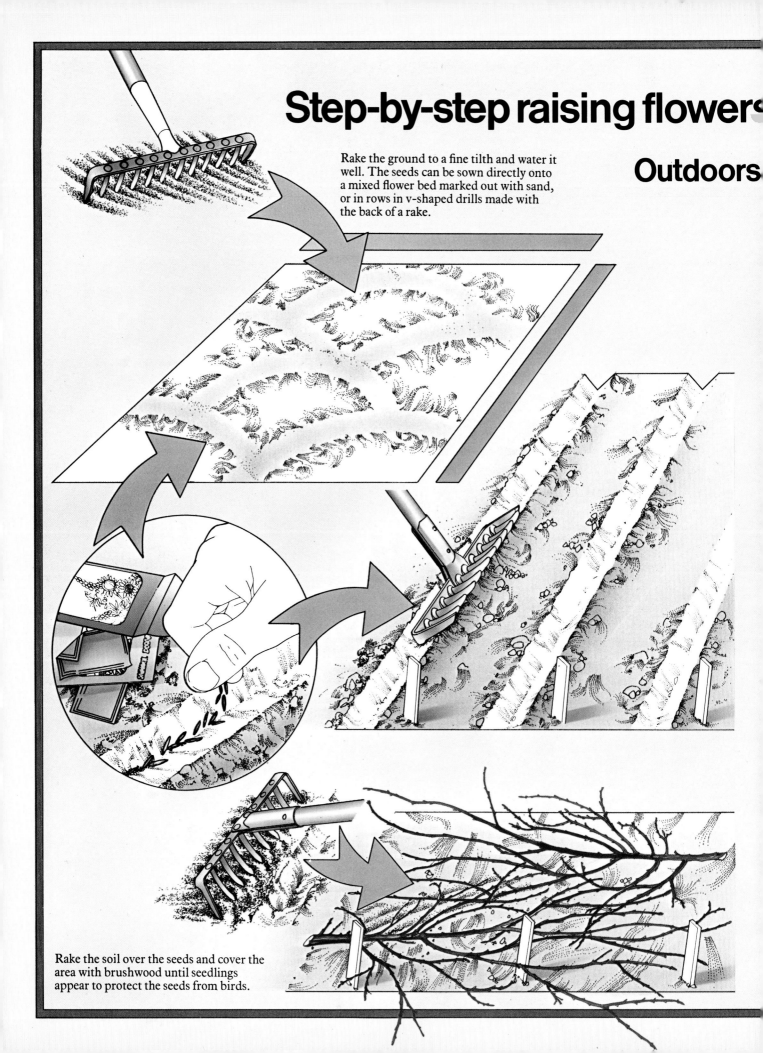

Step-by-step raising flowers

Outdoors

Rake the ground to a fine tilth and water it well. The seeds can be sown directly onto a mixed flower bed marked out with sand, or in rows in v-shaped drills made with the back of a rake.

Rake the soil over the seeds and cover the area with brushwood until seedlings appear to protect the seeds from birds.

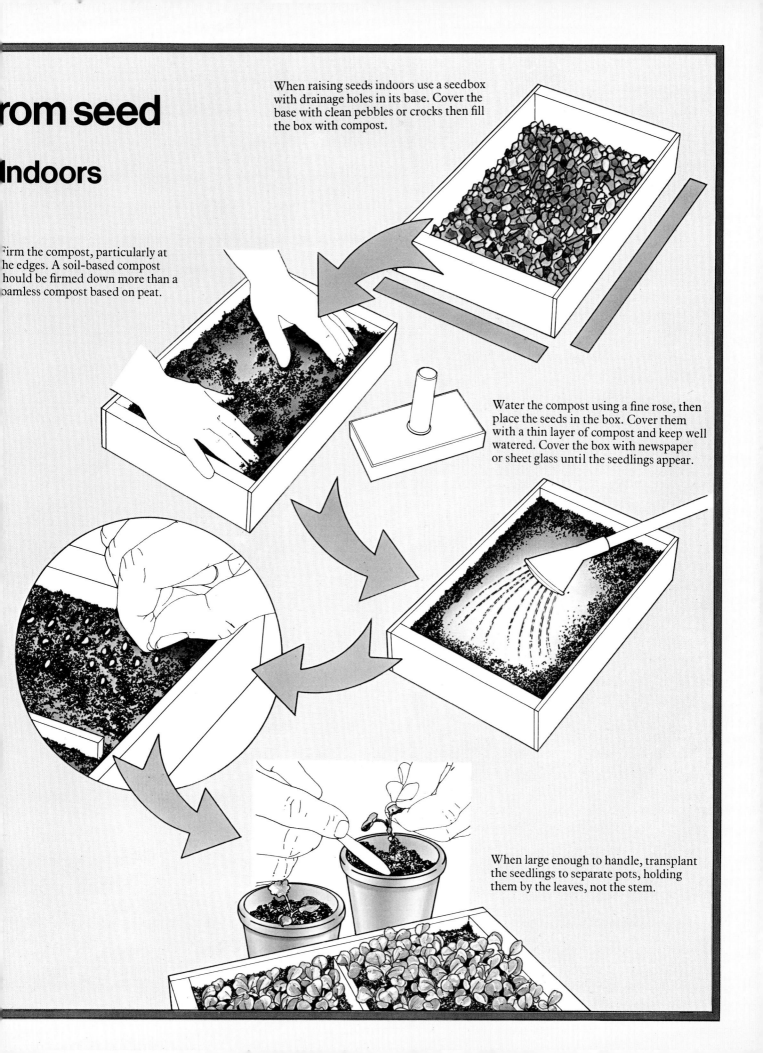

rom seed

Indoors

When raising seeds indoors use a seedbox with drainage holes in its base. Cover the base with clean pebbles or crocks then fill the box with compost.

Firm the compost, particularly at the edges. A soil-based compost should be firmed down more than a loamless compost based on peat.

Water the compost using a fine rose, then place the seeds in the box. Cover them with a thin layer of compost and keep well watered. Cover the box with newspaper or sheet glass until the seedlings appear.

When large enough to handle, transplant the seedlings to separate pots, holding them by the leaves, not the stem.

50 Easy to Grow Colourful Flowers

Illustrated Guide

Key

The first of each entry is the botanical term followed by the popular name. The plants are grouped according to habit – annual, biennial and perennial as a guide to their means of increase.

Plant height is indicated by the following letters

T = 1·2m (4ft) or over
M = between 30cm (1ft) and 1·2m (4ft)
S = normally less than 30cm (1ft)

Flowering season is denoted by the following

Sp = spring
Su = summer
Au = autumn
Wi = winter

Flower colour range is grouped into shades and is indicated by letters

R = Reds
P = Pinks
Y = Yellows and Oranges
W = Whites or creams
B = Blues
L = Lilacs and purples

Name	Size	Colour	Season
Hardy Annuals The following can be grown in a variety of positions, but are usually better in a bed on their own than mixed with other types of plant			
Calendula officinalis Pot Marigold	M	Y	Su
Centaurea cyanus Cornflower	S or M	P W B L	Su
Clarkia elegans Clarkia	M	P R	Su
Coreopsis tinctoria Calliopsis	M	Y	Su
Delphinium consolida Larkspur	M	P W B	Su
Eschscholzia californica Californian Poppy	S or M	Y	Su
Godetia grandiflora Godetia	S or M	R P W	Su
Papaver nudicaule Iceland Poppy	M	R P Y	Su
Half Hardy Annuals These are suitable for use in flower beds where the plants are changed a minimum of twice a year			
Antirrhinum majus Snapdragon	S or M	R P Y W	Su
Callistephus chinensis China aster	M	R P Y W L	Su or Au
Gazania hybrida Gazania	S	P Y	Su
Lobelia erinus Lobelia	S	P W B	Su
Matthiola incana Stock	M	R P Y W B L	Sp or Su
Nicotiana affinis Tobacco plant	M	R P Y W	Su
Petunia hybrida Petunia	S or M	R P Y W L	Su
Phlox drummondii Phlox	S or M	R P W L	Su

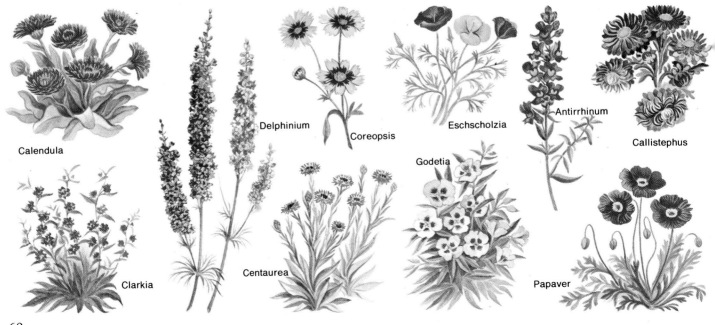

Calendula

Delphinium

Coreopsis

Eschscholzia

Antirrhinum

Callistephus

Godetia

Clarkia

Centaurea

Papaver

Name	Size	Colour	Season
Salvia splendens Salvia	S or M	R P	Su
Tagetes erecta African marigold	M	Y	Su
Verbena hybrida Verbena	S or M	R P W L	Su
Hardy Biennials			
Cheiranthus cheiri Wallflower	M	R P Y L	Sp
Dianthus barbatus Sweet William	M	R P W	Su
Digitalis purpurea Foxglove	M or T	P R W L	Su
Matthiola incana Brompton Stocks	M	R P Y W L	Sp
Myosotis alpestris Forget-me-not	S	P W B	Sp or Su
Oenothera biennis Evening Primrose	M	Y	Su to Au
Half Hardy Perennials			
Begonia tuberhybrida Tuberous begonias	S or M	R P Y W L	Su to Au
Chrysanthemum morifolium Florists chrysanthemum	M or T	R P Y W L	Su to Au
Dahlia variabilis Dahlia	S M or T	R P Y W L	Su to Au
Fuchsia hybrids Fuchsia	S M or T	R P W L	Su to Au
Impatiens hydrids Busy Lizzie	S or M	R P W L	Su to Au
Pelargonium zonale Zonal pelargonium	S or M	R P W L	Su to Au
Penstemon hartwegii Penstemon	M	R P W	Su to Au
Viola wittrockiana Garden Pansy	S	R Y W B L	Sp, Su, Au

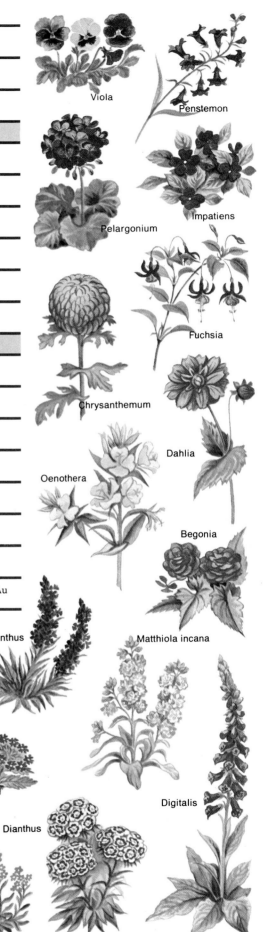

Viola

Penstemon

Pelargonium

Impatiens

Fuchsia

Chrysanthemum

Dahlia

Oenothera

Begonia

Nicotiana

Petunia

Matthiola

Gazania

Phlox

Tagetes

Salvia

Lobelia

Verbena

Myosotis

Dianthus

Cheiranthus

Matthiola incana

Digitalis

Name	Size	Colour	Season
Hardy Perennials The following list of herbaceous perennials includes plants which, with one or two exceptions, can be left undisturbed for 2 or 3 years. They can be used in herbaceous and shrub borders, rock gardens, and island beds.			
Achillea filipendulina Yarrow	M	Y	Su to Au
Alyssum saxatile Gold Dust	S	Y	Sp
Anchusa azurea Anchusa	M or T	B	Su
Aquilegia vulgaris Columbine	M	R P Y W B	Su
Aubrieta deltoidea Blue Rock	S	P B L	Sp
Campanula glomerata Globe campanula	S or M	B L	Su or Au
Delphinium elatum hybrid Delphinium or Perennial larkspur	M or T	W B	Su
Dianthus caryophyllus Border carnation	S or M	R P Y W	Su
Dianthus plumarius Pinks	S or M	R P W L	Su
Erigeron speciosus Fleabane	S or M	P B L	Su
Gaillardia aristata Blanket flower	M	R Y	Su to Au
Gladiolus hybrids Sword lily	M	R P Y W L	Su to Au
Kniphofia hybrids Red hot pokers	M or T	R Y W	Su
Lilium tigrinum Tiger lily	M or T	O	Su
Lupinus polyphyllus Lupin	M or T	R P Y W B L	Su
Lychnis coronaria Rose campion	M	P	Su
Primula vulgaris elatior Polyanthus	S	R P Y W B L	Sp

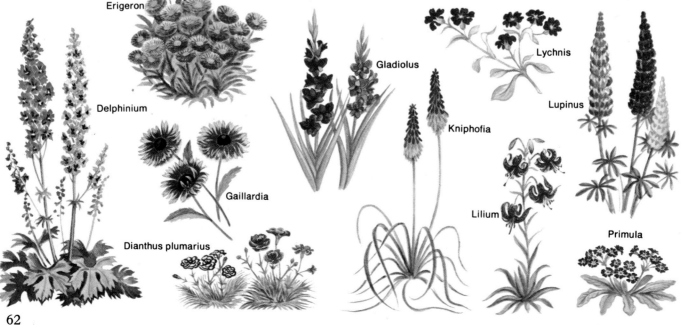

Maintenance of the flower garden

Weed control

Undisturbed weeds compete with garden plants for food and moisture and can be a source of pests and diseases. Among flowers, shrubs, fruit and vegetables, they can be prevented or controlled by cultivation or chemical means.

Cultivation is the most convenient method in the average garden. In summer, use the hoe regularly to chop off seedling weeds and leave them to wither in the sun. Do this job as early in the day as you can. In winter, dig in the weeds. Large weeds among flowers are best dug, cut off or pulled out, and the remaining small weeds hoed off or dug in as appropriate.

Chemical methods Use weed killer on paths or drives. Aminotriazole or simazine are suitable materials when used according to maker's instructions and are effective in most conditions.

Staking and tying

Flowers grown for display or cutting, such as dahlias or chrysanthemums, need to be staked and should be supported as unobtrusively as possible. Short pea sticks are useful and will be concealed by the supported plants. Push the sticks into the ground, and allow the flowers to grow between and above them. Large individual blooms for show purposes are best tied to separate canes. Support flowers which grow in clumps such as phlox, with a triangle of canes, using a loop of green twine to hold the stems. If you have an unobtrusive spot in which to grow flowers for cutting they can be held in place with horizontal nylon or wire mesh netting attached to posts. Young plants, especially those in pots, can be well supported by a split cane and tie or proprietary twist-grip.

1 and 2 twigs for plants to grow through; 3 and 4 horizontal netting; 5 large blooms supported by canes; 6 stopping; 7 and 8 deadheading; 9 thinning out surplus shoots; 10 disbudding.

Stopping and disbudding

Stopping means removing the growing point after four or six true leaves have formed. (The first 2 seedling leaves to appear do not count as 'true' leaves.) This causes the plant to make 'breaks' or shoots and to bear more blooms in a bushy rather than a tall form. Plants that respond well to this treatment include sweet peas, Brompton stocks, early-sown antirrhinums, chrysanthemums, dahlias, fuchsias and geraniums. Some varieties produce more shoots than can be supported and bloom to perfection, but by judicious thinning better quality, earlier flowers can be produced.

Disbudding Carnation, chrysanthemums, and dahlia blooms can be increased in size and quality by rubbing out the flower buds immediately below the terminal (or main) bloom bud.

Dead-heading

This term describes the cutting back of stems after they have flowered. The aim is to encourage another flush of flowers and improve appearance. Roses, delphinums, salvias, verbascums and bedding plants all benefit from dead-heading.

Step-by-step propagation

Division is carried out after flowering, and most plants which can be increased by this method are autumn flowering and therefore divided in spring, such as michaelmas daisies.

Layering is the method of increase for border carnations and is carried out in mid summer. Make a slit between joints and peg the cut portion into sandy soil. Once it has rooted, it can be cut from the parent plant.

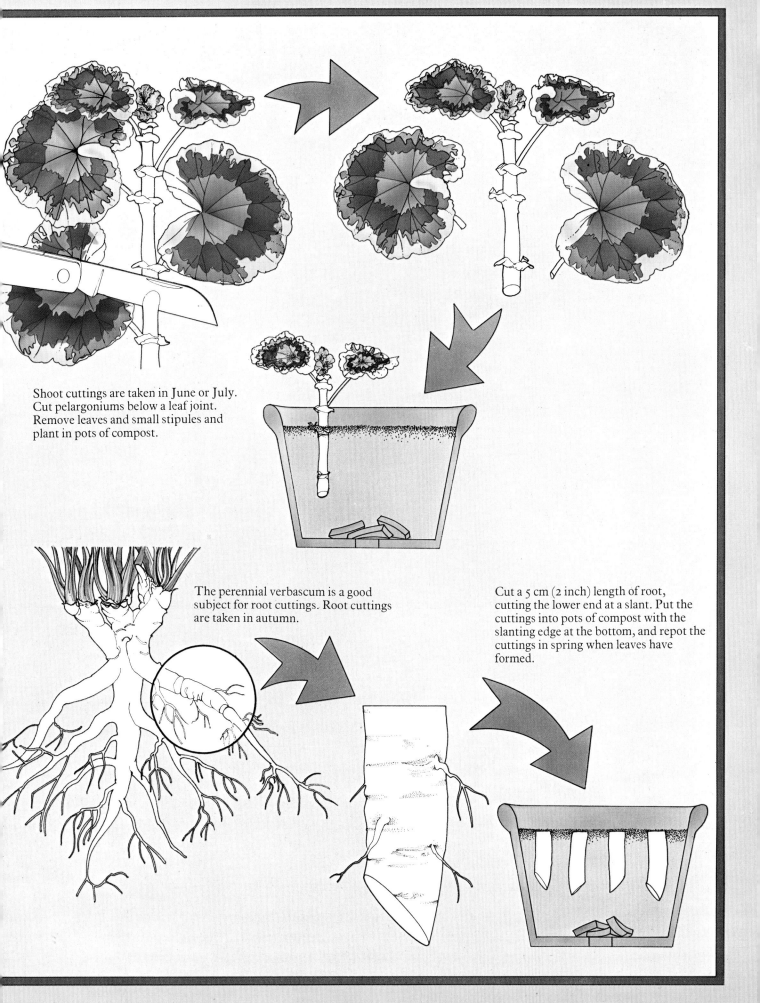

Shoot cuttings are taken in June or July. Cut pelargoniums below a leaf joint. Remove leaves and small stipules and plant in pots of compost.

The perennial verbascum is a good subject for root cuttings. Root cuttings are taken in autumn.

Cut a 5 cm (2 inch) length of root, cutting the lower end at a slant. Put the cuttings into pots of compost with the slanting edge at the bottom, and repot the cuttings in spring when leaves have formed.

Bulbs and corms

Bulbs and corms take their names from their form during the winter resting stage. These fattened or swollen parts of plants store plant food for the production of flowers and shoots until more favourable conditions return in spring. Bulbs and corms have a superficial resemblance to each other when viewed from the outside. However, if a bulb is cut cleanly in half from top to base, it will be seen to consist of layers of leaf scales. A corm cut in the same way reveals solid tissue. The significant difference from the growing viewpoint is that some bulbous plants (lilies, for example) can be increased by means of these leaf scales.

Tulips and daffodils are grown from bulbs; gladioli and crocus produce corms. Tubers occur in a number of forms, of which the two best known examples are the dahlia and the tuberous forms of begonia. Dahlias form a number of swollen finger-like roots radiating from the central stalk. With begonias, the tubers appear as flattened, rounded, hard tissue, slightly indented on one (mostly the upper) side. Tuberous plants are usually increased by means of cuttings (see the step-by-step guide to propagation).

Flowering season

There are very few weeks in the year when one or another member of this group is not in bloom and, aided by a cold frame and a window sill, they can provide year-round colour. Daffodils, hyacinths and tulips flower from December to May; begonias, gladioli and lilies continue the succession to late October, followed by crocus and cyclamen round to December again.

Colour and scent

The brilliant hues of this group include blues and pinks of hyacinths, reds and yellows of gladioli, and the peach,

ABOVE Underplanting of crocus.
ABOVE RIGHT A hyacinth bulb and a gladiolus corm. The cross-section of the bulb shows its leaf-scale formation.
RIGHT Daffodils make for easy spring gardening as they come up year after year.

Bulbs and Corms – species and colour

Note Catalogues of reliable suppliers are best consulted for named varieties because these change with great rapidity from season to season

Species or Kind	Common Name	Colours
Anemone appenina	Windflower	Blue, red, purple and white
Anemone De Caen hybrids	Single Poppy Anemone	Blue, red, purple and white
Anemone St Brigid hybrids	Double Poppy Anemone	Blue, red, purple and white
Anemone fulgens	Scarlet Windflower	Scarlet
Anemone hortensia	Garden Anemone	Blue, red, purple and white
Chionodoxa luciliae	Glory of the Snow	Blue and white
Colchicum autumnale	Autumn Crocus	Purple
Convallaria majalis	Lily of the Valley	White and pink
Crocosmia x crocosmii-flora	Montbretia	Orange-crimson
Crocus biflorus	Scotch crocus	Lavender
Crocus chrysanthus	Golden crocus	Orange-yellow
Crocus corms and hybrids	Dutch crocus	Lilac, violet, white and yellow
Cyclamen coum	Spring Sowbread	Red
Cyclamen neapolitanum	Autumn Sowbread	Pink and white
Eranthis hymalis	Winter Aconite	Yellow
Erythronium dens-canis	Dog's-tooth Violet	Rose
Fritillaria imperialis	Crown Imperial	Yellow
Fritillaria meleagris	Snake's head Fritillary	Chequered purple, yellow and white
Galanthus nivalis	Common Snowdrop	White
Gladiolus Dutch hybrids	Dutch or Garden Gladioli	Red, pink, yellow, white, scarlet
Gladiolus orimulinus	Small Sword Lily	Red, pink, yellow, white, scarlet
Hyacinthus orientalis	Hyacinth	Red, pink, blue, white and purple

Corms

Species or Kind	Common Name	Colours
Iris reticulata	Reticulate Iris	Violet, purple and yellow
Iris Xiphium hybrids	Dutch, English and Spanish Iris	Blue, yellow, purple and white
Leucojum aestivum	Summer Snowflake	White and green
Lilium regale	Regal Lily	White, yellow throat, pink reverse
Muscari armeniacum	Grape Hyacinth	Blue
Narcissus poeticus	Poet's Narcissus	White
Narcissus pseudo-narcissus	Trumpet Daffodil	Yellow and white
Narcissus triandrus	Angel's Tears	Yellow
Oxalis adenophylla	Pink Sorrel	Rose-pink
Scilla siberica	Siberian squill	Blue and white
Tigridia pavonia	Tiger Flower	Red, yellow, purple and white
Tulipa various	Tulips	Red, white, yellow, scarlet, pink, orange, purple and some black throated

BELOW *Crocosmia masonorum.*

Planting bulbs and corms

Spring bedding Daffodils, hyacinths and tulips can be planted in beds in autumn, together with plants such as wallflowers and forget-me-not, to provide spring colour. Lift and replant them in an out-of-the-way bed after flowering to make room for other bedding plants.

Summer bedding Tuberous begonias and gladioli can be used to transform ordinary flower beds into scenes more reminiscent of hotter climates. To achieve this they should be started into growth in March by being placed in shallow boxes containing a mixture of equal parts sand and peat in frost-free frames or similar protection. Transplant outdoors when a small shoot (about 12mm (½in)) has developed.

Note: Catalogues of reliable suppliers are the best source for named varieties as these change with great rapidity from season to season.

Borders The colour and interest of herbaceous shrub borders can be enhanced by the use of day lilies, various types of true lilies, iris and crocosmia.

Grass planting Drifts of bulbs and corms naturalized in grass look very striking, but are best suited to little-used areas. Autumn and spring crocus, daffodils, narcissi and snowdrops are excellent for this purpose. To plant, lift an area of turf and fork up the soil beneath. Work in some peat and bone-meal before planting the bulbs or corms and then replace the turf.

ABOVE *Eranthis tubergiana.*

crimson and orange shades of begonias. Jonquil, hyacinth and lilies are renowned for their scent.

Hardiness and ease of culture

Bulbs such as snowdrops, crocus, winter aconite and hyacinths are very hardy and provide a profusion of flowers when no other plants are in bloom.

With a minimum of care and attention crocus, daffodils, crocosmia and many lilies, once planted increase in number and strength, blooming year after year. Many bulbs and corms can be grown in confined spaces, such as town gardens and containers in places where it would be difficult or impossible to obtain colour from other kinds of plants.

Newly purchased bulbs and corms contain food reserves which have been built up over a number of years, and have the embryo flower already formed. They require a minimum of space, and adequate warmth, moisture and light for the flowers to emerge and open.

Bowls and pans Winter or spring-flowering bulbs can be placed in containers of bulb fibre during September or October to flower the following spring. Water the bulbs and place them in a cool dark cupboard or cellar, or cover them with a 10cm (4in) layer of peat in a shaded spot out of doors. Keep the container moist. Bring the bulbs indoors and into the light about 10-12 weeks after potting, when roots have formed and the shoots are developing.

Rock garden There are several varieties of spring-flowering anemones and also chionodoxa, colchicums, crocus, iris, muscari and narcissus which can be placed in pockets of soil to extend the flowering season.

o denotes suitability
x denotes unsuitability

Bulbs and Corms – Planting

Name	Tulipa	Tigridia	Scilla	Oxalis	Muscari	Lilium	Leucojum	Iris	Hyacinthus	Gladiolus	Galanthus	Fritillaria	Erythronium	Eranthis	Cyclamen	Crocus	Crocosmia	Convallaria	Colchicum	Chionodoxa	Anemone
Height (cm)	10-75	30-60	7-45	3-15	15-20	45-240	10-30	15-60	15-30	30-120	15-30	30-90	15	7-10	7-10	10	15-120	20	20-25	15	15-45
Planting depth (cm)	10	7	7-10	2-7	5-10	10-12	10	7	12	10	5	10-15	7	5	4	7	7	7	7	7	7
Spacing (cm)	15	12-15	7-10	10-20	2-5	15-30	7	7-15	15	15	2	15-20	5	5	7	5	5	7	7	2	15
Flowering Season	Win-Spr	Sum	Spr	Spr-Sum	Spr	Sum-Aut	Spr-Aut	Spr-Sum	Win-Spr	Sum-Aut	Win-Spr	Spr	Spr	Spr	Aut-Spr	Aut-Spr	Sum	Spr	Aut	Spr	Spr-Aut
Bedding use	o	o	o	x	o	o	x	o	o	o	x	x	x	x	x	o	x	x	o	o	x
Border use	o	o	o	o	o	o	o	o	o	o	o	o	o	o	o	o	o	o	o	o	o
Cut flower use	o	o	o	x	o	o	x	o	o	o	o	o	x	o	o	x	o	o	x	o	o
Naturalizing in grass	x	x	x	x	x	x	x	x	x	x	o	x	x	x	o	x	x	o	x	o	x
Growing in container	o	x	o	o	o	o	x	o	o	o	o	x	x	x	o	o	x	o	x	o	o
Container size Minimum pots (in)	5	–	3	5	3	8	–	5-7	4	7	3	–	–	–	5	4	–	5	–	3	5
Planting season	Aut-Spr	Spr	Sum-Aut	Aut-Spr	Sum-Aut	Sum-Aut	Sum-Aut	Sum-Aut	Aut	Spr	Aut	Aut	Sum	Aut-Win	Sum	Aut-Win	Spr	Aut	Sum	Sum	Aut-Spr
Rock garden use	o	x	o	x	o	o	x	o	o	o	x	o	o	o	o	o	x	o	o	o	o

Trees, shrubs and climbers

sensitive to smoke and grime. In built-up areas, the only scope for greenery in many gardens is upwards, and climbing plants provide welcome relief. This group includes not only the familiar ivy and Virginia creeper, but also clematis, jasmine, cotoneaster, and pyracantha, all useful for covering walls.

Tree forms:
ABOVE Columnar
BELOW Weeping
ABOVE RIGHT Pyramid
RIGHT Round
FAR RIGHT Compact upright

The skilful disposition of trees, shrubs and climbers forms the backbone of many outstanding garden designs. Trees and shrubs heighten flat sites and give scale and character to any planting scheme. The play of light and shade, the movement and rustle of leaves in the wind, or the reflection on still water can be turned to great advantage.

The opportunities for planting large trees and shrubs in the small or medium-sized garden, are necessarily restricted and it is important that the plants are carefully chosen and maintained. The town-dweller's choice is further limited by the fact that many conifers and evergreens are particularly

One or two trees, with some well-placed, wisely-chosen shrubs and a climber, can be the making of a labour-saving and easily-managed garden. To this basic framework the enthusiastic gardener can add as much or as little as time and inclination allow.

There are trees, shrubs and climbers for all purposes and situations, ranging in size from a few centimetres to tens of metres in height and breadth. They can be columnar, pyramidal, rounded, compact, or open and spreading.

The variety of small trees and shrubs permits a planting scheme that will be in scale with any setting. A flowering cherry or magnolia gives an annual display of colour for a modest outlay, and heathers and dwarf conifers provide year-round colour and interest in a rock garden.

In all but the most severe climates, it is not only possible but practical to provide year-round colour with trees, shrubs and climbers.

Trees

Your choice of tree is governed by the conditions prevailing on the intended site – climate, soil type, and aspect – and also the habit (growth characteristics) of the tree itself. A limited space requires a columnar shape, whereas a bushy tree will suit a larger area. Trees

take nourishment from the soil appropriate to their size, and inevitably provide heavy shade, so it is unlikely that any other substantial planting will thrive in their presence. Vegetable and fruit plots should certainly be well away from large trees.

Choice of trees

This seemingly simple question triggers off others. What colour of foliage or flowers do you prefer? At what time of the year do you want the tree to be at its best? Do you want it to provide shelter from the wind and sun? Is there a rock garden or pool that you want the tree to blend with? The illustrated table

on page 74 lists a variety of trees which will be appropriate to most situations and are not too demanding to grow. Having decided which tree you would like, buy it from a reputable nurseryman or garden centre.

The correct naming of plants often puzzles the beginner and it is very frustrating to find out too late that you have bought the wrong variety. Ornamental deciduous trees (those which shed their leaves each year) are usually bought at stages classified as standards, half standards, bush forms and 'whips' or maidens. *Standard trees* have a clear stem for about 1.8m (6ft) below the branches. *Half-standards* have about

1m (3ft 6in) clear stem. *Bush trees* have a short leg of about 60-75cm (2-2ft 6in) before the stem divides. *Whips* or *maidens* are single unbranched shoots, and are the cheapest to buy but take longer to mature and train.

Grading for quality

Instant or semi-mature trees are the largest and most expensive and give an immediate effect but they require considerable attention and the chance of survival is not high.

Heavy nursery stock trees have better developed root systems, stems, and head or branch framework than the standard or ordinary nursery stock,

which is the grade most commonly available. In the measurement of standard and half-standard trees, the diameter of the stem is taken 1m (3ft 4in) above ground level.

Stock plants for transplanting are commonly available in one of four presentations:

Bare root plants have been lifted and all the soil removed from in and around the roots. This obviously puts a severe strain on the subject as the vital fibrous (very fine) roots can dry out irrevocably. Roses and some shrubs seem to recover but it exposes trees to severe shock.

Balled plants are trees which have been lifted from their growing position with a ball of earth holding together in and around the roots. This is satisfactory for small plants such as whips.

Balled and wrapped trees are balled plants with secure wrapping round the root and earth ball. This is necessary if the young tree has to travel any distance between lifting and planting.

Container grown trees are, as the name implies, those grown in some form of receptacle. These trees can be moved and planted at any time of year without disturbance provided the ground is not frozen or waterlogged. Trees planted during summer require substantial watering. Container-grown trees are more expensive than others.

LEFT Flowering trees give character to both town and country gardens and provide a glorious show of colour in spring.
BELOW Broom and flowering crab apple in a small town garden.

Feeding trees

This topic is usually given scant attention, because it is argued that if trees grow well in the wild without being pampered, why should they need special care in gardens? However, the conditions which trees have to contend with in most gardens are far removed from those in the wild. Starvation is one of the more common causes of failure among established specimens.

Trees need nourishment if they are to flourish, and this can be considered in three stages.

Before planting It is much harder to improve and to feed soil after planting. A base dressing of bonemeal at 130g/m² (4oz per sq yd) worked into the bottom spit (spade's depth) of the planting hole, with a similar quantity of a good balanced fertilizer well mixed up in the top spit of soil, is adequate pre-planting preparation for most garden trees.

Routine feeding can be given as an annual mulch of organic matter (peat or manure) plus 65g to 130g/m² (2oz to 4oz per sq yd) of balanced fertilizer dressing in spring. Give the heavier dressing where peat or pulverized bark is used. If there is excessive shoot growth (more than 45cm (15 to 18ins) per year) at the expense of flowers, reduce the mulch by half, and in the case of dwarf conifers, to one quarter.

Rejuvenation Starvation is a major cause of debility in old trees, but those making little or no growth can often be induced to make new shoots. Remove the turf covering the roots. Lightly fork the ground from the trunk to just beyond the drip line (tips of the longest branches) and apply a 7.5cm (3in) layer of fresh soil and rotted manure. Gently fork a top dressing of balanced fertilizer into the soil and manure mixture at the rate of 65g/m² (2oz per sq yd). This mulch is best carried out in the spring.

Pruning

The object of pruning is to create a shapely, balanced framework of branches that will admit adequate light and air evenly in young trees and subsequently to keep trees the desired size and shape; to regulate growth and check and prevent pests and diseases; and to rejuvenate old trees.

The principles of pruning can be expressed quite simply: prune hard for vigorous growth; prune lightly to encourage flowering and fruitfulness. If growth is excessive and lush through generous feeding, prune lightly. Poor growth resulting from under-feeding requires hard pruning to promote vigour.

Pruning in practice Buy trees with a basic framework of branches from a reliable supplier, and in most cases subsequent pruning will be only minimal.

If you prefer to establish the basic framework yourself you should buy a whip or maiden. In the first autumn, cut the stem of whips or maidens slightly higher than the point at which you want branches to form; cut or rub out any growths lower down. In the second year, three or more shoots should have formed; shorten these to one-quarter or one-third of their length. In the third year, if growth is only moderate, prune the branches again, this time to one-third their

length. For a pyramidal shape, allow a central leader (or shoot) to develop, and shorten or summer-prune any side-shoots.

Each autumn, remove inward-growing branches and shorten crossing branches which touch one another. Cut back dead or broken shoots to healthy wood. Trim trees to the desired shape and thin out any thickets of shoots as necessary.

Conifers need only the occasional trimming to shape. However, those which are to be transplanted should be root-pruned in the spring before the move. This is done by cutting the outside roots with a spade to encourage a ball of fibrous roots to develop. The distance of cut is a circle 15cm (6in) beyond the outmost shoots or drip line. The moving of large conifers about 1.5-2m (5ft-6ft) is best left to professionals.

Any cut over 2.5cm (1in) diameter must be painted either with lead-based paints or a proprietary plant-wound sealer.

The lopping of large tree branches is best carried out in autumn. Before starting, check to see that the branch will fall somewhere safely. First a cut is made on the underside, followed by a matching cut on the upper surface to avoid splitting the branches.

ABOVE LEFT Crown raising (left) – remove lower branches to show off bark or when underplanting. Crown thinning (right) – remove some branches to promote flowering.
ABOVE Root pruning a dwarf conifer.
LEFT *Malus floribunda elwesii*.
RIGHT Flowering trees and shrubs, contrasted with a columnar conifer.

Trees for small gardens

Key	
	A = Acid
	N = Neutral
	C = Chalk
	T = Suitable for town use
	E = Evergreen
	S = Coast suitability
	All measurements are average and approximate at ultimate size

Name	Soil	Site	Size m ht × wth	Size ft ht × wth	Season and nature of interest
Acer palmatum Japanese Maple	Moist A N	T Sheltered	4·5 × 3·6	15 × 12	Spring to autumn Colourful foliage
Betula pendula Silver Birch	A N	T Open or shade	15·0 × 6·0	50 × 20	All year Graceful leaves and branches
Cercis siliquastrum Judas Tree	A N C	T Sun	7·5 × 4·5	25 × 15	Spring pink flowers Summer purplish seed pods
Crataegus coccinea plena Double Crimson Thorn	N C	T Sun, open	6·0 × 4·5	20 × 15	Spring crimson flowers
Laburnum vossii Laburnum	A N C	T Sun	6·0 × 4·5	20 × 15	Spring and early summer yellow flowers
Magnolia soulangeana alba Magnolia	A N Moist	Sun	6·0 × 4·5	20 × 15	Spring striking white flowers
Malus tschonoskii Flowering Crab Apple	N C Rich	T Sun	6·0 × 3·6	20 × 12	Spring pinkish white flowers. Autumn scarlet and yellow fruits
Populus alba Abele or White Poplar	N	S Sun open	15·0 × 7·5	50 × 25	Summer and autumn White undersides of leaves
Prunus cerasifera nigra Black-leaf Plum	N C	T Sun	6·0 × 4·5	20 × 15	Spring, pink flowers Summer and autumn dark leaves

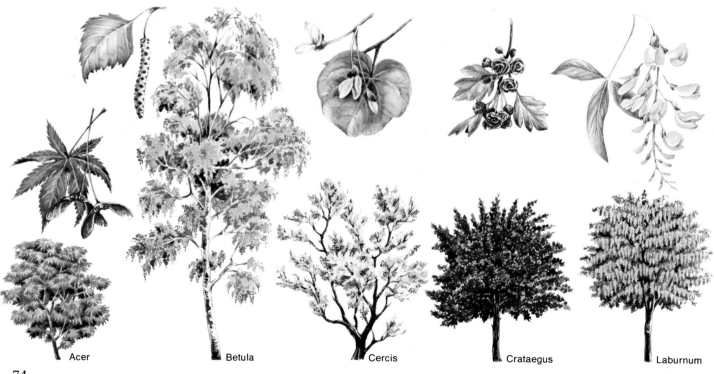

Acer   Betula   Cercis   Crataegus   Laburnum

Name		Soil	Site	Size m ht × wth	Size ft ht × wth	Season and nature of interest
Prunus serrulata purpurascens Japanese cherry Kanzan		N C	T Sun	7·5 × 5·4	25 × 18	Spring, masses of pink flowers
Pyrus salicifolia pendula Willow-leaved Pear		N C	Sun	6·0 × 6·0	20 × 20	Spring, white flowers Summer and autumn, grey-white leaves
Rhus typhina Stags Horn Sumach		N	Sun	6·0 × 4·5	20 × 15	Summer, large green leaves autumn leaf tints and brown fruits
Robinia pseudoacacia bessoniana False Acacia		A N C	Open T	15·0 × 6·0	50 × 20	Summer, whitish flowers delicate foliage
Sorbus aria Whitebeam		N C	Open T	9·0 × 7·5	30 × 25	Autumn red berries White underside to leaves
Sorbus aucuparia Rowan or Mountain Ash		A N Light Sandy	Sun Open T	6·0 × 4·5	20 × 15	Autumn clusters of red berries
Chamaecyparis lawsoniana pottenii Lawsons Cypress	E	N	Open	12·0 × 3·0	40 × 10	All year round blue green foliage
Cupressocyparis leylandii Leyland Cypress	E	A N C	Open Sun	12·0 × 3·6	40 × 12	All year round green finely divided foliage
Juniperus chinensis The Chinese Juniper	E	N C	Open Sunny	6·0 × 1·2	20 × 4	All year round green foliage
Juniperus communis The Common Juniper	E	N C	Sun	7·5 × 3·0	25 × 10	Year round grey green foliage
Pinus mugo Gnom Mountain Pine	E	A N C Light loam	Open Sun	0·75 × 0·75	$2\frac{1}{2} \times 2\frac{1}{2}$	All year green foliage
Thuya occidentalis holmstrupensis American Arbor-vitae	E	A N C	Sheltered Sun	3·0 × 1·5	10 × 5	Attractive bright green foliage all year round

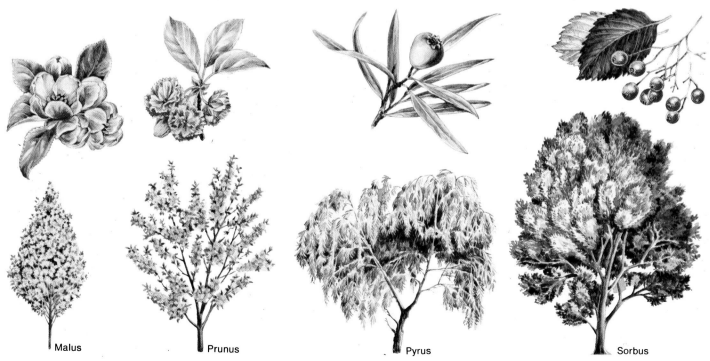

Malus   Prunus   Pyrus   Sorbus

Step-by-step planting a tree

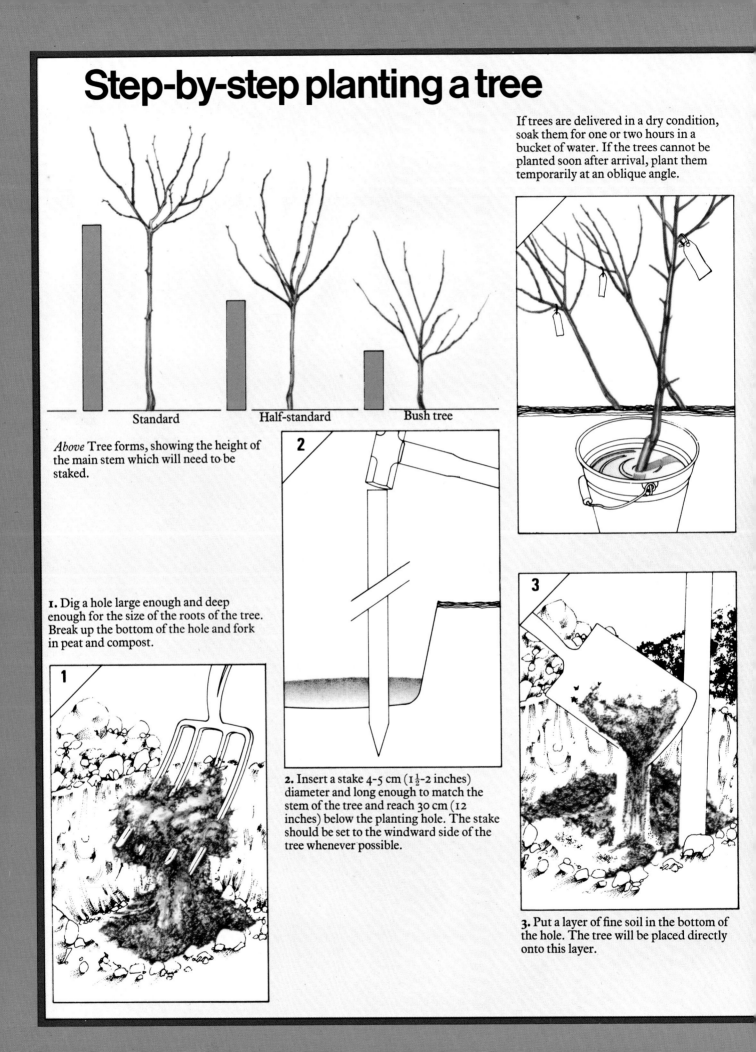

If trees are delivered in a dry condition, soak them for one or two hours in a bucket of water. If the trees cannot be planted soon after arrival, plant them temporarily at an oblique angle.

Standard   Half-standard   Bush tree

Above Tree forms, showing the height of the main stem which will need to be staked.

1. Dig a hole large enough and deep enough for the size of the roots of the tree. Break up the bottom of the hole and fork in peat and compost.

2. Insert a stake 4–5 cm (1½–2 inches) diameter and long enough to match the stem of the tree and reach 30 cm (12 inches) below the planting hole. The stake should be set to the windward side of the tree whenever possible.

3. Put a layer of fine soil in the bottom of the hole. The tree will be placed directly onto this layer.

3a. The tree is placed on a layer of fine soil so that the soil mark on the stem aligns with the level of the surrounding ground. The soil dug from the hole is firmed around the roots as the hole is refilled.

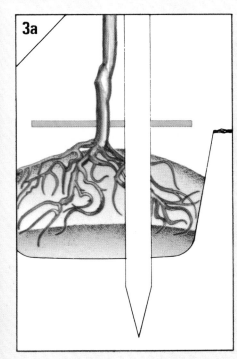

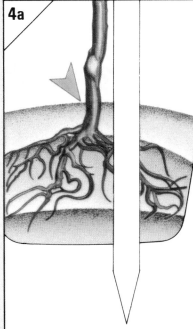

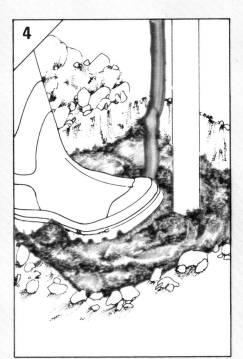

4a. Fill the remainder of the hole with topsoil, rounded above the soil mark. The soil will soon pack down to the surrounding ground level.

5. Fasten the tree to the stake with a tree tie and spacer and then prune back the branches to encourage vigorous growth.

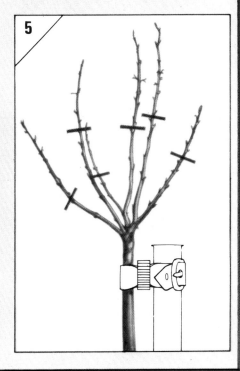

4. Firm the soil around the roots with your feet as you fill in the hole until the roots are covered.

Shrubs, hedging plants and climbers

Shrubs, hedges and climbers also occupy the ground for a long time, so good soil preparation is necessary. Before planting you should provide adequate land drainage, dig over the planting spot, apply manure and fertilizer, establish a minimum depth (30cm (12in)) of weed-free soil, break up the sub-soil and check the soil acidity (pH) adding lime if necessary.

Select species which are suited to your district and soil, healthy, and of a manageable size, and varieties that will provide colour and interest at a suitable season. As with trees, wrapped-and-balled, container or pot-grown plants will suffer a minimum of check to growth. Hedging plants sold with bare roots can, however, soon become established. Suitable subjects are thorn and hornbeam, both of which will provide inexpensive functional barriers.

Planting season
Conifers and evergreens are best moved in September-October or April-May unless pot or container-grown, in which case planting can take place at any time, as long as the soil is not frozen or waterlogged. Deciduous plants can be safely set out between October and March, or at any time with containerized subjects, again in land that is not frozen or too wet.

Marking out and spacing
To save time and effort mark out plant positions with short sticks for indicators before digging out any holes. Spacing will vary according to the vigour of the variety and the method of planting. When plants of the same kind are grouped together, distances can be reduced to allow the branches of one plant to intertwine with another.

Measurements for individual shrubs, hedging plants and climbers are given in the illustrated tables below.

Planting
Wait for ground conditions to improve if the land is frozen or waterlogged. Plants which have dried out in transit should be stood in water for several hours before planting. Dig a hole wide and deep enough to take the spread-out roots. Place a moist peat layer 2.5cm (1in) deep in the base of the hole and fork this in. Position the plant, spread out the roots and cover them with fine soil, working this between the roots,

and firm the earth. The finished level of the soil surface should correspond to its nursery position and will be seen by the soil mark on the stem. Unless the land is very moist, water the plants to settle the surrounding soil.

With the possible exception of pot or container-grown subjects, plants which are moved invariably lose some roots. In order to restore the balance between root and shoot, some pruning is needed. With deciduous subjects shorten new growth by one half, but only trim conifers and evergreens lightly.

Some form of protection, especially with evergreen subjects, is helpful to plants placed in exposed situations. Choice conifers can be sheltered on the windward side with hessian or sacking supported on light posts. Chestnut paling secured to posts will shield hedges until they become established.

ABOVE Providing shelter for a conifer with a hessian windbreak.

Mulching In the spring following planting, a 5cm (2in) layer of compost or peat spread on the ground around the plants to cover the root area will reduce moisture loss. Water as necessary in a hot dry season, with a good soaking rather than frequent dribblings. Further mulching is advisable in subsequent years and it will also help to smother weed growth.

Feeding An application of 65g to 130g/m² (2oz to 4oz per sq yd) of a good balanced fertilizer can be given at the

same time as mulching in the second and later years, unless growth is too vigorous.

Pruning shrubs
For pruning purposes, there are four main groups of shrubs, each needing different treatment.

Slow growing deciduous shrubs require little or no regular pruning, and are best left alone except for the occasional cutting back of untidy, weak or dead shoots. Examples include *Daphne mezereum*, (mezereon), *Hibiscus syriacus*, azaleas and lilacs.

ABOVE Part-pruned forsythia. Cut back the stems which have flowered to new growth.

Evergreen and coniferous shrubs require no pruning, but need an occasional trim to keep them neat and compact.

Spring and summer-flowering subjects which bloom on the previous season's growth should be pruned as soon as the flowers fall. Deutzias, forsythias, kerrias, philadelphus (mock orange) and weigelas are best treated in this way.

Cut the flowered stems back to new growth or plump buds.

Summer and autumn-flowering shrubs which carry their flowers on the current season's growth, usually during late summer and autumn, should be pruned during winter or spring by cutting out old flowered shoots annually. Where shrubs have reached the desired size and spread, cut the new growth back to within a bud or two of the older wood. Where a shrub is required to grow larger remove only half the length of new growth to build up a larger framework of shoot-bearing wood. Subjects pruned in this manner include: *Buddleia davidii*, fuchsias, hypericums and *Tamarix pentandra*.

Any plant with damaged, diseased or dead branches should be cut back to firm healthy wood or growth.

RIGHT Broom flowers on the previous season's growth. To prune, cut back flowered stems to new growth as soon as the flowers fall.

ABOVE Part-pruned tamarisk. Cut back hard in winter or spring.

Trimming hedges
Trim hedges early in life at the sides and top to encourage thick, bushy growth at the base. Clip hedges so that they narrow towards the top, never the reverse, to admit more light to the lower areas and prevent them becoming bare. There will also be less opportunity for snow to lodge on the hedge top and force the branches outwards, spoiling the shape. Cut rapid-growing subjects like privet and *Lonicera nitida* two or three times a year to keep them tidy. Cut beech and hornbeam in July.

Formal hedges of regular outline such as yew, box or *Lonicera* need cutting each time they make 15 to 20cm (6 to 8in) of growth. This promotes branching and makes a denser hedge.

Cut informal hedges of *Berberis stenophylla* and escallonia less frequently during the formative stage, lightly topping them at each 30cm (12in) increase in height to thicken them out. Thereafter an occasional clipping will keep them in shape.

Once any type of hedge has reached the desired size it will need only an occasional trim to prevent it getting out of hand.

Training climbers
The principles of shrub pruning also apply to climbing plants. These vary in their methods of support: twiners like clematis hang by tendrils, as do some vines; others, like ivy, cling with aerial roots, and virginia creeper (*Parthenocissus*) with small suction pads.

The two latter types of climber can be damaging to brickwork, unless kept severely under control. Most climbers are best trained against a lattice frame fixed to a wall, with a 5cm (2in) gap separating wall and frame. Wood or wire mesh lattice frames are cheaper than the cost of renovating stone or brick walls.

ABOVE Training a climber against a lattice frame.

Propagation
One of the easiest methods of increase is from seeds, but the range of good woody plants raised this way is limited as most shrubs, hedging plants and climbers are named varieties which do not come true from seed. Division, layers and cuttings are the methods generally used.

Some shrubs, such as some of the cotoneasters, plain-leaved hollies, and thorn used for hedging, can be raised from seed quite successfully, although they require a good deal of patience.

79

Raising shrubs from seed Shrub seeds usually ripen in autumn. They can be stored but are best sown straight away. Many kinds of woody plants do not germinate immediately they are sown, and need to be subjected to frost or cold to break their dormancy. This can be done by stratification: place freshly collected seed mixed with a small quantity of sand in pots or seed pans which have peat in the bottom, to prevent the mixture coming out at the base. Put the containers outside, sink them to the rims in sand and cover them with fine mesh netting to keep out birds and vermin, leaving the seeds to the action of frost and snow.

In spring, sow the seeds and sand in prepared pots or seedpans. Seeds of shrubs such as brooms and hypericum can be bought and sown without stratification.

The method of preparing seed containers and subsequent treatment is described in the section on flowers (see step-by-step guide to propagation) and also applies to stratified seed. Prick out the seedlings into containers of potting compost as soon as they are big enough to handle.

BELOW *Clematis jackmanii.* The best method for increasing clematis is by half-ripe cuttings.

Division is a good method for beginners to increase plants, and is suitable for shrubs like kerria or euonymus, berberis, erica and spiraea.

Division is usually carried out in autumn or spring and consists of lifting the plant, teasing away and cutting off a rooted piece, which is replanted in prepared ground.

Layering is another easy method of multiplying plants and can also be used with success on many of the more difficult subjects such as quince.

The main requirement is that one or more branches can be pulled down to ground level. Select a healthy branch and make a slanting incision halfway through the stem. Peg this into prepared earth about 5cm (2in) deep at the cut area, and tie the tip in an upward position to a stick or cane. Lift the buried section when it has formed roots, about a year later; separate it from the parent plant, and replant. Rhododendrons, *chaenomeles* (Japanese quince) and many others can be raised in this way.

ABOVE LEFT Division of Aster.
LEFT Layering. The branch can be held down with a peg or a stone.

Cuttings Of the many ways of taking cuttings, four straightforward types will serve to increase the majority of garden shrubs and climbers.
Half-ripe cuttings consist of firm non-flowering new shoots, taken in summer and cut just below a leaf joint. The length of cutting varies from about 2.5cm (1in) in the case of heathers, to 10–15cm (4–6in) with buddleias.

Remove the lower leaves to half the length of the cutting. Dip the cut end in hormone rooting powder, insert the cutting to one third its length at the edge of a pot filled with cutting compost and firm it. Water and cover with a polythene bag and place in the shade or in a propagator. If a quantity of cuttings are needed, a garden frame can be used with a 7.5cm (3in) layer of cutting compost, well firmed, levelled and watered. 10cm (4in) pots can take four to six cuttings: cover the drainage holes with clean crock or gravel; fill the pot with cutting compost; firm with a presser to leave the surface 1cm ($\frac{1}{2}$in) below the rim of the pot for watering and finally dust the surface with sharp sand.

Hardwood cuttings can be taken in two ways: with a heel – a portion of stem attached – or as node cuttings which are cut just below a leaf joint or scar. Take 25 to 35cm (10 to 14in) lengths of firm new growth in autumn, removing any remaining leaves on deciduous subjects. Cut cleanly below a leaf scar, or trim the heel; and cut the top end above a bud to leave the finished cutting about 20 to 30cm (8 to 12in) long.

In a sheltered spot make a narrow trench about 15cm (6in) deep and 5cm (2in) wide. Fill this with sandy cutting compost and insert the cuttings about 15cm (6in) deep and about 10cm (4in) apart. Tread the soil down to press it against the cuttings. Never let cuttings dry out. They can usually be transplanted a year from the time they were taken. Forsythia, weigela and escallonias are raised successfully from hardwood cuttings.

Root cuttings A few fickle subjects such as *Rhus typhina* (the stag's horn sumach) and *Daphne genkwa* can be raised from root cuttings, usually taken in winter or spring. Root cuttings from shrubs are taken in the same way as for flowering plants, see page 65.

BELOW LEFT AND RIGHT Taking heel cuttings.

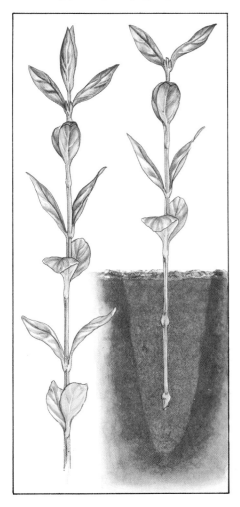

LEFT Taking a node cutting.

ABOVE Shrubs and climbers in a small garden.
Ceanothus (blue flowers), *Eccremocarpus* (orange flowers) and *Philadelphus* (white flowers).

81

Colourful Shrubs

Name	Soil	Site	Size m ht × wth	Size ft ht × wth	Season and nature of interest
Azalea Swamp Pink	Moist A	Light shade	wide range		Spring and summer, flowers colours various including scarlets, reds and flame
Berberis thunbergii Barberry	A N C	Sun	1·2 × 0·9	4 × 3	Spring, yellow flowers, summer and autumn red berries Flame, red and yellow foliage
Buddleia davidii Butterfly Flower	A N C	Sun Open	3·0 × 2·4	10 × 8	Summer and autumn, flowers shades of purple, mauve, pink and wine
Calluna vulgaris Ling or Heather	A N	Open Full sun	0·6 × 0·6	2 × 2	All year foliage, golds, greys, greens and rusts. Summer and autumn flowers, shades pink, purple, wine, white, lavender
Camellia williamsii Donation Camellia	A N	West facing sheltered	3·0 × 2·4	10 × 8	All year gloss green foliage spring, pale pink semi-double flowers
Caryopteris clandonensis Blue Spiraea	A N C	Sun	0·9 × 0·6	3 × 2	Summer and autumn, lavender blue flowers
Cornus alba sibirica Red-barked Dogwood	Moist A N C	Sun light shade	2·4 × 1·8	8 × 6	Autumn and winter, red coloured young shoots
Cytisus scoparius Broom	N	Open sun	1·8 × 1·2	6 × 4	Spring and early summer gold, cream, buff, yellow and reddish flowers
Daphne mezereum Mezereon	A N C	Light shade sun	1·2 × 0·6	4 × 2	Winter, early spring, fragrant, pink, mauve and white flowers
Deutzia scabra Deutzia or snowflower	A N C	Open sunny	2·4 × 1·5	8 × 5	Summer, white or white-tinged purple flowers
Erica carnea Heaths	A N C	Open sun	0·3 × 0·3	1 × 1	Year round foliage-various. Winter and spring flowers, pink, carmine, white and wine
Fuchsia magellanica Lady's Ear-drops	A N C	Light shade or sun	1·5 × 0·9	5 × 3	Summer and autumn flowers, purple and scarlet
Hibiscus syriacus Tree Hollyhock or Shrubby Mallow	A N C	Open sun	2·4 × 1·5	8 × 5	Summer and autumn flowers, blue, maroon, pink rose-purple and white
Hydrangea macrophylla Hydrangea	A N C	Sun	1·8 × 1·2	6 × 4	Summer and autumn flowers, pink, red, carmine, white and blue
Hypericum patulum St Johns Wort	A N C	Light shade or sun	0·9 × 0·9	3 × 3	Summer and autumn Golden-yellow flowers
Philadelphus hybridus Mock Orange	A N C	Sun Open	1·8 × 1·2	6 × 4	Summer, white, cream or whitish flowers

Key

1	Azalea	9	Hypericum
2	Buddleia	10	Caryopteris
3	Camellia	11	Lonicera
4	Hibiscus	12	Erica
5	Hydrangea	13	Cotoneaster
6	Clematis	14	Wistaria
7	Fuchsia	15	Chaenomeles
8	Spiraea	16	Pyracantha

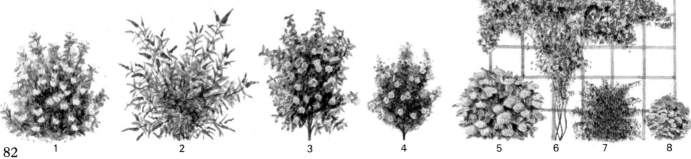

1   2   3   4   5   6   7   8

Name	Soil	Site	Size m ht × wth	Size ft ht × wth	Season and nature of interest
Potentilla fruiticosa Shrubby Cinquefoil	A N C	Sun	1·2 × 0·9	4 × 3	Summer and autumn flowers, yellow and orange shades
Rhododendron hybrids Flame Flower	A	West aspect light shade	Various	Various	Year round foliage, winter spring and summer flowers pink, flame, scarlet, purple
Spiraea bumalda Garden Meadowsweet	A N C	Sun or light shade	0·9 × 0·2	3 × 2	Summer flowers, pink
Syringa vulgaris Lilac	A N C	Open sun	3·0 × 2·1	10 × 7	Summer, fragrant flowers, white, pink, violet, crimson, purple, lilac
Viburnum tinus Portugal Laurel or Laurustinus	A N C	Sun Light shade sheltered	3·0 × 1·8	10 × 6	All year foliage, winter and spring flowers, pinkish buds scented white flowers
Weigela florida Diervilla	A N C	Open sunny	2·4 × 1·8	10 × 6	Spring and summer flowers, creamy white, pink and crimson shades

Key   A = Acid
N = Neutral
C = Chalk

Climbers

Name	Soil	Site	Size m ht × wth	Size ft ht × wth	Season and nature of interest
Chaenomeles speciosa Japonica	A N C	Sunny Southern aspect Sheltered	2·4 × 1·8	8 × 6	Spring flowers, shades of pink, red and scarlet
Clematis 'Laserstern' and 'Nelly Moser' Clematis large-flowered hybrids	N C	Sunny South or West aspect	Various	Various	Summer and autumn flowers, tones of pink, purple, red, carmine, white and violet
Cotoneaster horizontalis Herring-bone Cotoneaster	A N C	Sun or shade Open	1·8 × 1·8	6 × 6	Summer flowers, pink Autumn and winter red berries
Lonicera caprifolium Honeysuckle	A N C	Sun or light shade	4·5 × indefinite	15 × indefinite	Summer, creamy white or pinkish scented flowers
Pyracantha atalantioides Firethorn	A N C	Sun or shade	4·5 × 3·0	15 × 10	Summer flowers, white. Autumn berries red or yellow
Wistaria sinensis Wistaria	A N C	Sun. South aspect Sheltered	indefinite	indefinite	Summer flowers, scented, mauve or white

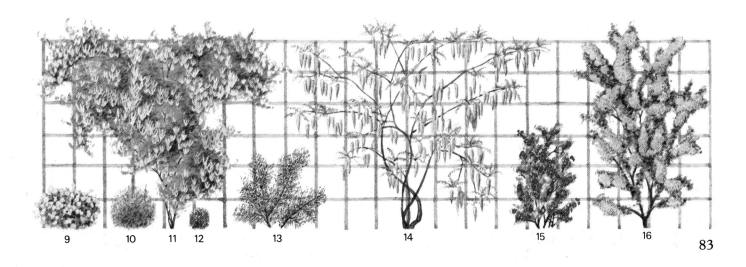

9   10   11 12   13   14   15   16

Roses

The uses and range of rose species and varieties are very wide. Roses are popular in formal beds, and for less-regimented planting, in borders or shrub beds. Climbing and rambling species can be used to disguise hard walls, to screen undesirable views, to cover pergolas and to scent the air. Roses can be used in rock gardens to cover the ground with colour, or to climb through trees. They are good for cutting and floral arrangements. Such diversity of function and such a wealth of species in the rose family provide a bewildering choice.

Varieties of roses:
1 Shrub rose
2 Miniature rose
3 Hybrid tea
4 Floribunda
5 Climbing rose

Classification of roses

A full classification of roses would be very complex but the five simple groupings given here can help selection from rose-growers' catalogues.

Shrub roses include many types, most of which flower less profusely than the hybrid teas and floribundas. The blooms are usually single or semi-double, and are attractive not only for their flowers, but also for the hips, or seed cases. These roses are mostly used in shrub borders, hedging and informal situations.

Miniatures These diminutive roses can be used in rock gardens, pots and even window boxes. They grow to a height of about 22 to 37cm (9 to 15in) and have double or semi-double flowers, ranging in size from about 1 to 4cm ($\frac{1}{2}$ to $1\frac{1}{2}$in) across.

Hybrid tea roses are the most popular for the majority of purposes and include those with large, well-formed fully double flowers having one main flower per stem. These are found in most colours, are highly fragrant, and are excellent as cut flowers for floral arrangements. Members of this group bloom more or less continuously in summer.

Floribunda roses are of more recent origin than hybrid teas and of a rather more vigorous habit than the former. They carry clusters of flowers, double, semi-double and single and are very popular.

Climbers and ramblers are invaluable for providing necessary cover. Climbers have a permanent framework from which side shoots develop, while ramblers have their main growth from the base of the plant. Ramblers have only one annual flowering period. Flower shape and form can be of the hybrid tea, floribunda, or shrub type. There are climbing forms of just about every kind of garden rose.

Acquiring roses

It is a good idea for the new grower to look at the catalogues of two or three leading rose-growers and select varieties common to each. If two or three producers sell the same variety, it is likely to be reliable. A collection of good, named varieties can be obtained from top growers early in the planting season, as these are unlikely to be available in end-of-season clearance offers. To get the best quality it is necessary to go to the actual grower.

Budded or grafted plants provide better rootstock. Some rootstocks produce many suckers which are undesirable shoots of the root variety and they should be removed with secateurs. The fault often lies not in the rootstock itself but in its preparation in the nursery.

Form Roses can be obtained in various shapes and sizes according to their purpose. Standards have a bushy head on a tall stem of 1.2m (4ft), the crown of which may be upright or weeping in habit. Half-standards are similar to the above, but have a shorter leg with about 75cm (2ft 6in) of clear stem.

The other forms are the bush and climbing roses.

Pest and disease resistance Where possible, it is helpful to see the varieties of your choice actually growing, and note if they suffer from blackspot or mildew, as both diseases can be difficult to control in bad years. The former occurs as dark spots on the leaves, the latter as a white powdery covering on leaves and flower buds.

The Care of Roses

Firming and mulching In the spring following planting and subsequent springs, firm the soil round the roots if winter winds and frost have loosened them. Lightly prick up the soil between plants with a fork after pruning the roses, removing any weeds as you go.

In well-prepared soil feeding will not be necessary until the second year, when 100g/m² (3oz per sq yd) of a high potash balanced fertilizer should be applied before lightly forking the soil. After feeding, spread a 2.5 to 5cm (1 to 2in) thick covering of compost, peat or similar mulch around the plants, to conserve moisture in summer and smother seedling weeds. This improves the soil and produces better flowers as a result.

Cultivation and weed control If the soil has been mulched all over, little cultivation will be required until autumn when a light forking-over should be given. Remove any weed growth. Keep the hoe moving to kill weeds and create a dust mulch where there is no mulch cover. Water occasionally during any prolonged drought after planting. Climbers and ramblers need tying in as they grow, which requires regular attention during the growing season, as plants can be loosened and damaged in strong winds.

ABOVE Dead-heading roses.

Disbudding and dead-heading The practice of disbudding is used mainly for exhibition blooms. Where large single blooms are required, one flower bud on a stem is selected and the remainder removed. If a cluster of flowers is required, the central bud only is removed, causing a number of flowers to open simultaneously.

Dead-heading involves the removal of old flower heads and should be done as soon as blooming finishes. Where hips are required, as in the case of shrub roses, dead-heading is not carried out. Cut back the old flower head and half the length of the flower stem to a good bud or leaf and reduce this to one quarter as the season progresses. In flower clusters, the dead heads only are removed, until all the flowers in a group have finished blooming. The cluster is then cut out in its entirety. Cut back dead or seriously diseased stems and shoots to healthy tissue.

Carry out routine measures of pest and disease control, especially at the first sign of trouble. Insecticide and fungicide sprays are usually needed for aphids, blackspot and mildew.

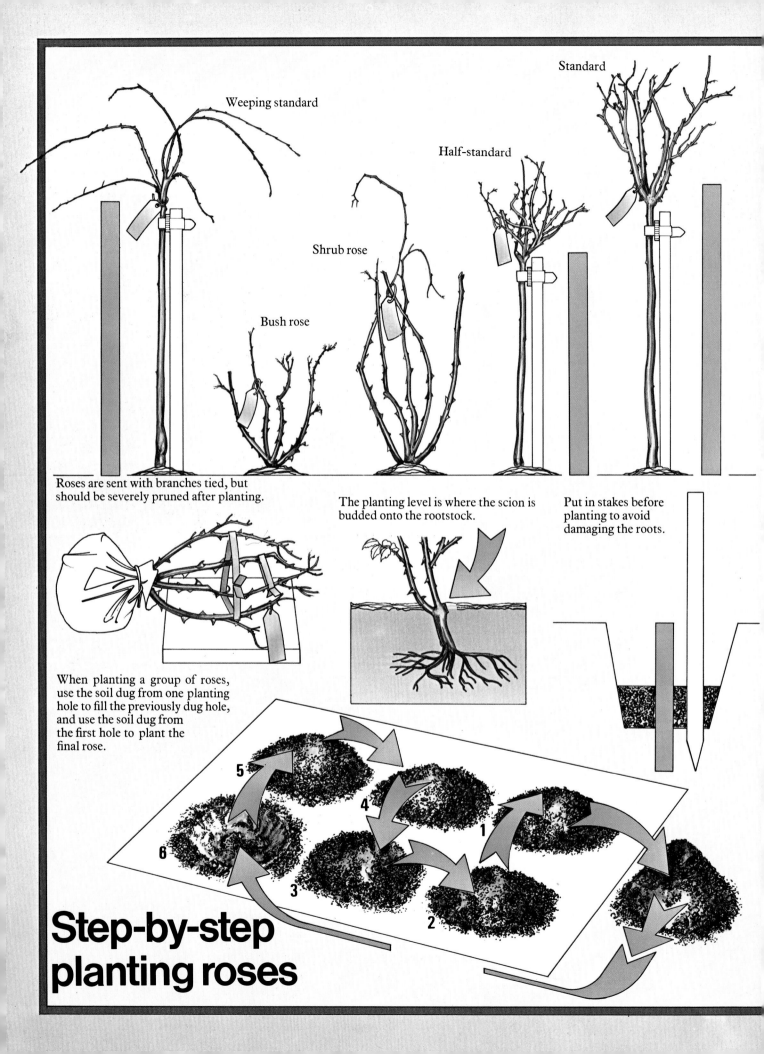

Weeping standard

Standard

Half-standard

Shrub rose

Bush rose

Roses are sent with branches tied, but should be severely pruned after planting.

The planting level is where the scion is budded onto the rootstock.

Put in stakes before planting to avoid damaging the roots.

When planting a group of roses, use the soil dug from one planting hole to fill the previously dug hole, and use the soil dug from the first hole to plant the final rose.

5

6

4

3

2

1

Step-by-step planting roses

Cut back a hybrid tea bush rose to 2 to 3 buds on the old wood (10 cm or 4 inches off the ground) each spring.

Always prune roses back near an outward facing bud. Dead-heading should be carried out after flowering but the main pruning takes place in March or early April.

A standard or half-standard hybrid tea should be treated in the same way as the hybrid tea bush rose.

Cut back a floribunda bush rose to 5 or 6 buds on the old wood.

Prune climbing roses by cutting back some side shoots to 6 or 7 buds, and others to 2 or 3 buds, leaving the main stems unpruned.

Leave a framework of a few growths on weeping roses.

Vegetable growing

The tending of a skilfully managed vegetable garden contributes to the household economy and is a source of satisfying exercise.

Basic requirements for vegetables

Essential tools for the average plot are fully described in chapter 3. They should include a spade, fork, rake, hoe, trowel, a measuring stick and garden line. A medium-sized plot for three people requires an average of 3-4 hours weekly work. This will however depend on many factors: the size of the plot, the kind of crops grown, the type of soil and the method of cultivation.

Poor feeding and general neglect of the soil will be reflected in the performance of the vegetables. Keep vegetables sufficiently warm, well-fed and watered and carry out tasks as they arise. Follow the rules and reap the results.

Cost

The cost of seeds, manures, fertilizers, tools, pesticides and weedkillers varies widely. Compare prices before making purchases and you will avoid much needless expenditure. Savings can also be made on purchases of manures, sundries and seeds by several gardeners joining together to buy in bulk.

Once your land is in full production, keep the weeds down. Good husbandry and crop rotation reduce bills for weed-killers and pesticides to a minimum. Crop failure is due as much to the ravages of pests and diseases as any other cause.

Size of site needed

This is determined by the number of people there are to feed, their tastes, and whether the aim is to meet all or only part of those requirements from the garden. The following table gives a guide to the approximate area required to feed three people.

Crop		Row length (m)	Row width (cm)
Group A (Seed and stem crops)	Beans– Broad	d4.5	67
	Beans– French	s6.0	40
	Beans– Runner	d4.5	60
	Cucumber	s2.25	60
	Celery	d3.0	40
	Leek	s9.0	30
	Lettuce intercrop	s9.0	30
	Marrow	s2.25	60
	Onions	s22.5	30
	Pea	s9.0	80
	Shallots	s4.5	30
	Spinach	s4.5	30
	Spinach Beet	s4.5	40
	Sweet Corn	d2.7	90
	Tomato	s2.7	45
Group B (Root Crops)	Beetroots	s9.0	30
	Carrots	s13.5	30
	Parsnips	s4.5	45
	Potatoes early	s9.0	60
	Potatoes maincrop	s27.0	67
	Swede garden	s9.0	45
Group C (Greens)	Broccoli, sprouting	s4.5	60
	Brussels Sprouts	s13.5	67
	Cabbage, Autumn planted	s13.5	45
	Cabbage, Spring sown	s9.0	50
	Cabbage, Savoy	s9.0	60
	Cauliflower, Autumn use	s4.5	60
	Cauliflower, Winter use	s4.5	60
	Kale	s4.5	45
	Turnip intercrop	s4.5	45

s = single,   d = double

LEFT A small vegetable garden. Flowers for cutting are also grown here.

The area of groups A, B and C should be equal in the interest of good cultivation with a regular rotation of crops to prevent a build-up of disease in the soil.

Supposing in Group A that the family prefer French beans to peas. The area of beans can be increased at the expense of peas.

Revised areas

Crop	Original	Revised
French beans	6.0m × 40cm	13.5m × 40cm
Peas	9.0m × 50cm	4.5m × 80cm

BELOW Preparing the vegetable plot for next season's crop.

Similar adjustments can be made between other crops, but any re-arrangements should be made between crops within the same group, otherwise the rotation benefits may be lost.

The area of land required to feed one person under poor conditions may be 90m² (100 sq yd), but in good circumstances the requirement can be half that figure.

Until the capabilities of your soil, the climate, and the appetites of your family are known, start off with the lower figure, which is based on a plot size of 13.5 × 9m (45 × 30ft). In very small gardens, the problem will be to reduce the area still further and cut out plants that need a lot of space, such as maincrop potatoes, peas and Brussels sprouts.

Preparation of the plot

Vegetables need richer soil than any other group of garden plants. They are also vulnerable to many pests, diseases and weeds. Vegetable crops are usually considered in three categories for the purpose of soil treatment:

Group A the seed and stem crops such as peas, beans, onions and leeks.

Group B the root crops, potatoes and parsnips.

Group C the brassicas (greens) such as cabbages and Brussels sprouts.

Divide the vegetable garden into three plots of equal size, using pegs or markers for permanent reference. Label these plots A, B and C, and treat each one to a basic programme of autumn and winter cultivation. This programme incorporates clearing weeds, top growth and old crops; digging, ridging or trenching, and allowing frost, wind and rain to weather the land; and forking to break up and tilth the soil in spring or summer.

The manurial, fertilizer and liming treatment for each group of plants varies according to their respective needs, and depends on the availability of manures and garden compost.

In the first year of cropping, grow plants in Group A on Plot A, Group B on Plot B and Group C on Plot C.

Group A Give priority to the seed and stem crops in this group for available farmyard manure, garden compost, or other forms of organic material like peat.

Apply well-rotted manure or compost at the rate of about 3kg/m² (7lb per sq yd), or a 2.5cm (1in) layer of peat, working this in when digging, preferably in autumn or winter.

Check the pH level, liming if the soil is acid to a pH reading of about 6.5. Apply a good general fertilizer at 70g/m² (2oz per sq yd) where farmyard manure or well-made compost has been used. Double this amount of fertilizer where peat or pulverized tree bark is used instead of manure and apply preferably 7-10 days before sowing or planting.

Group B Do not apply manure to the ground for the root crops in this group as it can cause split and mis-shapen roots. Avoid liming soils for root crops unless the pH is below 5.5, and then only give sufficient to raise the pH reading to about 6.0. Do not apply lime where potatoes are to be grown or potato scab disease will result. Apply a balanced, high-potash base fertilizer at the rate of 140g/m² (4oz per sq yd) and work this in a few days before sowing or setting.

Group C The cabbages, cauliflowers and Brussels sprouts in Group C benefit from an application of lime before planting if the soil has a pH reading of less than 6.8-7.0, which is neutral. The significance of liming and neutralising soil is that club root, a devastating disease of the cabbage family, is usually much worse under acid conditions than neutral or alkaline. Give balanced fertilizer dressings at the rate of 140g/m² (4oz per sq yd) for spring or summer planted crops, and half to three-quarters of that amount for autumn-sown or planted subjects.

Each one of the three plots receives a different treatment each year for three years then the cycle is repeated. Take plot A as the example.

Year 1: prepare the plot for the plants in Group A by applying manure and fertilizer.
Year 2: give fertilizer only for those of Group B.
Year 3: lime and fertilizer only is applied for the greens in Group C. The arrangements and sequences are shown in the diagrams of a 3-course rotation.

Crop protection

Vegetables are attractive to many pests and diseases and are also vulnerable to the vagaries of site and situation. Crops can suffer from problems which are caused by one or more of three types of agency: pests, diseases, or some imbalance in plants or their surroundings.

Prevention is the best form of defence against any disorder, but in some cases such as the virus diseases, potato or tomato mosaic, there is no cure for the damage.

Overcrowding, warm moist conditions and stagnant air will weaken plants and favour pests and disease. Strong growing plants are naturally more resistant to troubles. Balanced feeding and watering, avoiding excess nitrogen, and thinning are good safeguards.

Preventive measures

You can discourage pests and diseases by avoiding conditions which suit them and by destroying the organisms at source.

Never allow dead, diseased or damaged plant material to lie around for one moment longer than need be. Burn it immediately. Do not make compost of infected plant remains. Before sowing or planting, dig up and destroy any pest or disease-ridden weeds and remove any litter, which can harbour undesirable organisms.

When starting off any new crop, one good insurance is to obtain correctly named varieties of seeds or plants which have been well-tested and proved, and are from a reliable source. Potatoes for planting should be stock and ministry-certified as free of eelworm and virus diseases – potatoes are planted under a national scheme to provide healthy plant material. Never plant cabbage seedlings that have swollen and evil-smelling roots, as this is the distinctive symptom of club root.

Rotation cropping, when correctly carried out, has been proved to be one of the best answers to plant ailments. It ensures that no crop is grown more frequently than one year in three on the same ground and provides the best growing conditions for each group.

Disorders such as flower-dropping of beans, due to some imbalance such as poor light, are most likely to occur in out-of-season growing. These problems are caused not by living organisms but by growing conditions. When attacks by pests or diseases are likely, protect crops with applications of suitable dusts or sprays. Seeds or seed beds can be treated against damping-off (a disease which attacks seedlings) with fungicidal dusts such as thiram or benomyl. Potatoes can be sprayed against blight disease.

Remedial measures

Once plants are affected there are two or three courses of action. If an attack of pest or disease is slight, immediately remove the affected parts (such as the tops of broad beans infested with blackfly). If the trouble is likely to spread such as celery blight, quickly apply a spray to prevent further infection, and check on the growing conditions. Where plants are severely damaged or dying, as with root rot of beans or potatoes, remove and burn the entire plant.

	Plot A	Plot B	Plot C
Year 1	A	B	C
Year 2	B	C	A
Year 3	C	A	B

■ Group A
■ Group B
■ Group C

ABOVE Chart to identify which crop will grow on each plot over 3 years of the 3 course rotation. A 'year' refers to the growing cycle of plants, not a calendar year. Leeks, for example, will be on Plot A in Year 1, from June until the last are harvested by April of Year 2. In Year 2 on Plot A, a vegetable from Group B will be planted from May, after the leeks have been harvested.

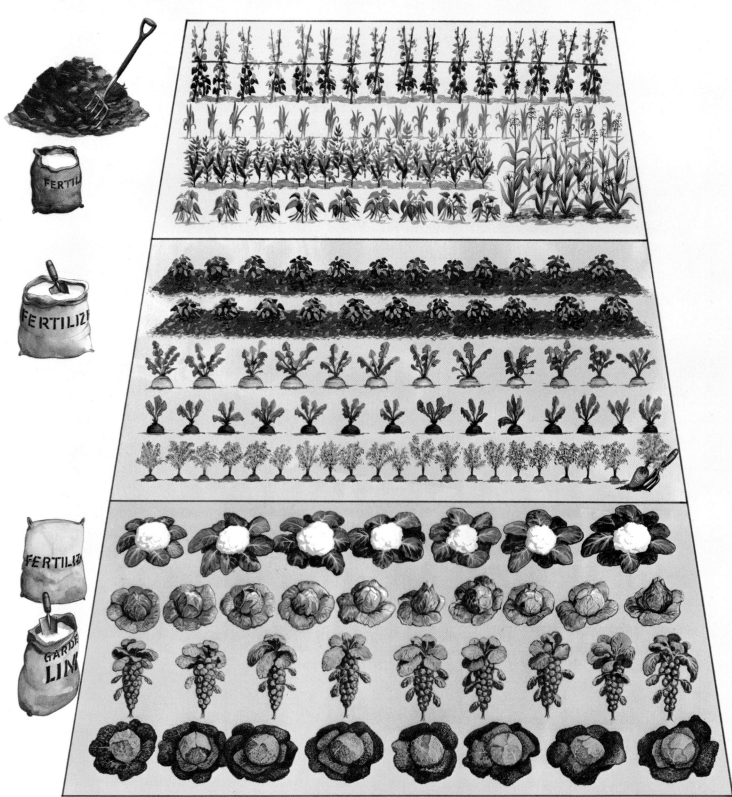

ABOVE From top to bottom, Groups A, B
and C of the 3 course rotation plan. Group
A require manure and fertilizer; Group B
require fertilizer, and lime if the pH
reading is below 5·5; Group C require
fertilizer and lime.

Step-by-step sowing, thinnin

1. Before sowing, mark the line of the drill with pegs and string. A v-shaped seed drill for small seeds is made with the draw hoe.

2. A flat-bottomed drill for planting potatoes is made with the side edge of the draw hoe.

3. A wide flat-bottomed drill is for seeds such as garden peas which are sown two or three abreast in the drill.

4. A ridge, used particularly on wet soils, is drawn up with the draw hoe.

5. A v-shaped drill on the ridge is made with the back of a rake.

6. A deep hole for long-rooted crops on shallow soils is made by twisting a crowbar round in the soil. The hole is filled with compost or fine soil, and raised slightly as it will soon pack down to ground level.

7. Sow about 5 small seeds per 2.5 cm (1 inch) run by hand in the v-shaped drill.

8. Set potatoes in a flat-bottomed drill 10 cm (4 inches) deep with the sprouts pointing upwards.

9. Cut off the top of onion sets when planting as birds are likely to pull at them when nest-making. Plant onion sets 10-15 cm (4-6 inches) apart in rows 30 cm (12 inches) apart using a trowel.

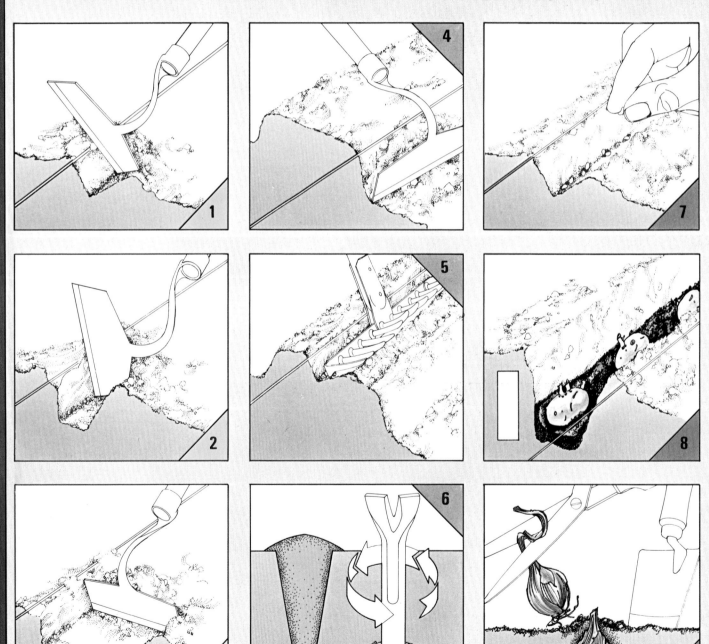

nd transplanting vegetables

10. Cover seeds with fine soil if the ground is rough and cloddy. Otherwise rake them in to give them a good covering.

11. Thin out seedlings by chopping, using a narrow draw hoe 10-15 cm (4-6 inches) wide, or pull them out by hand.

12. Lift cabbages and sprouts with a fork for transplanting after thoroughly watering them.

13. Seedlings for transplanting: lettuce with round-balled roots (left); cauliflower grown in pots overwintered in cloches (centre); trench or self-blanching celery (right).

14. Transplant seedlings with a dibber, levering the dibber to firm the soil against the roots.

15. Transplant trench celery into a wide flat-bottomed trench, and earth up with a trowel.

16. Trim the leaves of leeks and transplant into dibber holes. Do not firm soil, but water in so the growing plant can swell more easily.

17. When transplanting cauliflower, make a hole with a trowel and test it for size before knocking the plant out of the pot.

18. Test cabbage to see that it is firmly planted – a small portion of the leaf should tear away without shifting the plant.

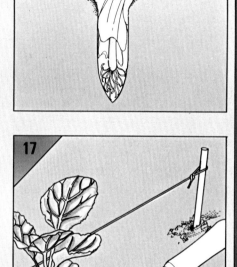

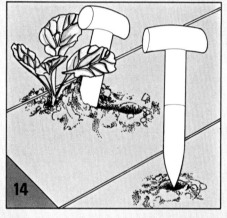

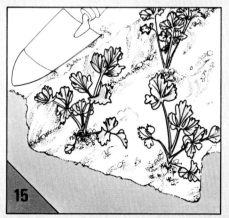

Popular vegetables

These have similar soil requirements and places in crop rotation and are considered individually in their respective groups.

Group A: Seeds and stems

Vegetables in this class require a general application of organic material such as farmyard manure or peat before cropping, plus 140g/m² (4oz per sq yd) of a balanced fertilizer. The soil should be slightly acid, with a reading of pH 6.5. The pea and bean crops of this group revitalize soil after the cabbage family have exhausted the food reserves of the land. Lettuce, onion and spinach are included in this group as their requirements are similar to seed and stem crops.

This group should precede root crops in the rotation as liming the land for gardens often renders the soil too alkaline for potatoes. A further consideration is that crops of carrots, parsnips and beetroots can be spoiled if fresh manure is applied immediately before sowing.

Each crop is given the same soil preparation unless stated to the contrary.

Broad beans Waterlogged soil, acidity or deficiency of phosphates or potash should be corrected. Although this crop is quite hardy, it will grow

Broad beans

better on an open, sunny spot, sheltered from freezing, spring winds. Sow beans on well-prepared land between November and April, in double staggered rows, 22cm (9in) apart leaving 20cm (8in) between plants and 60 to 90cm (2 to 3ft) between the double rows. A 4.5m (15ft) double row will

need approximately 225g (8oz) of seed. Hoe the ground to keep weeds down during the growing season. Provide supports and string for the taller varieties. Remove the top 5 to 7cm (2 to 3in) of growth when the bottom pods set (develop from flowers), to control blackfly. The beans will be ready to harvest in 16-30 weeks after sowing. Pick before they are mature and hard.

Those sown in autumn take longer to grow.
Suitable varieties: Aquadulce for autumn sowing: Windsor and Longpod types for spring sowing; The Sutton dwarf is suitable for small plots.

French beans like deep friable, well-manured and non-acid land supplied with fertilizer and drained. Select a sheltered spot, which is warm and out of the wind. Sow outdoors between late April and early July or set out suitably

French beans

hardened, indoor-raised plants in May or June, in rows 60cm (2 ft) apart with 25cm (10in) between plants. Sow seeds 12.5cm (5in) apart and thinned to a final 25cm (10in). Provide twigs to support plants.

Hoe and water the plants in dry weather. Bait slugs as necessary. After hot days, when the pods are setting, syringe plants with water to assist fruit set. Harvest the pods before seeds swell and harden.
Suitable varieties: The Prince for heavy cropping; Kinghorn Waxpod, stringless and of excellent flavour; Chevrier Vert, an excellent all-round variety, can also be dried as haricot beans.

Runner beans are more demanding than other beans. Grow them in well-manured trenches, preferably prepared in autumn. Avoid heavy clays, sandy or wet soil. Apply fertilizer a week before sowing or planting. Reserve a warm, sunny and sheltered area. Set out indoor-raised beans or sow seeds in May or June, in double rows 37.5cm (15in) apart, and 22cm (9in) between plants, in 45cm (18in) wide shallow

trenches. Seed needed to sow a 4.5m (15ft) long row is approximately 225g (8oz). Provide tall sticks to support the plants, stopping them by pinching out growing point when they reach the top. Water copiously in dry weather, and syringe with water in the evenings to help flowers to set. Give liquid feed of balanced fertilizer in July and August.

Harvest pods while they are young and before seeds harden. Prevent plants running to seed by removing the old flowers or pod formation will cease.
Suitable varieties: Enorma, excellent for flavour and freezing; Fry, a prolific stringless type; Achievement, very good quality maincrop variety; Kelvedon Marvel and Sunset, both dwarf types.

Celery, whether self-blanching or not, needs fertile, well-prepared ground on a sunny, well-drained site. Manure the beds for self-blanching celery or trenches for the trench variety in April, and rake in a balanced fertilizer before planting. If raising plants from seed, sow in pots in March and keep in a warm greenhouse. Harden off in cold frames before planting. In May/June set out plants of self-blanching celery

Celery in trenches

in level beds spaced 22 × 22cm (9 × 9in) apart and trench types in double rows 30cm (12in) apart 25cm (10in) between the plants. Water copiously and feed generously with balanced liquid feeds during summer. Remove sideshoots. Earth up trench celery to blanch the stems, and remove any leaves with brownish blisters from either type, and spray with malathion. Put down slug bait as a preventative measure. Harvest self-blanching sorts when the stems or crowns are large enough. Dig out

trench varieties 8-9 weeks after the final earthing.
Suitable varieties: Golden Self-blanching requires no earthing up; American Green, similar to the Golden, but with green stems. Gold and Green varieties mature quicker than trench varieties but are less hardy. The best trench varieties are Giant White, Giant Pink, and Giant Red.

Leeks need soil that has been well dug and manured and has had fertilizer added before planting. Correct water-logged, acid conditions. Leeks are very hardy, but prefer an open sunny spot sheltered from freezing winds. Sow seed in drills in a sheltered spot or in frames during late March or April for planting out in June. Space the plants out 30cm (1ft) between rows and 20cm (8in) apart. Make planting holes with a dibber, drop the seedlings in and water well. The water will bring soil close up around the plants so there is no need to firm them in. Keep weeds down, and

Lifting leeks with a fork

hoe or cultivate the land to prevent it becoming compacted. Earth up leeks slightly to blanch the stems. Water and give balanced feeding in summer for increased size.

Harvest leeks as you need them, starting if necessary before they reach full size to extend the season. Leave in the ground until needed in most situations.
Suitable varieties: The Lyon (syn. Prizetaker), a good early variety; Musselburgh, excellent and well tried; Winter Crop, very hardy and stands well.

Lettuce For best results the land should be well-manured, weed-free and moisture retentive. It should also be well-drained, have received fertilizer before sowing or planting and

have a good tilth. A sheltered sunny position out of the wind is very important.

For the earliest outdoor lettuce, set out well-hardened indoor-raised plants in April or early May. You will need 2g ($\frac{1}{16}$oz) seed for a 4.5m (15ft) row. On well-prepared land, sow lettuce between late March and early July. Transplant or thin lettuce to stand 22cm (9in) apart or 30cm (12in) for larger crisphead varieties, with similar spacing between rows.

Use black threads or bird scarers to keep birds off, and control slugs by

Curly lettuce

baiting. Keep lettuce well watered, hoed and weed-free. Spray with malathion at the first sign of aphid attack. If grey mould appears, pick off affected leaves, or destroy badly infected plants and spray or dust the crop with benomyl or thiram fungicides.

To harvest, cut lettuce in the morning or evening. Discard plants with a central flowering shoot because these have gone to seed and will taste bitter.
Suitable varieties: Four kinds of lettuce are commonly grown: Butterheads, which are soft, smooth-leaved, hearting and quick growing. Of these Unrivalled is excellent, and Avondefiance is good for June sowing. The latter is mildew resistant. Good Crispheart varieties include Webb's Wonderful and Windermere. Cos types have an upright habit, with narrow leaves and good flavour; Lobjoits Green Cos is an excellent large lettuce, and Winter Density is smaller and suitable for spring or summer sowing. Curly lettuce is a non-heartening type. Instead of picking the whole plant, simply remove as many leaves as you need at one time. Salad Bowl produces tender curled leaves, and is a good variety.

95

Marrow Dig out a 30cm (12in) hole and replace the soil with a compost of 1 part well-rotted manure and 2 parts of soil, plus 30g (1oz) of balanced fertilizer well mixed in. Leave the planting area about 7cm (3in) above the surrounding soil. Choose a warm and sunny spot sheltered from wind. Plant out well-hardened plants on the mounds, spaced 60cm (2ft) apart and 90cm (3ft) between rows, after all danger of frost has passed, in late May or June. Marrows from outdoor sowings in May or June tend to be late fruiting.

Water as necessary to keep the roots moist, and syringe freely in hot weather. Pinch out the growing point when plant is 35cm (14in) high. Fertilize the female flowers (those sitting on small marrows) with a male flower: cut off a male flower, remove the petals and push into the female flower. Feed the plants at 10–14 day intervals with a balanced liquid feed when the fruit swell. Place a slate under swelling fruit to protect the marrows from soil and dirt. Harvest marrows while they are young to encourage continuous cropping.

Suitable varieties: Bush types: Green Bush is one of the best; White Bush, creamy white, early maturing; Prokor F1 Hybrid, green, early and prolific. Trailing: Long Green Striped, vigorous and excellent for winter storage; Long White is the best long white variety and stores well. Courgettes: Golden Zucchini, yellow-skinned and productive; Zucchini, bushy habit, early maturing dark green fruits.

Pollinating marrow

Onions need rich well-prepared land that has been autumn dug, manured, consolidated and given a dressing of balanced fertilizer. Select a warm, open sunny situation.

Trim back the dried stems of onion and shallots which attract birds, and using a trowel, plant in March or April. Plant autumn-sown onions and shallots from late February to early April, in rows 30cm (12in) apart and 15cm (6in) between plants or sets. Indoor spring-sown plants are set out in April, and are planted slightly closer for average purposes, same spacing between rows by 12cm (5in) apart.

Sow salad or spring varieties from March or April to September in rows 30cm (12in) apart. These are not generally thinned. Outdoor spring-sown bulb onions are thinned to the same spacing as those sown indoors in spring.

Hoe regularly to kill weeds and remove flower stems as they appear. Water in dry weather but do not water when the bulbs start to ripen. When the crop begins to mature and the tops start to fall over, bend over the remainder to assist ripening, and leave for two or three weeks. On a fine day lift the roots with a fork, and place on netting or shelving to dry.

Ripening onions

Suitable varieties: Ailsa Craig, a large variety of good flavour; Bedfordshire Champion, an excellent keeper; Sturon, heavy yielding; Express Yellow, heavy and early cropping, good for autumn sowing. White Lisbon, a reliable spring onion. Paris Silver skin is a good pickling variety. Stuttgart Giant, suitable for growing from sets.

Shallots: Giant Yellow, Dutch Yellow, and Dutch Red are reliable and heavy cropping varieties.

Seed required: Sow about 4g (⅛oz) onion seed to a 4.5m (15ft) row, or 0.75kg (1½lb) of onion or shallot sets.

Peas require deeply dug, well-manured land that is adequately drained. Rake in a dressing of balanced

Peas ready for picking

fertilizer before sowing, on land that has been rested from peas or beans for at least two years. Choose a sunny site, sheltered from the prevailing winds.

Rake out flat seeds drills 10–15cm (4–6in) wide, 5–7cm (2–3in) deep, and space the seeds 5–7cm (2–3in) apart, covering them with fine soil to the same depth. You will need 225g (8oz) of seed to sow a 4·5m (15ft) row. Water the bottom of the drills before sowing in dry ground. Cover the seedlings with wire netting to keep birds off, and provide pea sticks for support as soon as the plants make growth. Kill weeds with frequent hoeing. Give plants adequate water in hot weather and spray with fenitrothion 10 days after flowering starts to prevent peas becoming maggoty.

Pick pods regularly before the peas in them touch each other.

Suitable varieties: Round-seeded: Meteor, suitable for cold districts; sow November to January; height 45cm (18in). Pilot, early, heavy cropper; sow January to March; height 90cm (3ft). *Wrinkle-seeded* (for second, early and maincrop): Onward, sow March, stands poor conditions, heavy cropper, height 60cm (2ft). Hurst Green Shaft, very prolific cropping; mildew and wilt resistant; height 67cm (2ft 3in). Kelvedon Wonder, suitable June/July sowing, mildew resisting, fine flavour, height 45cm (18in). The wrinkle-seeded varieties named here are all suitable for freezing.

Spinach grows best on well-drained, deeply-dug and limed land enriched with fertilizer before sowing. Grow summer spinach in the light shade of tall crops like peas and beans. Winter spinach needs a sheltered spot.

Sow round-seeded varieties from March to July and prickly-seeded winter varieties in August and September, in rows 30cm (1ft) apart, plants thinned

Perpetual spinach

to 7.5cm (3in), and later, to 15cm (6in) apart. Sow perpetual spinach between March and July in similar row width and 22cm (9in) between plants. Space New Zealand types as for the perpetual and sow outside in April or May.

A 4.5cm (15ft) row needs about 8g (¼oz) of seed. Control weeds by hoeing, and water plants in dry weather. Protect winter spinach from November to February with cloches in cold areas. Spray with malathion if greenfly is troublesome.

To harvest, start with the outside leaves and pick regularly to promote fresh growth.

Suitable varieties: Greenmarket, large-leaved winter type; sow September, March and April; mosaic-resistant; Sigmalea, a round-seeded variety for summer use; sow autumn or spring; good long-standing qualities. Long-standing Round, quick growing, good colour. Long-standing Prickly, for winter use, quick growing and stands well, sow from June to September.

Tomato crops need deeply-dug land with peat and high-potash base fertilizer incorporated before planting. Alternatively, plants can be grown in pots or growing bags. For both, choose a sunny sheltered position or unshaded south-facing wall.

Set out hardened-off plants in rows 75cm (2ft 6in) apart, with 45cm (18in) between plants, in June after all

Ripe tomatoes

danger of frost has gone. Provide tall or standard varieties with stakes and ties. Tie plants into supporting canes or overhead strings as they grow at 20cm (8in) intervals. Remove sideshoots (growths between leaf and stem) as they form. Cut out the growing point two leaves above the fourth or fifth truss (cluster of fruits) in July when the fruit has set. Place straw under bush fruits to keep them clean. Give weekly liquid feeds with a balanced fertilizer when the tomatoes are swelling. Place a peat mulch around plants in the ground.

Harvest tomatoes as they ripen. When frosts threaten, remove remaining fruit, and bring indoors to ripen.

Suitable varieties: Standard type: Alicante, green-back resistant, good quality; Harbinger, early maturing, good flavour; Moneymaker, heavy cropper, good quality, later ripening. Bush type: Sigmabush F1 Hybrid, outstanding for earliness and yield. The Amateur, early and well tried; Tiny Tim, small fruited, suitable for window boxes.

Group B: Root crops
Members of this class need fertile, deeply worked soil that is moderately acid (pH 6), and well supplied with phosphate and potash.

Manure should not be given to root

crops except for potatoes, because this can cause forked and badly shaped roots.

Increased yields of potatoes usually result from a dressing of well-rotted material at the rate of 3 kg/m² (7lb per sq yd).

Avoid liming for this group unless the soil is very acid, and then only add sufficient to raise the pH to 6.

Before sowing or planting apply 140g/m² (4 oz per sq yd) of a balanced high potash fertilizer.

On land where clubroot is a problem, swedes and turnips should be treated as for Group C.

Sweet corn is included in this group to make up the size of group B for rotation with groups A and C.

Beetroot must have well-worked land manured for a previous crop. Apply a balanced fertilizer before sowing in an open, unshaded situation. Sow seeds in drills 30cm (1ft) apart in March–July for round kinds, and April–May for long varieties. You will need 4g (⅛oz) seed for a 4.5m (15ft) row.

Beetroot

Keep the soil stirred and free of weeds. Water regularly in dry weather. Thin out young plants to allow 10cm (4in) between seedlings. Harvest young roots as required and carefully lift maincrop, twisting off the leaves to leave about 5cm (2in) of stem. Store in layers of dry peat or sand in an airy frost-proof place.

Suitable Varieties: Round: Early Bunch, for early sowing only. Globe, excellent flavour; Boltardy, good colour, slow to run to seed. Long: Cheltenham Greentop, longest-keeping variety, first-class colour.

Carrot This vegetable succeeds best in a deep, well-worked, rich, light loam, manured for a previous crop. Apply a balanced fertilizer dressing before sowing, together with a soil insecticide to control carrot root fly and wireworms. Select an open, sunny position.

Sow all varieties in rows 30cm (1ft) apart, early sorts in February to March and again in July, maincrop in April and May. Allow 4g ($\frac{1}{8}$oz) seed for 4-5m (15ft) row.

Thin early kinds to 7cm (3in) between plants and maincrop to 12cm (5in) apart. Water dry soil; thin when the ground is moist, firm in the remaining roots and burn or use the thinnings. Hoe to keep down the weeds, and water during dry weather conditions.

Harvest small carrots as needed. To store, lift, clean and cut off the foliage to leave about 2cm (1in) of growth. Store the roots between layers of dry peat or sand in boxes in a dry frost-free place, or in outdoor clamps.

Stump-rooted carrots

Suitable varieties: Early: Amsterdam Forcing, excellent flavour, cylindrical shape. Early Nantes, small cylindrical roots, very early. Parisian Rondo, small quick-growing, round in shape. Maincrop: Chantenay Red Cored, a heavy-yielding stump-rooted kind of high quality. New Red Intermediate, a long tapering carrot, of good quality and colour, excellent for winter storage.

Parsnip This vegetable requires a deep, well-worked friable soil that has been well manured for a previous crop and limed if necessary. Heavy or shallow soils are unsuitable. Add fertilizer before sowing. An open sunny situation is preferable, but a light shade is

tolerated. Sow parsnips as soon as soil conditions allow in March, in rows 45cm (18in) apart. A 4.5m (15ft) row will take 4g ($\frac{1}{8}$oz) seed.

Thin seedlings to 20cm (8in) apart. Hoe to kill weeds and keep the soil loosened. If the celery leaf fly should attack, causing small blisters on the foliage, squash these and spray plants with malathion. Grow resistant types to combat canker disease.

Parsnips

Suitable varieties: Improved Hollow Crown, good flavour, white flesh, maincrop. Avonresister, short-rooted, suitable for difficult soils, canker-resistant. Tender and True, one of the best all-round varieties, good for exhibition and resistant to canker.

Potatoes will grow successfully on many different types of soil, but prefer medium loam. It is a good crop for breaking up new gardens, mostly because it calls for thorough digging of the soil before planting. In effect, you do most of the work, not the potatoes! Dig in manure or peat deeply in autumn if not previously manured. Apply fertilizer to the drills at planting time, but do not give lime. A sunny open position away from shade is best.

You will need 1.2kg (2lb 8oz) of seed potatoes for each 4.5m (15ft) row. Buy certified stock from a reliable supplier. Place the seed potatoes in a single layer with the eyes uppermost in shallow boxes, in a light airy frost-free place to form sturdy shoots.

In early April, set early varieties for the 'new potatoes' in June. Plant in drills 12cm (5in) deep, 60cm (2ft) apart, spacing the tubers 30cm (1ft) between each. Cover the drills with fine

earth. Maincrop varieties are planted in April but spaced 67cm (2ft 3in) between rows with 37cm (15in) between tubers.

If frosts still occur as shoots emerge, cover them with a 2.5cm (1in) layer of fine soil for protection. Earth up the plants when the growth is 15-20 cm (6-8in) high, drawing fine soil around the stems, to form a 12-15cm (5-6in) high ridge. A second earthing up is usually required. In July in wet seasons, spray the foliage with a copper or other fungicide against blight disease.

Harvest early sorts as the flowers die, leaving the main crop until the tops (haulm) die.

Chitting (sprouting) potatoes

Suitable varieties: Early—those grown for 'new potatoes'—Arran Pilot and Duke of York are both reliable for most situations and soils. Foremost is very popular, and crops heavily. Maincrop: King Edward, coloured skins, widely grown. Majestic, an older variety, also popular. Golden Wonder, rated the finest-flavoured potato, but yields are light. Pentland Crown, an outstanding newer variety.

Sweet corn require deeply-dug land that is well broken up, and has been manured for a crop in previous years, and with a dressing of general fertilizer at 100g/m² (3 oz per sq yd) raked in 10-14 days before sowing.

Choose a place in the sun, out of shade.

In all but the warmest southern districts, where seeds can successfully be sown outside, use indoor pot-grown plants. Plant sweet corn in blocks of 12 or more rather than long rows as it is

98

wind-pollinated and the plants need to be near each other. Plant after the danger of frost has passed in late May to June.

For sowing direct, place two seeds at each station at similar spacings in May about 1 to 2 cm (½ to 1in) deep. After germination, discard the weaker seedling at each station. For indoor raised plants, sow two seeds to each 7.5cm (3in) pot of seed compost. You will need 8g (¼oz) of seed for each 4.5m (15ft) row.

Thin seedlings, whether pot or direct-sown, to one at each position. Hoe the ground. Avoid deep cultivation or the shallow roots may be damaged. Keep the plants well watered, and give a balanced liquid feed as the cobs swell. Stake tall plants as necessary.

To harvest, test the cobs for ripeness, when the silky tassels turn brown, by pushing a fingernail into one or two of the grains. If a creamy fluid oozes out, they are ready for use. If watery or

Planting sweetcorn

doughy and hard, either they are too early or too late.
Suitable varieties: First of All, F1 Hybrid: John Innes, F1 Hybrid: both are early and compact. North Star is suited to northern districts, Kelvedon Glory for the south.

Turnip and swede need firm ground, limed if necessary, (swede are vulnerable to club root), and preferably manured for a previous crop. Grow both crops on ridges if the land is inclined to be wet, choosing an open sunny situation if possible. Apply and rake in fertilizer before sowing. You will need

4g (⅛oz) of seed for a 4.5m (15ft) row. Sow turnips from March to July in drills 37cm (15in) apart. Sow swedes 45cm (18in) apart and sow in May and June.

Hoe regularly and keep the plot weed-free. Thin early turnips to stand 15cm (6in) apart, with maincrop turnips and swedes at 25cm (10in). Water all crops in dry weather. Dust seedlings with derris against flea beetle.

Turnips

Harvest early turnips when little bigger than golf balls. Lift maincrop turnips in autumn and store between layers of peat or sand in boxes, placed in a frost-free and dry place. Leave swedes in the ground until required.
Suitable varieties: Early turnips: Jersey Navet, white flesh and attractive flavour, Golden Perfection, quick-growing. Snowball, early good all-round type.

Maincrop turnips: Golden Ball, compact, round with fine flavour, hardier than white-fleshed varieties, good keeping quality. Green Top White, both roots and tops are edible.

Swede: Purple top, fine flavour, quick growing; Chignecto, club root resistant and of excellent flavour.

Group C: Greens

Greens or brassicas grow best on rich well limed soil that is firm.

Ideally vegetables in this group follow well manured potatoes relying on the manurial residues of that crop.

Brassicas, other than autumn-planted cabbage, will benefit from a light dressing of rotted farmyard manure at a rate of 2kg/m² (3lb per sq

yd) where the preceding crop (carrots for example) were unmanured.

Lime the land if necessary to raise the pH to 7.

Before planting incorporate 140g/m² (4oz per sq yd) of balanced fertilizers, reducing this by half for autumn planting.

Brussels sprouts should be grown in an open spot away from shade and out of the wind on firm ground, with a pH reading of 7. Rake in a dressing of balanced fertilizer at 100g/m² (3oz per sq yd) before sowing or planting.

In March or April sow seeds in a seed bed and transplant seedlings to their final positions in May to June at 67cm (2ft 3in) square. For 3 4.5m (15ft) rows you will need 2g (1/16 oz) seed.

Protect from birds if necessary with scarers or netting. Hoe regularly, and water plants in dry weather. Earth up plants as winter approaches to prevent them toppling over. The canopy of leaves at the top helps protect the sprouts from rain. Spray plants with malathion if aphids are present.

When harvesting, start picking firm buds from the stem base, snapping them off with a downward pull.
Suitable varieties: Peer Gynt, F1 Hybrid, dwarf, good for small gardens, matures October. Market Rearguard, first class late sprout, crops December to March. Fillbasket, mid-season, produces large solid buds. Red, colour as name, decorative and good flavour.

Brussels sprouts

Cabbage should be grown on firm, well-limed soil containing plenty of manurial residues from a previous crop. Rake in fertilizer at 100g/m² (3oz per sq yd) before sowing or planting, reducing the quantity by half for autumn-planted cabbage. Avoid shaded areas, but select a sheltered spot for spring cabbage.

For summer, autumn and winter cutting sow on prepared seed beds from March to July. Sow cabbage for spring cutting in late July and early August. In April plant indoor-raised small summer varieties at 45cm (18in) square. Set the larger outdoor-sown types including Savoys 60cm (2ft) square.

Space spring-maturing sorts at 45 × 22.5cm (18 × 9in). All cabbages should be firmly planted.

Hoe carefully until the crop itself is big enough to smother weeds. Pick every other plant for use as Spring cabbage to leave a final spacing of 45cm (18in) square. Water plants in dry weather and give liquid feeds as the heads mature. Re-firm any plants which frost has lifted out of the ground. Spray with malathion if aphids, caterpillars or white fly appear.

Harvest mature heads as needed. The time of harvesting will depend on the type of plant.

Suitable varieties: Spring cabbage: Harbinger and Wheelers Imperial, compact, suitable for small gardens. Durham Early, one of the best. Summer cabbage: Hispi, F1 Hybrid, quick maturing and compact. Greyhound, early and compact, but sown indoors. Autumn and Winter cabbage: Progress and May Express are both suitable for succession sowing (sown in small quantities at intervals to ensure a continuous supply). Winnigstadt, tight and compact hearts, matures in August to October. Autumn Supreme, dark green semi-ball head. January King, very hardy, use December to April. Savoys: Best of All, Autumn Green and Rearguard can provide a succession from August to April.

Cauliflower needs to be grown quickly in a sheltered sunny site. Deeply-dug and manured land is best, well-cultivated, limed if necessary and allowed to settle before planting. Hoe in a dressing of fertilizer at 100g/m² (3oz per sq yd) before planting.

As only 2g ($\frac{1}{16}$ oz) of seed will sow a 13.5m (15yd) row, it is a good idea to share seed with another gardener. In March to April set out the earliest plants from indoor-sown seedlings. Sow outdoors in April and May for transplanting to final positions in June to July. Space the rows 60cm (2ft) apart and the same distance between plants in the rows.

Water in dry spells, and give the occasional liquid feed. Bend a leaf or two over each curd (the white head) as they mature, for protection from sun or frost.

Cut the earliest heads of each batch when small, to prolong the season.

Suitable varieties: Early types: Arcturus, the earliest and Snowball, pure white, are both suitable for April planting from indoor raised plants. Autumn types (sow April to May outdoors to cut in autumn). Kangaroo, excellent for general and exhibition purposes. All the Year Round, reliable general purpose variety.

Winter types (sow April to May to cut February to June): Thanet, hardy, good quality; matures April. Late Queen, dwarf, compact, hardy, matures May. June Market, large size head, good in North, ready in June.

BELOW Cabbages at different stages of development as a result of successional sowing.

Crop	Month	Space between	
	J F M A M J J A S O N D	Rows	Plants
Beans, broad		60cm*	20 × 20cm
Beans, dwarf		45cm	25cm
Beans, runner		1·5m	25cm
Beetroot		30cm	12cm
Broccoli, sprouting		60cm	45cm
Brussels sprouts		75cm	70cm
Cabbage, spring sown		50cm	22/44cm
Cabbage, summer sown		50cm	40cm
Cabbage, savoy		60cm	50cm
Carrot		30cm	10cm
Cauliflower		60cm	45/60cm
Celery		1·2m**	20cm
Cucumber		90cm	60cm
Kale		60cm	60cm
Leek		30cm	20cm
Lettuce		30cm	22cm
Marrow		90cm	60cm
Onion, bulb		30/45cm	12cm
Onion, spring or salad		30cm	2cm
Onion, sets		30cm	12cm
Parsnip		45cm	20cm
Peas, round seeded		60cm***	5cm
Peas, wrinkled		1·2m	5cm
Radish		25cm	1cm
Shallots		30cm	15cm
Spinach, summer		30cm	25cm
Spinach, winter		30cm	25cm
Spinach, perpetual		30cm	25cm
Swede		45cm	25cm
Sweet corn		75cm	45cm
Tomato		60cm	45cm
Turnip		35cm	12cm

Key

▬ = Outdoor sowing	* = Distance between double rows
▬ = Indoor sowing	** = Self-blanch type only needs 25cm
▬ = Harvest	*** = Narrow space is for dwarf varieties

Growing vegetables in containers

Contrary to expectations, container grown vegetables can and do out-yield some crops grown in the ground. Container cultivation enables the owner of a small or town garden to grow plants on patios, in porches, on window sills, balconies, roof tops and other difficult places.

The range of vegetables which can be grown easily and successfully depends largely on the size of receptacle, type of compost, and the subsequent care and attention. When choosing suitable containers, the main points to bear in mind are the needs of the plant, ease and convenience of cultivation and appearance.

The principal needs of a plant are: space and depth to develop, adequate food and moisture, suitable anchorage and support, avoidance of extremes of temperature, and freedom from poisons, pests and diseases.

Watering should not be messy nor should containers dry out too rapidly, and training the growing plants should be a fairly easy task.

Appearance is important in conspicuous places: there are many types of container to choose from and they should be reasonably accessible. Plastic pots and troughs are clean, lightweight, and easy to handle and the more ornate ones look quite attractive. Growbags are practical and convenient for out-of-the-way places or for use in place of diseased soils. Timber tubs and window boxes are made in various sizes and though pleasing to look at, they have two possible defects: their weight, and the fact that, unless treated with preservatives, they will rot. Glazed earthenware containers are the best but very expensive. Unfortunately the porous type stain.

Although loam-based or soilless potting composts suit most subjects, those of the all-peat type are less satisfactory for beetroot and carrots, where a preparation containing a fair proportion of sand or 25% or more gravel aggregate is better.

Unless you have the facilities to raise them from seed, tomatoes, cucumbers, courgettes and marrows are best bought in young plant form. Other vegetables can be sown directly into their final pots and thinned out as necessary, or raised in seed pans on the window sill, as with lettuce. Water carefully and give developing plants a balanced diluted liquid feed. Spray plants with derris or malathion if aphids appear. Pick off and burn any dead, dying or diseased foliage.

Train climbing beans, courgettes or marrows in tubs, over a wigwam of canes, tying in new growth as necessary with soft string. Pinch out the plants when they reach the top of the supports.

Grow potatoes, dwarf beans and carrots in deep containers, supporting potatoes and dwarf beans with twigs to prevent them falling over. Container growing requires careful choice of varieties. Choose dwarf, compact, early-maturing types from the following list:

Dwarf bean–Masterpiece
Beetroot–Boltardy
Carrot–Parisian Rondo, a round type, or Early Nantes, stump-rooted
Courgette–Zucchini
Cucumber–Patio-Pak F1 Hybrid
Lettuce–Tom Thumb
Marrow–Smallpak
Onion–White Lisbon
Peas–Mangetout Dwarf de Grace
Potato–Foremost
Radish–French Breakfast
Shallots–Dutch Yellow
Tomato–Tiny Tim, or Sub-arctic Plenty

ABOVE Lettuce in a proprietary growing bag.
LEFT Tomatoes in pots on a balcony.
RIGHT Vegetables in the flower garden.

Vegetables in the flower garden

In small gardens, where a lack of space prevents the allocation of an area exclusively to vegetables, the idea of growing flowers and food together is attractive. It is particularly important in these circumstances to prepare the ground well and look after the crop attentively.

Observe rotation requirements as in an ordinary vegetable garden: Wallflowers and arabis also suffer from the club root that affects cabbages. Control pest or diseases as soon as any signs of trouble appear, by spraying or dusting.

Display vegetable plants so that their decorative qualities are shown to advantage and their utilitarian nature masked by the overall effect. Do not separate flowers from vegetables, interplant them: carrots, for example, among gladioli.

Not all vegetables will thrive in the flower garden, but the following combinations have proved successful.

Display the red-flowered runner bean (Scarlet Emperor) as a screen or backing to a flower bed, or grow them in clumps, stopping them at 1.5m (5 ft) and using a cane wigwam of that height

for support. They are then less over-powering among other flowers.

The dark red leaves of beetroot 'Globe' or the 'Ruby' Swiss chard make a useful contrast of foliage texture and colour dotted among geraniums or begonias in summer bedding. Leeks with their strap-like foliage make a quite useful substitute for ornamental sweet corn when dotted among African marigolds, antirrhinums and French marigolds. Lift the leeks when the summer bedding is pulled out. 'Musselburgh' is a good choice for this situation.

Parsley ('Imperial Curled') can be grown as an edging round flower beds.

The salad onion 'White Lisbon' makes a delicate division between different groups or blocks of low-growing plants such as *Phlox drummondii*, or *Begonia semperflorens* instead of the more common blue-green fescue grass.

Sow carrots of the 'Concord' variety among summer-flowering anemones – both have similar foliage – and interplant with gladioli to give height, each complementing the other.

Chives make useful edging or dot plants and produce an attractive crop of pink flowers. Plant various thymes in a sunny position in a window box or in a rockery in association with other plants. Sow a clump or two of the purple-podded peas among herbaceous border plants for contrast. Dwarf kales, either coloured for summer use or curled green used as dot plants among early flowering daffodils and forget-me-not can be effective, but it is important that dead or discoloured leaves are removed as soon as possible.

Nasturtiums provide a good display of summer colour and the leaves add piquancy to any salad. When their fruits have set, pot-grown sweet peppers can be planted among bedding plants to provide colour and interest especially when decorative plants such as nemesia have finished flowering. Some of the small bush types of tomato can be grown among flowers. The variety Sub-arctic Cherry grows happily even in hanging baskets, producing a profusion of small bright red fruits. Harvest the various crops of plants, pods, or roots gradually, so that the decorative effect or general appearance is not ruined by the sudden gaps or loss of colour.

Harvesting and storing vegetables

The time and cost of producing good wholesome home-grown food can be wasted unless crops are gathered in the right conditions and properly kept until they are required for the table.

When to pick crops

Vegetables have to be harvested at the right stage of development before they become too tough for eating, and the maturing process must be slowed down by storing the crop until it is required.

The swollen roots of root crops are organs for storing plant energy and unless growth is arrested will continue to develop, form fibre and be tough to eat. To be tender and succulent, salads like lettuce should be used as soon as they are ready; their storage life cannot be extended beyond a few days. Stem and leaf crops like celery and spinach also have a limited life once picked, but will stand on the plant for a few weeks

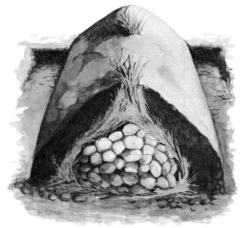

ABOVE Potato clamp.

in cold winter weather if protected from severe frosts.

Seed and pod crops can be used when tender, green and fresh, or they can be frozen or dried. Peas, beans and sweet corn can be preserved for quite a long time in excellent condition when quick-frozen, as can cauliflowers and broccoli. Their life in the fresh state cannot be easily extended beyond a week or so. Hearted cabbages and mature marrows will last for several weeks if they are hung up in nets in a cool airy place.

During the coldest months of the year hardy vegetables like leeks, parsnips, Savoy cabbage and kale can remain in or on the ground without coming to much harm, provided pigeons and other birds are prevented from eating them.

Storing in boxes or clamps

In autumn, before the severe frosts arrive, lift and trim crops such as turnips, carrots and beetroot and place them in a frost-free shed between layers of dry sand or peat in boxes. Store larger quantities in clamps outside. Place the roots on beds of clean straw and cover them with straw 10cm (4in) thick. Finally, cover with a layer of soil 15cm (6in) thick, leaving a straw plug for ventilation to prevent sweating and rotting.

Harvesting individual crops

Broad beans: Pick the pods before the beans harden, and use fresh or freeze for future needs.

French and runner beans: Pods are ready for picking if they snap when bent and before the seeds swell. Use fresh and freeze the surplus.

ABOVE Twisting leaves of beet.

Beetroot: Pull small roots for immediate use, twisting off the leaves. Do not cut them off or the beet will 'bleed' and be useless. In autumn lift large roots, twist off the leaves, and store in boxes or clamps.

Brussels sprouts: Start picking sprouts from the base when firm and solid, but before they begin to open. Mid-season and late varieties will keep on the plants for several weeks in cold weather. Freeze surplus buttons.

Cabbage: Hearting types will stand for a week or two in summer or several weeks in autumn or winter. Cut solid heads and store in airy nets hung up in a cool place out of direct sunlight.

Carrots: As for beetroot.

Cauliflower: Protect curds by bending a leaf or two over the developing head to avoid sun or frost damage.

Celery: Use self-blanching types when ready and before the frosts. Dig trench celery as required. When blanched, from about October, they can be left standing in the ground until February.

Kale: Pick over each plant removing a few leaves each time, starting at the centre and working down. Since it is very hardy, this crop will usually stand outside for weeks in winter.

Leeks: Lift carefully as required, leaving the remainder in the ground.

Lettuce: Begin cutting when young to avoid a glut. In summer, lift plants with roots and stand two or three in a shallow bowl of clean water in a cool airy place to give an extra few days' life.

ABOVE Carrots stored in sand.

Marrows and Courgettes: Start cutting when small. Allow marrows to mature at the season's end, cut and store in suspended nets in a cool airy place.

Onions: As the bulbing onions mature and the stems fall over, bend the remainder down, lift, and dry off three weeks later on slatted or wire mesh trays. To store, tie up in ropes or spread thinly on trays for drying in a cool airy place. Use thick-necked bulbs first. Lift salad onions as needed.

Parsnips: Lift roots as required when the leaves begin to die down, leaving the crop in the ground. In February, dig up the remainder and store in layers of sand or peat in boxes.

Peas: Pick when the pods are almost filled and before they change colour or turn pale. Freeze surplus peas.

Potatoes: Dig and use early or new varieties when the flowers die. Lift maincrops when the foliage dies off. Dry for an hour or two after lifting. Store in boxes in a dark airy frost-free place or in a clamp.

Shallots: Lift, divide and dry on wire trays as for onions when the foliage dies down in summer.

Spinach (all types): Pick regularly as soon as leaves are large enough to use.

Swedes: Leave in the soil and dig up as required.

Sweet corn: Test seed between fingernail and thumb when the silks or tassels turn brown. Pull cobs with seeds of a creamy consistency. Leave ones with watery sap for a few days. Freeze surplus cobs.

Tomatoes: Pick fully ripe fruit with green calyx attached. Remove trusses of green tomatoes at the end of the season and ripen indoors in a warm dark place.

Turnips: Lift early types young when about golf ball size. Dig up maincrop, twist off leaves, store in boxes in layers of peat or sand protected from frosts or in clamps.

Herbs

Members of this group have been grown for a long time but they are only now beginning to be more widely appreciated.

Many people know only mint, sage, parsley and thyme. Without spending a great deal of time and money, many other interesting herbs can be added to this list. Most herbs take up little space, and can be used in seasoning food, in herb vinegars, herb breads, tisanes and as garnishes.

Cultivation

Make your herb plot conveniently close to the kitchen, preferably in a sunny, well-drained spot. A south or east-facing aspect with light shade for part of the day will suit them admirably. Choose a semi-shaded spot for parsley, chervil, basil and mint. A poor soil in a dry and warm position promotes improved and stronger flavour and scent.

BELOW Well stocked and attractive small herb garden.

Angelica *A. archangelica*
Biennial; 1.5 to 1.8m (5-6ft) height. Prefers semi-shaded site, and a deep moist soil. Sow seeds in summer, transplant in autumn or spring; allow 60cm (2ft) for each plant. Remove immature flowers to prolong life.

Balm *Melissa officinalis*
Perennial; 60 to 90cm (2 to 3ft) height. Prefers warm, sunny situation and ordinary soil. Sow in spring or divide plants in autumn. Allow 30cm (1ft) between each plant. Cut and dry stems before flowering.

Sweet basil *Ocimum basilicum*
Annual; 30 to 60cm (1 to 2ft) height. Prefers sunny position and a light well-drained soil. Sow indoors in a warm place in spring, harden off and plant out in May, allowing 30cm (1ft) for each plant.

Bay *Laurus nobilis*
Perennial bush or small tree 10cm-3m (4in-10ft) high. Place in a sunny sheltered spot in well-drained soil, in border or tubs. Increase by cuttings in summer, layers in early autumn or buy rooted plants. Gather leaves for drying in summer.

Chervil *Anthriscus cerefolium*
Annual; 30 to 37cm (12 to 15in) height. Grows in sun or partial shade in ordinary well-drained land. Make succession sowings in spring and summer. Grow in beds, pots or window boxes. Allow 20cm (8in) between plants.

Chives *Allium schoenoprasum*
Perennial; 15 to 25cm (6-10in) height. Place in semi-shade or sun in fertile porous loam. Sow in spring, or divide clumps in spring or autumn every two or three years. Space clumps 25 to 30cm (10 to 12in) apart in beds, window boxes or grow in pots.

Dill *Peucedanum graveolens*
Annual; 75 to 90cm (2ft 6in to 3ft) height. Grow in sunny situation in **fertile, well-drained soil**. Sow seeds in spring, thin the plants to stand 22 to 30cm (9 to 12in) apart. Pick leaves before the plants set seed.

Fennel *Foeniculum vulgare*
Perennial, grow as annual; 0.9 to 1.5m (3 to 5ft) height. Sow in light, well-drained fertile soil in a warm sheltered place in the sun. Thin plants to stand 45cm (18in) apart. Remove the flower heads unless seeds are wanted.

Marjoram *Origanum marjorana*
Perennial; 45 to 60cm (18in to 2ft) height. Succeeds best in dry, ordinary loam soil in a sunny situation. Sow outdoors in April, or root cuttings under cold frame in April to May. Thin seedlings or plant rooted cuttings to allow each plant about 25cm (10in). Grow in pots or window boxes for early and late picking. Cut and dry the flowering stems for winter.

Mint
There are two common varieties of mint. Mint spreads rapidly so to avoid this it is best to plant it in containers.

Apple Mint *Mentha rotundifolia*
Foliage hairy, rounded leaves, light coloured. 60 to 90cm (2 to 3ft) height.

Spearmint *Mentha spicata*
Mid-green leaves. 45 to 60cm (18in to 2ft) height. Plant both types in deep moist, fertile soil in semi-shade in clumps 30cm (12in) apart. Increase by lifting and dividing roots in spring or cuttings placed in unheated frames in April to May. Cut and dry the sprigs in summer and store in glass jars.

Parsley *Carum petroselinum*
Treat as an annual. 30 to 60cm (1 to 2ft) in height. Thrives in deep, moist rich soil in sun or light shade. Sow in spring or about July. Be patient if germination is slow. Thin or plant to stand at 20cm (9in) spacing. Protect plants with cloches, or lift a few roots into pots to put in frames or bring indoors for winter use in cold districts.

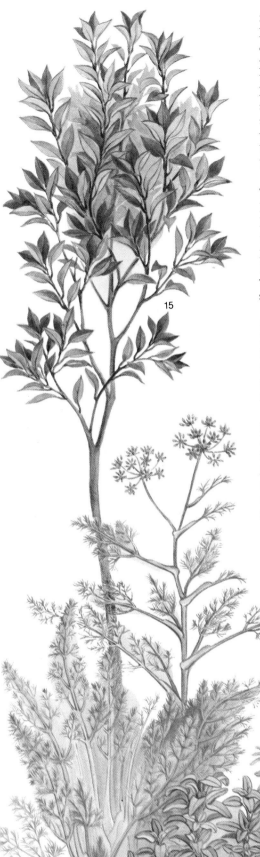

Sage *Salvia officinalis*

Perennial. 60cm (2ft) high. Prefers a dry soil in a warm sunny position. Raise plants from heel cuttings (see page 81) taken in September and rooted in un-heated frames, or sow seeds indoors in spring and harden off. Plant out in late spring, allowing 37cm (15in) space between each plant. Grow sage in pots, boxes or in beds. In summer, cut bunches, tie up and dry.

Tarragon *Artemisia dracunculus*

Perennial 45 to 60cm (18in to 2ft) high. Prefers deep-dug light soil in a warm sunny position. Increase by dividing plants in spring, space divisions 20cm (8in) apart. Protect against severe frost with cloches. Cut and dry leaves in summer before flowers appear.

Common Thyme *Thymus vulgaris*

Perennial evergreen. 10 to 20cm (4 to 8in) high. Both lemon and common thyme succeed best in warm light dry soils in sunny situations, but grow well in pots or window boxes.

Common thyme can be increased by seeds sown outdoors in late spring. Both thymes can be raised from cuttings or by division in May. Allow space between plants of 22 to 30cm (9 to 12in) for both varieties. Dry or freeze summer shoots although fresh leaves are best.

Key
1 Balm
2 Parsley
3 Marjoram
4 Thyme
5 Chervil
6 Dill
7 Angelica
8 Fennel
9 Sage
10 Tarragon
11 Chives
12 Apple Mint
13 Spearmint
14 Sweet Basil
15 Bay

Fruit growing

The trend towards increasingly smaller gardens and the need for quick results have brought about many changes in home fruit-growing. Modern high-yield compact trees and plants can be grown in confined spaces and bring home-grown, vitamin-rich fruits within the grasp of a wide public.

Climate, soil and site are as important in fruit-growing as in other crops. Rootstocks, pollination, varieties and pruning are of particular significance for promoting rich crops.

Fruit in the small garden

Growing fruit, flowers and vegetables close to walls and buildings can present problems. To cultivate these successfully and maintain an attractive appearance in a small space demands considerable forethought.

When considering plans to plant fruit, it is useful to bear the following points in mind. Firstly, if you do not grow it, can you obtain such fruits in season? If not, is it necessary or just a luxury? For instance, cooking apples, pears or plums can usually be bought more cheaply than good dessert varieties, which may be more difficult or impossible to obtain. Good dessert fruit of any type is more expensive than cooking sorts, and may lack the flavour of fruit ripened on a bush or tree. In the smallest spaces, grow cordon or trained forms of hard and soft fruits. Dwarf pyramid and dwarf bush types produce a greater weight of fruit per plant than cordons, but need more space.

Siting and aspect

Cordon and similar forms of tree make useful screens and can be sited in a north/south or east/west direction. In southern districts reserve sunny south facing walls for dessert pears.

Use east or west facing walls for dessert plums, gages and pears, or red currants.

All fruits thrive in a sheltered, sunny situation but crops such as raspberries, blackcurrants, gooseberries, blackberries, loganberries and early cooking apples will crop on north-facing walls in the South. The results will obviously be inferior to similar varieties grown in more favoured positions.

In gardens north of the River Trent position dessert apples against south-facing walls, and cordon cooking apples, currants and gooseberries on east or west-facing aspects.

Avoid planting fruit where it may be covered regularly with sea spray, or in heavy shade under trees. Trees in grass are the most likely to suffer from drought and starvation and need a clear 30cm (12in) minimum width of earth around each stem. Keep the grass short to reduce the competition for summer moisture.

LEFT Cordon-trained gooseberry bushes take up little space and are useful in small gardens.
ABOVE Spring mulching of a blackcurrant bush to preserve moisture.
RIGHT Fruit bushes hide the vegetable plot from the view of the house in this small garden.

Rootstocks

Apples, pears, plums and many other kinds of fruit trees consist of two or more plants—a scion, or fruiting wood, which is budded or grafted on to the rootstock.

There are various combinations of these and the home gardener should select grades which have vigour, resistance to pests and disease, and a strong formation of stem or trunk.

Healthy dwarf-growing rootstocks are most useful for the production of small-sized fruiting trees and bushes. Outstanding examples of this are the apple rootstocks M1X and M26 which not only enable small trees to be grown in confined spaces, but induce earlier and heavier cropping.

Pollination

In most years healthy fruit trees of named varieties produce an abundance of blossom, but certain sorts of cherry and plum in particular, and some apples and pears, may fail to set fruit. This problem can be overcome by planting two different but compatible varieties together which flower at the same time.

Variety

New and improved varieties have brought increased crop yields, a longer season and a greater resistance to disease than many kinds grown a century ago. Many home gardens are more concerned with quality than quantity, and Cox's Orange Pippin apples, for example, are still preferred to the heavier-cropping newer varieties, which are of inferior quality.

The more exotic fruits such as figs, apricots, peaches, nectarines, and grapes are best left until some gardening experience has been gained. These are specialists' subjects and also take up a fair amount of space.

Training

This is an important part of fruit growing. It is closely bound up with manuring and feeding, and is essential for intensive production.

The training of different forms of tree, such as standards, bush forms, cordons, pyramids and any other, is inseparable from pruning and feeding and pest and disease control.

Even when a framework of branches has been formed, pruning remains necessary to regulate the amount of fruiting wood and to counteract any tendency to biennial cropping (heavy fruiting in alternate years) rather than a reliable annual crop.

The principles of feeding are much the same for fruit as any other plants. Nitrogen promotes growth of leaf and shoot, phosphates encourage good root action and earliness, and potash increases hardiness, improves quality and resistance to disease.

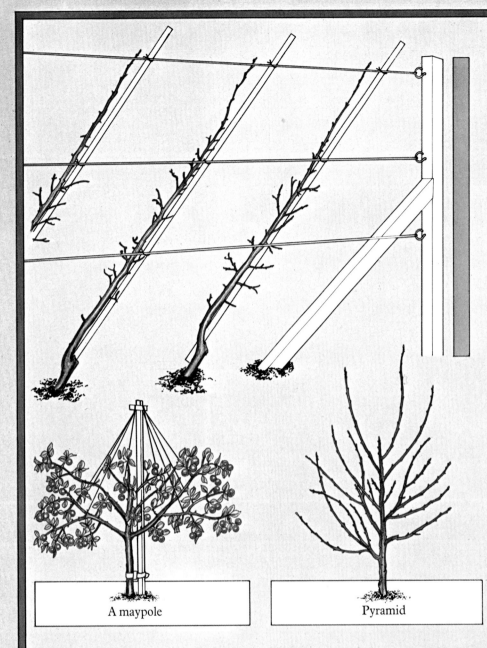

To train cordon apples, tie stakes at an oblique angle to horizontal wires. The stakes need not be driven deeply into the ground. Tie the growing tree to the angled stake.

A maypole (below left) safeguards small bush trees from breaking their branches under the weight of the fruit. Attach wires to the main stake and loop these round fruiting branches. Protect the branches with strips of hessian to stop the wire from digging into the bark.

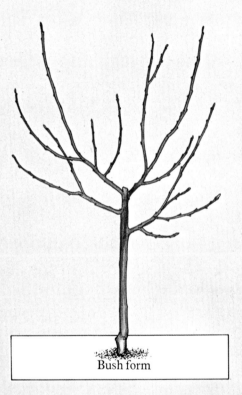

A maypole

Pyramid

Bush form

Gooseberries – double upright cordon (left), triple upright cordon (right). Prune fruiting spurs but never cut main stems unless diseased or damaged.

Blackcurrants – cut back to 16 cm (6 inches) off the ground after planting and remove one third of the old wood after fruiting.

Redcurrants – like gooseberries, prune only fruiting spurs and leave the main framework uncut.

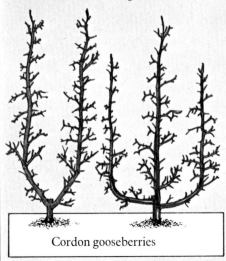

Cordon gooseberries

Blackcurrant

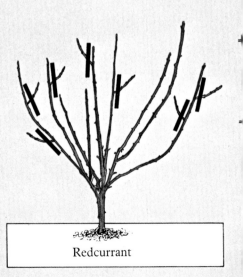

Redcurrant

Step-by-step training and supporting fruit

Pruning a tip bearer – prune back only
half the number of shoots.

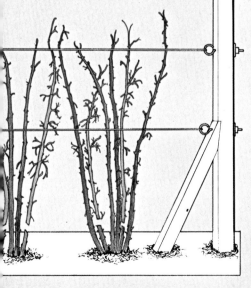

spberries – cut out old shoots after
iting, and tie in young canes.

Spur-pruning cordon apples – cut back
fruit spurs each autumn.

Table of popular varieties of Apples/Plums/Pears

season of use

Varieties of Apples	Pollinator	Jul	Aug	Sept	Oct	Nov	Dec	Jan	Feb	Mar	Apr	May	Jun
Culinary													
Crawley Beauty							■	■	■	■			
Discovery			■	■									
Emneth Early		■	■										
Bramley Seedling						■	■	■	■	■			
Rev. W. Wilks				■	■	■							
Grenadier			■	■									
Dessert													
Geo Cave			■										
Worcester Pearmain				■	■								
James Grieve				■									
Laxton's Fortune				■	■								
Egremont Russet					■	■	■						
Cox's Orange Pippin						■	■	■					
Newton Wonder						■	■	■	■	■			
Idared						■	■	■	■	■			
Crispin							■	■	■				
Tydeman's Late Orange										■	■		
Varieties of Pears – All dessert													
Fondante d'Automne				■	■								
Williams Bon C				■									
Bristol X				■	■								
Fertility Improved				■	■								
Beurré Hardy					■								
Louise Bonne					■								
Conference					■	■							
Marie Louise					■	■							
Doyenne du Comice						■	■						
Winter Nelis						■	■	■					
Plum Varieties	**Pollinator**												
Dessert													
Early Laxton	Czar/Victoria		■										
Early Transparent Gage	s.f.		■										
Denniston's Superb	s.f.		■										
Victoria	s.f. Czar		■										
Coe's Golden Drop	Early Transparent Gage			■									
Damsons													
Farleigh Damson	Warwickshire Drooper			■									
Merryweather	s.f.			■									

Key s.f. = self-fertile – will pollinate its own variety.

5-year plan for fruit in your garden

A planting scheme should be based on two important questions: What are your favourite fruits? How much growing space is available? If there is not enough space to grow them all, then you must also decide which fruits are to be given priority.

Group together plants which have broadly similar requirements. Apples and pears are related to each other and require similar feeding, spraying and pruning treatment. Stone fruits, such as cherries, plums and gages (and peaches in warmer areas with rich soil) are best treated collectively. Members of this group break into growth earlier than apples and pears and the timing of their sprays, pruning and cropping has to be adjusted accordingly. Cherries, plums and gages suffer more severely than apples and pears in winter and in summer from bird damage. It is wise to provide protection against birds in some form of netted cage for soft fruits such as redcurrants and gooseberries in particular.

One important consideration in most households is the growing time. Strawberries give the quickest return, with raspberries, blackberries and loganberries in the next group, followed by blackcurrants, redcurrants, and gooseberries, then apples and pears, and finally plums and gages.

Year one

Plant apples, pears, plums, black, red and white currants, gooseberries, raspberries and strawberries in the autumn. Where space allows, plant blackberries and loganberries.

Peaches or nectarines can be planted in warm districts in a sheltered situation on a south or west-facing wall.

Stake and tie tree and cane fruits as necessary.

Fruit trees and bushes are pruned after planting.

Year two

Plant strawberries for a succession as they are of little value after three seasons.

Pick strawberries planted in year one.

Spray all fruits as necessary to control pests and diseases.

Mulch tree and bush fruits in spring.

Prune cordon apples and pears in summer and all tree, cane and bush fruits in autumn or spring.

Plant any replacements.

Year three

Increase strawberries by runners from healthy plants for planting this autumn.

Pick fruit from first and second-year planted strawberries, blackberries, loganberries, raspberries and blackcurrants.

Mulch and spray as for year two, but start feeding in spring.

Year four

Increase strawberries from healthy runners, planting these in autumn for succession.

Pick strawberries from runners planted in the first to third years and harvest all cane and bush fruits, cordon apples and pears.

Feed and mulch all fruits except new-planted strawberries.

Spray all plants as necessary to control pests and diseases.

Prune all trees, canes and bushes as needed, but cut plums as little as possible.

Clear first-year strawberries after fruiting.

Year five

Carry out the operations as for the previous year, grub out second-year strawberries and start to pick fruit from bush, pyramid or other forms of apples, pears or plums.

Take cuttings from healthy fruiting blackcurrant bushes as they will need clearing in two or three years' time. In the sixth year, soft fruit reverts to year one. For fruit trees see under individual fruits.

BELOW Fruit trees in a country garden can make an attractive feature.

Apples

Apples can be grown in most parts of lowland Britain. North of the River Trent, it is wiser to grow cooking varieties, because in most seasons the weather is too cool to ripen dessert apples. South of this line both sorts of fruit can be grown successfully with good cultivation. Tree space should be considered carefully in small gardens, and will depend on tree type, rootstocks and variety. Differences of climate, soil and cultural treatment have a bearing on growth. Warmth, moisture and high-nitrogen feeds all promote growth and cool, dry conditions inhibit it. Low-nitrogen nutrition lessens vigour.

Choice of tree

In confined spaces, the two most useful forms are the oblique cordon and the dwarf bush, both of which are also easier to manage. The oblique single cordon is a tree planted at an angle of 45 with one main stem which has short fruiting spurs along its length. The dwarf bush usually has a 60cm (2ft) clear stem.

There are four main groups of apple but only two, the dwarfing and the semi-dwarfing stocks are of real value to the amateur.

In the first category are Malling No 9 (M IX) and Malling 26 (M 26) which crop quickest and make the smallest trees.

In the second group are M VII and M 106. Variety influences tree size less than tree form and rootstocks, but vigorous varieties like Bramley's Seedling should not be planted in the smaller gardens.

The table below is an approximate guide to space requirements.

ABOVE Apple tree 'Discovery'.

Buy young plants from a specialist nursery or reputable garden centre. The new fruit-grower should obtain trees with an established basic framework of branches.

Apple trees are available as bare root or wrapped for planting in autumn and winter. Container-grown stock are more expensive but can also be planted between March and October.

Planting

A deep fertile well-drained loam is preferred but sound soil preparation is even more important. The land should be fertilized and ready to receive plants a week or two in advance of planting, which is best carried out in autumn.

Double dig the ground, and work well-rotted manure or peat into the top

Space for trees

Rootstock	M IX		M26		M VII and M106	
	Distance between trees	Distance between rows	Distance between trees	Distance between rows	Distance between trees	Distance between rows
Oblique Cordon	75cm (2ft 6in)	1.8m (6ft)	90cm (3ft)	2.1m (7ft)	90cm (3ft)	2.4m (8ft)
Dwarf Bush	3m (10ft)	3m (10ft)	3.6m (12ft)	3.6m (12ft)	4.5m (15ft)	4.5m (15ft)

(The distances given are for average conditions).

and second spit (or spade depth) together with 100g/m² (3oz per sq yd) of balanced base fertilizer.

The method of planting is described in the guide to tree planting on page 76.

Feeding

A sensible manuring and feeding programme is to mulch each tree in spring, applying a 2.5 to 5cm (1 to 2 in) layer of peat or manure. Scatter 70g/m² (2oz per sq yd) of balanced fertilizer before mulching with manure, or double that rate where peat is used.

Control weeds by cultivating (see page 63). Trees planted in grass should have a 30cm (12in) clean collar of soil to promote good growth. Close mowing of the grass is essential.

Pests and diseases

Pest and disease control is extremely important for best results. Preventative sprays can be applied when danger is imminent, or a routine pesticide spraying programme adhered to (see page 124 for fruit-spraying chart).

Pruning

Although of great importance, pruning is fairly simple for cordon and bush trees.

Cordons Cut any young fruit spurs back to within 2.5 to 5cm (1 to 2in) of the stem after planting and in following autumns, leave the main stem untouched until the top wire of the support is reached. Shorten the new tip growth to about 2.5cm (1in).

In summer, cut the tips back to four or five leaves of the new season's growth in July to encourage fruit bud formation.

Dwarf bush Following planting, prune the current season's growth to half its length, removing or cutting back any weak shoots to within 2.5m (1in) of the stem.

Summer pruning is not normally necessary with this type of tree.

Winter pruning follows one of two patterns; spur pruning as for cordons, or tip pruning. The main difference lies in the branches of bush trees and the central stem of the cordons. Treat varieties like Cox's Orange Pippin which fruit on short spurs in this way.

Tip bearers Worcester Pearmain forms fruit at the extremities of shoots. It is a tip bearer and needs different handling. In this method of pruning, cut back only half the number of shoots each autumn, leaving the remainder to fruit on the tips.

Fruit picking

When apples raised slightly into the palm of the hand and given a half twist part readily from the tree, they are ready to gather.

Apple Varieties – see table on page 112.

Pears

This fruit is more exacting than the apple, and cultivation north of the River Trent is problematical.

In Northern districts plant pears against a south-facing sunny wall or fence, but in southern areas in sheltered gardens such a favoured spot can be used for even more tender crops such as peaches. The size of a pear tree is governed by the same factors as for apples, but tree types and rootstocks present a few more problems. Tree types for small gardens are restricted to wall forms, such as cordons, which can be single, double or treble.

Pear trees trained as bushes tend to grow too large due to the vigour of many varieties, and to the absence of a dwarfing rootstock comparable to M-IX for apples. The dwarf pyramid form can be manipulated to remain within its allotted space, and closely resembles a bush, but has a central stem. Only two rootstocks are in common use:
Quince C semi-dwarfing, only suitable for fertile soils;
Quince A which is semi-vigorous and useful for soil that is poor or difficult to manage.

The minimum space requirements for pears both Quince A and Quince C rootstocks, are set out overleaf.

RIGHT Cordon pear, Fondante d'Automne, mulched to retain moisture in summer.

Space for trees
Rootstock-Quince C or Quince A

	Between trees	Between rows
Single cordon	90cm (3ft)	2.1m (7ft)
Dwarf pyramid	1.0m (3ft 6in)	2.1m (7ft)

RIGHT Conference pears.
BELOW Doyenne du Comice pears.

Many varieties of pear fail to set fruit unless planted with a pollinator. To overcome the need to plant two separate trees, some nurseries bud or graft two varieties into one rootstock, a main and a pollinator. These plants, with two or more sorts on a single rootstock, are sometimes referred to as family trees. Soil requirements, feeding and mulching, and pest and disease control are as for apples.

Pruning and training
Treat cordon pears as for cordon apples. After planting dwarf pyramid forms, cut back to the central or main leader to leave 20 to 25cm (8 to 10in) of new growth. In summer, shorten the branch tips, but not the central leader, to five or six leaves. Shorten laterals which arise from branches to three leaves, and sub-laterals to one leaf.

Subsequent summer pruning follows a similar pattern. In winter, shorten the central leader to leave 20 to 25cm (8 to 10in) of new growth. Cut back any secondary shoots which may have developed since summer pruning, to leave one or two buds on the new wood. In later years prune in winter until a height of about 2m (6ft 8in) is reached. After this, the new growth is cut each winter or spring to leave about 2.5cm (1in) of new wood.

Fruit picking Catch hold of and raise a fruit until the stalk is horizontal, giving it a gentle twist in the process. If the pear parts readily from the tree it is time to start picking. Place pears which require a ripening period in a cool, dull, frost-free place that is well ventilated. Varieties – see separate table on page 112, for details.

Plums
Bullaces, damsons, gages and plums are the hardiest of all stone fruits. One or other variety of plum is found in most counties. Dessert plums and gages need warmer conditions than cooking varieties and usually crop better when grown in the Midlands and South, or trained against a south-facing wall in sheltered situations in the North. Damsons are very hardy and make excellent and fruitful windbreaks. Plums flower earlier in spring than apples and pears and can easily be damaged by frost early in the year. Wall-trained trees in Northern areas can be protected with a muslin or plastic sheet. In the Midlands, plant dessert varieties against east or west-facing walls, saving those with a southern aspect for more tender fruits.

Plums are not yet grown as cordons and as a rule require more space than apples and pears, but they give heavier crops than cordon apples and pears. At present dwarfing rootstocks are not available and the trees most suitable for small gardens are pyramids and fan-trained forms (which produce excellent dessert plums) trained against a wall.

Most choice plums are budded or grafted on to a rootstock. Only two of these are suitable for growing plums in confined spaces: common plum and St Julien A, both of which are semi-dwarfing.

Two trees should be sufficient for an average family's demands, see page 125.

Space for trees

Rootstock—Common Plum or St Julien A

	Space between plants	Space between rows
Pyramid	3m (10ft)	3.6m (12ft)
Fan	4.5m (15ft)	— —

Plums will grow on most soils but for best results give them richer, moister ground than for apples. Plums and blackcurrants grow well together, since they both require more nitrogen than other fruits. Double dig, manure and fertilize the ground as for apples and pears.

Plums require lime but too much will result in yellowing leaves and stunted growth. Aim for a soil pH of 6.8 – just on the acid side of neutral.

The sequence and method of feeding, mulching and weed control are as for apples. When plums start to crop heavily, apply 35g/m² (1 oz per sq yd) of nitro-chalk in addition to the annual fertilizer dressing.

When buying young trees, it is advisable to get them ready-trained from a reputable source and worked on one of the semi-dwarfing rootstocks already mentioned. Use balled-and-wrapped trees for autumn planting, as they are cheaper; container-grown plants can be set out at other times. Plant as for other trees, first staking as needed (see page 76). Avoid deep planting or the dwarfing effect of the rootstock may be lost in scion-rooting, a condition in which the fruiting variety forms a root system of its own and is independent of the important restraining influence of the rootstock.

Crop thinning
In a good year plums set more fruit than can be supported or nurtured. Thin the crop to leave the fruits 5 to 7cm (2 to 3in) apart, and prop up the main branches of older trees.

Pests and diseases Routine measures are necessary for the control of various fungal diseases such as silver leaf disease and die-back.

Pruning
Pyramids: reduce the branches to about 20cm (8in) to a downward pointing bud each winter. In April each year cut back the main or central leader to one-third of the new growth, until it has reached 2.7m (9ft). In subsequent years remove all but 2.5cm (1in) of the new wood in May and any shoot which threatens to replace the main stem.

A three-year-old fan-trained tree should be pruned after planting by shortening the branches to within 60cm (2ft) of their base. Train the resulting growths as follows: tie in the topmost shoots to extend the branches; remove outward or ingrowing buds; allow lateral growths (side shoots on branches) to develop above and below branches at about 15cm (6in) intervals and tie these in, pinching out the growing tips if they encroach on other shoots.

A framework of horizontal wires with 15cm (6in) spacing makes training easier. In subsequent years after fruiting, cut out old laterals and tie in replacement shoots. Keep growths at least 10cm (4in) apart. In late spring, stop sub-laterals (side shoots on laterals) at the first leaf, and remove shoots growing into or away from the wall. Plum varieties – see separate table on page 112.

BELOW Plum 'Severn Cross'.

Picking plums Plums are ready for use when the flesh separates readily from the stone. Some varieties, like Coe's Golden Drop, can be stored for a week or two if picked on the point of changing colour, before becoming fully ripe. Store these in a cool place out of direct sunlight.

Strawberries
The strawberry is one of the most popular and widely grown of all garden fruits. Cultivation requires sufficient space (minimum 5 inch pot), adequate depth of soil, an open sunny aspect and protection from freezing winds, pests and diseases. Present-day strawberries are the product of much hybridization and, by using different types and varieties, the fruiting season can be extended from May to November. Strawberries give the quickest return of any fruit after planting.

There are several recognized ways of growing strawberries for at least four months of the year without the aid of a heated greenhouse: the early protected crop, the early outdoor crop; the main or mid-season crop, the late summer crop, the autumn outdoor crop, and the autumn protected crop, and the alpine crop.

Strawberries are generally planted in the ground, but in confined spaces they can be grown in containers. Strawberries require well-drained, porous soil that is moisture-retentive and drainage should be provided where the ground lies wet for long spells after rain. Incorporate sand with organic matter before planting on clay or heavy soil. Dig the ground 30cm (12in) deep, working in about 3kg/m² (7lb per sq yd) of well-rotted manure or peat well in advance of planting. Grow this crop in mildly acid soils; if the pH reading is below 6, add sufficient ground limestone to raise the pH to that figure. On chalk or limestone soils that are alkaline with a pH of 7 or above, apply a further 1kg/m² (2lb 8oz per sq yd) of peat. Fork in a dressing of 100g/m² (3oz per sq yd) of a balanced high-potash fertilizer about 7 to 10 days before planting. This application rate should be increased by half as much again where peat and not manure has been dug in.

To reduce attack by pests and diseases, give the land a minimum rest of two or three years between strawberry crops. Grow a different crop in the intervening period.

LEFT Picking strawberries. A bed of straw has been put down under the fruits to keep them clean.
BELOW Propagating strawberries by pegging runners into pots.
BELOW LEFT Pot-grown strawberries (Cambridge Vigour).

Planting

Best carried out between mid-July and late September, either just before or after rain. Set out vigorous, certified virus-free, pot-grown plants with 75cm (2ft 6in) between rows and 45cm (18in) between plants. A closer spacing of 30cm (12in) is adopted for protected crops when growing for one season only.

Use a trowel for planting. Make the hole deep and wide enough to take the roots comfortably without being cramped. Plant firmly, work fine soil around the roots and finish with the ground level flush with the top of the root ball. It is a good idea to grow a few plants for runner production (the production of young plants by pegging down embryo plants in summer and rooting them). Six plants will produce twenty or so. Water the plants in if the soil is dry.

Put plants into well-crocked 5 inch pots using loam-based or soilless potting compost, and plunge these pots up to the rims in sand or peat to overwinter in a sheltered spot.

Hoe regularly to keep weeds down. In dry weather, water the young plants as necessary. Spray with malathion if aphids appear. Cover the early protected crop with cloches in the first half of February, the late crop in September, to prevent frost damage.

Put down a bed of straw under the

swelling fruits before they are weighed down to soil level, to keep them clean. Strawing is practised with all strawberry crops, except for those grown in containers, where the fruit trusses are supported. Put down slug pellets.

Picking

Strawberries for dessert are picked with the green calyx attached, but those for making jam are gathered without. When harvesting is finished remove any cloches; clip off the leaves with a pair of shears and rake up the remains, pulling out weeds and cutting off runners in the process. Fork up the soil between rows, taking care not to disturb the plants. If the soil is dry, water

thoroughly. Apply a mulch of well-rotted manure or a 2.5cm (1in) layer of peat in a strip 15cm (6in) wide on each side of the rows of plants in autumn. Give a dressing of 70g/m² (2 oz per sq yd) of a balanced fertilizer before mulching where peat is used.

Grub out (dig up) all plants after three seasons of cropping.

Propagation

Select the strongest and earliest runners (small plants preferably from plants set aside for the purpose) pegging these into 7.5cm (3in) pots sunk into the ground. Keep the runners well watered and sprayed against aphids. Remove any growth beyond the runners after pegging them down. As soon as these runners have rooted, sever them from the parent strawberry and plant out as soon as possible.

Pests and diseases

Strawberries are prone to various ailments. Keep a watch for grey mould or botrytis which can quickly reduce the berries to a fluffy grey shrunken mass. Remove infected fruits as soon as these are noticed and spray or dust the crop with benomyl or captan fungicides.

Control aphids with malathion or derris preparations. Two other diseases which can ruin a bed of strawberries are mildew and leaf spot.

Mildew covers fruits and leaves with a powdery white dust unless checked: spray or dust with benomyl or dinocap.

Leaf spot appears as greyish spots surrounded by reddish-brown rings and unless controlled will seriously weaken plants. Cut off and burn affected leaves, especially after fruiting.

Suitable varieties
Early
Cambridge Vigour, early in the first year, subsequently with later growth so it becomes a 'maincrop.' Vigorous plants, upright habit, producing large conical scarlet fruit of fine flavour.

Gorella, produces wedge-shaped fruit of good size, colour and flavour. Resistant but not immune to mildew. Grandee, heavy yielder, produces very large fruit.

These varieties are suitable for covering with cloches as well as open air cultivation.

Maincrop
Cambridge Favourite, heavy cropping, reliable, makes large plant, producing big pinkish-red berries. Suitable for cloches and frames as well as outdoors; mildew resistant.

Redgauntlet, medium size spreading habit, large fruit, crimson conical or wedge-shape. Suitable for Northern districts, and produces a secondary autumn crop.

Royal Sovereign, moderate cropper of finest flavoured scarlet fruits. Suffers more than most varieties from disease. Early fruiting first year, later in subsequent seasons.

Late
Cambridge Late Pine, vigorous plants, suffer less from frost than many. Berries medium to large, sweet alpine flavour.

Domanil, heavy cropper, producing medium to large berries of good flavour. Elista, late, but heavy cropper. Produces small compact plants. Talisman, vigorous upright habit, large fruit. Produces second crop in autumn. Cover with cloches for late autumn crop.

Perpetual fruiting
Hampshire Maid has large conical or rounded berries of good flavour. Sparse runner production, and suffers from drought. Gento, heavy yielding, producing large conical fruits in summer and autumn.

Cane fruits
Raspberries, blackberries and loganberries come under this heading. In very small gardens it may be practical to grow only raspberries from this group as it requires less space.

Raspberries
This crop is second only to strawberries for giving a quick return after planting. Their flowering and fruiting season enables them to be successfully grown further north than many fruits. A further advantage is their heavy yield – about 1kg per metre (2lb 4oz per yd) run of row. Unlike strawberries, raspberries are not covered although they benefit from shelter from strong winds, especially during the winter months.

Raspberries will crop well in light shade as well as sun, provided the ground is fertile and moist.

When growing raspberries for the first time, buy Ministry-certified, virus-free healthy stock. It is a false economy to plant diseased stock which will cost as much to grow as healthy canes. Buy raspberry canes which have wrapped roots and plant them as soon as possible to prevent drying out. The usual planting period is November to February.

Planting
Raspberries require a fertile, deep, well-worked and manured soil to nourish their surface fibrous roots. As they are also deep rooting, prepare the land well. Excavate a spade-deep trench 45cm (18in) wide. Apply a 5cm (2in) layer of well-rotted manure, compost or peat and fork this into the bottom of the trench. Lime the soil if necessary but only to raise the pH to 6.5 – on the acid side of neutral. Where peat is used, apply 140g/m² (4oz per sq yd) of bone meal at the same time and work it in. Replace the top soil and break up any lumps of earth in the process. Scatter and lightly fork in 140g/m² (4oz per sq yd) of a balanced fertilizer before planting. Remove any perennial weeds when preparing the land.

BELOW Malling Delight, a mid-season heavy yielding raspberry cane.

Raspberries need some form of support, which can conveniently consist of posts and wires to which the canes are tied not less than 10cm (4in) apart. Hammer in posts of minimum length 2m (6ft 6in) spaced 3m (10ft) apart. Fix two horizontal wires to the posts, one at 90cm (3ft) high and the other at 1.5m (5ft) above ground level. Guy the end posts, using a straining wire and pegs, to prevent the posts being pulled in.

Plant raspberry canes 37 to 60cm (15 to 24in) apart, with 1.5m (5ft) between

rows where more than one row is grown. Use the closer spacing for varieties like Malling Jewel, which do not produce canes very freely.

Dig a V-shaped hole, at least 15 to 17cm (6 to 7in) deep and wide enough to take a raspberry cane. Insert cane upright and firm the soil by treading round each cane. After planting, cut each cane back to two or three buds above soil level. It is a mistake to take a crop (to allow it to fruit) the season after planting, because little or no new growth will occur, and future cropping suffers.

Keep raspberry beds clear of weeds, and mulch with manure, compost or peat in spring. This crop requires a cool, moist root run which a surface covering helps to create. Before mulching, apply a 100g/m² (3 oz per sq yd) dressing of balanced fertilizer each year from the second season onwards. Water the beds in dry seasons. Keep the space clean between rows, removing any growths which develop.

Pruning and training
The aim of any system should be to provide new growth to replace old

fruited canes. As new growth develops, train these above the fruiting rods, which should be cut out and burnt as soon as picking ceases. Unless new canes are temporarily tied above the old, there is a constant danger of drops of water carrying disease spores on to the young wood.

In the first autumn after planting summer-fruiting varieties, thin out the growths, and tie in the new canes to allow 7 to 10cm (3 to 4in) between each. In subsequent years remove all old fruited canes to ground level as soon as picking finishes. Thin and tie in new growth as in the first year, cut out weak and straggling shoots completely. In February trim the tips of the tallest canes to about 1.5m (5ft).

Autumn-fruiting varieties are treated in a similar manner to summer-fruiting varieties at planting time. In the first autumn loosely tie the canes to the wires to prevent them from being blown about. In the following February and every following year cut all growth down to the ground level. This produces strong shoots which fruit at their tips in autumn.

Propagation
It is unwise to save canes or spawn from old fruiting beds as these become increasingly infected with viral and other diseases. Raspberries can be increased by digging up healthy vigorous new canes from young stools in autumn or winter.

Pests and diseases
The most common pests are aphids, controlled by malathion sprays. Raspberry beetle, which lays grubs in the berries, can be controlled with a fenitrothion spray 10 days after the flowers open and again 14 days later.

Suitable varieties

Early Glen Clover, medium height, fine flavour, strong growing and one of the heaviest croppers.
Phyllis King, similar to the above, not always easy to pick.
Mid-season Malling Delight, a heavy yielder, producing large fruits, aphid resistant. Malling Orion, good cropper, fine flavour.
Late Malling Admiral, vigorous, good quality fruit, excellent for freezing and jam-making.
Autumn fruiting Norfolk Giant, good quality, attractive fruit, excellent for freezing and jam-making.

Blackberries and Loganberries
The climate, soil and site requirements of these two crops are similar to those of raspberries. Both require more space and are rather too vigorous for very small plots.

Start off with healthy, Ministry-certified virus-free plants. Treat the ground as for raspberries, giving similar amounts of manure, lime and fertilizer as necessary. Erect posts 3m (10ft) apart to support three horizontal wires at 0.9, 1.2 and 1.5m (3, 4 and 5ft) above ground.

Follow the planting instructions outlined for raspberries, but space blackberries at 3.6m (12ft) and loganberries at 2.4m (8ft) apart.

The same principles apply as for raspberries. Immediately after cutting out the old rods, tie young blackberry or loganberry canes into position, leaving more than will eventually be needed because some will not survive the winter.

In spring, after the danger of hard frost has gone, cut out dead or surplus canes.

Loganberries LY59 is a special selection of virus-free loganberry. It is of medium vigour and fruits are large, conical or rounded in shape, dull red and juicy.

Thornless Loganberry, very similar to the above but thornless, lighter green in colour, good cropper.

Propagation
Always bear in mind the importance of disease-free stock. Blackberries and loganberries can be increased quite simply by rooting the tips of young shoots ('tip layering').

In July or August dig a 10 to 12 cm (4 to 5in) deep hole, peg a tip into the hole and fill it up with sandy fine earth. Firm the soil. In late autumn or spring sever the rooted tips from parent plants, lift and plant in their fruiting positions.

Pests and diseases
Treat as for raspberry. Dig up and burn any virus-infected and seriously stunted plants.

Suitable varieties

Blackberries Bedford Giant, earliest, and produces the largest berries, fruiting in late July and early August.

Himalaya Giant, extremely vigorous, fruiting in August and September, heavy cropper.

Parsley-leaved or cut-leaf, moderate growth, good flavour.

Oregon Thornless is a thornless form of cut leaf type.

Currants and gooseberries
These are some of the best-natured and longsuffering plants which, with a minimum of attention, crop year after year. Although they are related, they differ in their requirements and cultivation. Currants and gooseberries can be grown in most parts of the country provided their modest needs are attended to.

Currants There are black and red varieties; white currants are a variety of the red form, and have similar needs.

The essential differences between black and red currants are the fruiting habit and the soil and moisture requirements. Blackcurrants bear the bulk of their crop on new wood, while redcurrants fruit on old stems. Blackcurrants require more generous feeding, higher nitrogen fertilizer and moister growing conditions.

For best results all currants and gooseberries need sunlight, good air circulation, shelter from intensely cold winds and protection from late spring frosts. However, they will all tolerate light shade in the absence of ideal conditions. Redcurrants will crop satisfactorily on east or west-facing walls, blackcurrants will even grow on a north-facing wall in the Midlands and the South.

It is important to obtain healthy and disease-free plants, so buy Ministry-certified stock from a reliable supplier. Blackcurrants in particular suffer from virus diseases, such as reversion, or nettle leaf.

Plants can be raised from hardwood cuttings (see page 80) or new shoots 25 to 30cm (10 to 12in) long, taken in autumn and rooted outside under the shelter of a wall or hedge.

The method of preparing the land is broadly similar for currants and gooseberries and is suitable for most soils.

These crops occupy the ground for a long period with limited opportunities to improve the soil after planting. Well in advance of planting, double-dig the land, simultaneously working in 3 to 4kg/m² (7 to 9lb per sq yd) of well-rotted manure or peat. Correct the soil acidity, liming if necessary to raise the pH to 6.5, or adding peat if the land is alkaline. Scatter and lightly fork in 140g/m² (4oz per sq yd) of a high potash fertilizer. Where the ground is of a sandy nature, add 35g/m² (1oz per sq yd) of sulphate of potash for gooseberries and redcurrants.

Planting
It is best to plant in autumn. Prune the bushes after planting (see below) and water if the ground is dry. Hoe to keep the weeds down and mulch currants and gooseberries with a 2.5 to 5.0cm (1 to 2in) layer of manure, compost or peat in spring. In future years, apply fertilizer dressing before mulching by giving blackcurrants 100g/m² (3oz per sq yd) of a balanced fertilizer, plus 35g/m² (1oz per sq yd) of nitro-chalk. Give redcurrants and gooseberries the same quantity of fertilizer plus 35g/m² (1oz per sq yd) of sulphate of potash, but without the nitro-chalk.

Pruning
Cut blackcurrants hard back to two or three buds above ground level immediately after planting. This promotes vigorous growth necessary for heavy cropping.

Shorten the branches of redcurrant bushes and gooseberries by about a half to an upward pointing bud. Cut any weak and spindly shoots back to the ground. When training cordon forms

Suitable varieties

Suitable varieties
Blackcurrants Mendip Cross, early, heavy cropper. Tor Cross, early, similar to Mendip Cross, good quality.

Seabrook Black, early to mid-season, suitable for northern districts.

Raven, early to mid-season, vigorous growth, fine flavour.

Wellington XXX, mid-season, crops heavily in southern conditions.

Brodtorp, mid-season, promising newer variety.

Baldwin, late, compact, heavy cropper in southern and western areas.

Redcurrants Earliest of Fourlands, early, vigorous habit, heavy cropper, small fruited, very good for jellies and preserves. Jonkheer van Tets, early, crops well, good quality fruit.

Laxton's No 1, early, moderate growth, excellent quality.

Laxton's Perfection, mid-season, given to wind damage, largest fruited variety.

Red Lake, early to mid-season, similar to Laxton's No 1 but larger fruited. Wilsons Long Bunch, late, good quality, large strings or bunches of fruit.

ABOVE A fruit cage for protection against birds. This cage would not be difficult to make at home.

of gooseberries or redcurrants, remove any surplus shoots and shorten the lateral growths to 2.5 to 5cm (1 to 2in) to form fruiting spurs on the old wood.

Once blackcurrant bushes are established, cut to soil level one-quarter to one-third of all the older shoots to encourage vigorous young fruiting branches. Where strong growths develop low down on old wood, prune back to those branches rather than cut them to soil level and lose fruiting wood. With established bush forms of redcurrants and gooseberries, shorten new tip growth of branches by half, for a year or two until these are 1.5 to 1.8m (5 to 6 ft) high. These form the main framework on which the fruiting spurs develop. Cut the young laterals or shoots back to 2.5 to 5cm (1 to 2in) to form fruit spurs. For cordon redcurrants and gooseberries, shorten the laterals as for the bush forms. Do not prune the main branch or branches until they are taller than required. When this occurs, cut back the new growth to within 2.5cm (1in) of the older wood.

Pest and disease control
See fruit-spraying chart, p. 124.

Gooseberries Keepsake, early, suitable for cooking if picked small, or dessert if left to ripen, pale green fruit.

Whitesmith, early to mid-season, good cropper, fine flavour, large yellowish-green berries.

Careless, early to mid-season, pick early for cooking or leave to ripen for dessert, fruit greenish white of good flavour.

Lancashire Lad, mid-season, red, moderate vigour, moderately flavoured berries.

Leveller, mid-season, yellowish-green fruit, best flavoured, large berries, dessert variety.

Whinhams Industry, mid-season, large red berries, very fine flavour.

Lancer, late, yellowish-green, good-sized dessert fruit.

White Lion, late, whitish green, very fine flavour, pick early for cooking but leave to ripen for dessert.

BELOW LEFT Redcurrants
BELOW RIGHT Blackcurrants
RIGHT Gooseberries

Fruit-spraying chart

When to spray	Pest or disease	Spray material
Apples and pears		
Winter (Dormant)	Egg stages of aphid, red spider and other pests	Tar oil
Spring	Aphid, caterpillar and other, plus scab disease	Malathion, derris or fenitrothion plus captan or benomyl
Mid-Spring (Pink bud of apple or petal fall of pear)	Scab and mildew if woolly aphid present	Benomyl plus dimethoate
Late Spring (Petal fall of apple, post-blossom of pear)	Scab and/or mildew	Benomyl
Early June	Red spider and aphid	Malathion and derris
Late June	Red spider and aphid if scab is present	Repeat malathion and derris and add captan to spray
Early July and repeat 14 days later	Aphid, codling and red spider	Fenitrothion
Plum		
December (Dormant)	Eggs of aphid, red spider and other	Tar oil
March	Aphid and caterpillar	Derris, malathion or fenitrothion
Early June (post-blossom)	Aphid and red spider	Derris, malathion or dimethoate
Blackcurrant		
Winter (Dormant)	Eggs of aphid, red spider and other	Tar oil
Late March, early April (start of flowering) and repeat after 21 days	Big bud	Lime sulphur
When seen	Aphid and red spider	Derris, dimethoate or malathion
Gooseberry		
Winter (Dormant)	Eggs of aphid and other and disease spores	Tar oil
April	American Gooseberry mildew	Lime sulphur
May (After flowering)	American Gooseberry mildew	Lime sulphur
When seen	Aphid and caterpillar	Derris or fenitrothion
Strawberry		
April	Aphid	Malathion
Early May	Aphids and mildew	Malathion plus benomyl
Mid-May (first flowers open)	Aphids and botrytis	Malathion plus benomyl or thiram

When to spray	Pest or disease	Spray material
Raspberry		
Winter (Dormant)	Eggs of aphid and disease spores	Tar oil
March (Bud burst)	Cane spot	Copper spray
June (10 days after flowering)	Raspberry beetle	Derris, malathion or fenitrothion
21 days after flowering	Raspberry beetle	Derris, malathion or fenitrothion

Note: many of these sprays can be mixed to provide combined control for pests and diseases.

Crop yields

Crop	Planting distances Between plants	Between rows	Yield
Apple–cordon	75cm (2ft 6in)	1.8m (6ft)	3kg per tree (7lb)
Apple–pyramid	1m (3ft 6in)	2.1m (7ft)	5kg per tree (12lb)
Apple–bush	3m (10ft)	3m (10ft)	10kg per tree (25lb)
Pears	similar to apples		
Plum–pyramid	3m (10ft)	3.5m (12ft)	8kg per tree
Plum–fan	4.5m (15ft)	—	7kg per tree (18lb)
Blackcurrant	1.5m (5ft)	1.8m (6ft)	4kg per tree (9lb)
Redcurrant–cordon	37.5cm (15in)	1.5m (5ft)	1kg per bush (2lb 4oz)
Redcurrant–bush	1.5m (5ft)	1.8m (6ft)	3kg per bush (7lb)
Gooseberry–cordon	37.5cm (15in)	1.5m (5ft)	1.3kg per bush (3lb)
Gooseberry–bush	1.5m (5ft)	1.8m (6ft)	4kg per bush (9lb)
Blackberry	3m (10ft)	1.8m (6ft)	0.6kg/30cm of row (1lb 4oz/12in)
Raspberry	45cm (18in)	1.8m (6ft)	450g/30cm of row (1lb/12in)
Loganberry	3m (10ft)	1.8m (6ft)	0.6kg/30cm of row (1lb 4oz/12in)
Strawberry	45cm (18in)	75cm (2ft 6in)	150g per plant (5oz)

TOP Early transparent gage (Laxton).
BOTTOM Apple (James Grieve)

Crop yields

These vary widely according to season, climate, soil, site, variety and standard of cultivation and any indications can only be approximate. The table left gives details of suitable spacing and approximate yield of various fruits, assuming dwarfing rootstocks are used and given a good standard of cultivation.

(N.B. Figures given for yields are for plants in full bearing (at their peak of production) and are approximate only.)

Special-purpose gardens

The special gardens discussed here are designed to suit peculiarities of site or personal circumstances or preferences. The differences of style and methods of application are merely modern adaptations of old concepts; water gardens, for instance, have been in existence for thousands of years. The only comparative newcomer is the busy man's garden below, designed for minimum time spent on upkeep.

The busy man's garden

The aim here is a garden which serves its purpose and can be kept neat and tidy for 52 weeks of the year with a minimum of attention. The busy owner can solve this by paying someone else to look after the garden or by streamlining the work. Here we consider the latter alternative.

With time at a premium, reduce or eliminate time-consuming repetitive tasks. Annual bedding schemes, climbers and plants require constant tying and attention and should be kept to a minimum. Where the aim is primarily to keep the garden tidy and presentable, incorporate labour-saving surfaces and avoid fussy planting.

Lawns should be formed of finer grasses like fescues and bents, or a blend of these and special hard-wearing rye grass. Avoid farm grass mixtures which require heavy mowing. Changes in level are best dealt with by the use of retaining walls, or shrub and grass banks, or terraces, all of which are much less demanding than rock gardens, unless these are heavily planted with permanent subjects.

Plants and planting

A few well chosen and carefully sited plants can look most attractive as well as being easy to manage. Select slow growing perennial plants, preferably evergreen, such as dwarf conifers, heathers, and hollies. The herringbone cotoneaster and pyracantha are both useful for covering walls. Colourful bush roses require little care.

Keep planting in lawns to a minimum to cut out obstacles to mowing.

Lawn edges should be as straight as the site will allow. Hard kerbs round beds and borders will reduce grass edging problems.

Trained forms of fruit, like cordon apple and pear trees or cordon gooseberries and redcurrants, require more attention than bush forms. Fan-trained trees are best avoided as they require considerable attention. Vegetable growing is also time-consuming. As a guide, a vegetable plot requires about ten times as much attention as a comparable area of lawn. On the other hand, perennial herbs such as sage, thyme, mint, and chives require little attention or space.

Avoid container-grown subjects, which need regular watering. Crocus, snowdrop, muscari and daffodil are excellent bulbs for this type of garden. They can safely be left year after year, apart from the occasional lifting, dividing and replanting.

For surfaces, use flagstones, concrete or other easily-brushed materials, which are longer lasting and less trouble than gravel, loose chippings or even grass. Confine your equipment to basics, stored under cover and well maintained.

Formal and town gardens

Modern gardens, which are mostly small, of regular outline and dominated by buildings, are well suited to formal treatment.

As with the wall and herb garden, these gardens are typically bounded by straight sides and laid out in geometric patterns such as squares, rectangles and circles. The plants are generally naturally compact or severely pruned and trained to conform to the character of the architectural environment. Although regimented straight lines are not everyone's choice, the horizontal and vertical lines of buildings considerably influence the design of the town garden.

Town gardens are much restricted by size and are often overwhelmed by walls and buildings. The main difficulties are drab surroundings, pollution and shade.

Only the hardiest evergreens such as laurel and skimmia can survive the combination of these conditions. Although many towns are not as grimy or

dirty as even ten years ago, many evergreens look jaded when compared with the fresh green leaves of deciduous plants as they unfold in spring.

In these surroundings, where colour is so important, spring bedding plants or bulbs like tulips and daffodils, or summer pelargoniums and begonias stimulate the eye. As these plants are raised in nurseries in good conditions of light and air, their accumulated food reserves are useful for flowering in the less congenial conditions. Hardy deciduous shrubs like forsythia, winter flowering jasmine, and flowering currants or lilacs are invaluable for town gardens.

Paved surfaces are harder wearing than grass. Changes in level are better solved by steps, terraces and retaining walls in confined areas. Drainage must be checked for flooding in your own garden and neighbouring gardens.

Formal gardens are not confined to towns and can be used in country areas. Features include clipped hedges, hard surfaces, paved or flagged floor area, terraces and beds, borders or pools of regular shape. Bush roses are often planted in square or rectangular beds in lawns or surrounded by paving, a formal setting which seems to suit them.

Plants for town gardens resemble those listed for container gardening and roof gardens, together with the following trees: Amelanchier; Betula; Crataegus; Ilex; Laburnum; Malus; Prunus; Pyrus; Robina; Sorbus. Recommended shrubs include: Aucuba; Berberis; Buddleia; Chaenomeles; Cotoneaster; Escallonia; Forsythia; Hydrangea; Hypericum; Magnolia; Mahonia; Philadelphus; Pyracantha; Rhododendron; Ribes; Rosa; Spartium; Spiraea; Syringa; Tamarix; Weigela.

LEFT The busy man's garden can be kept neat and tidy with a minimum of attention. Particular features are hard surfaces and labour-saving plants such as azaleas, greyleaf plants and lavender.
RIGHT An alternative treatment for a small town garden has a formal patio and pathway and is largely planted with foliage plants.

Herb gardens

Herb gardens can be little more than a window box providing household needs or, on the other hand, may have an area devoted exclusively to them. A collection of herbs laid out as a formal garden with separate beds or panels for individual groups can make an interesting and highly fragrant feature but their lack of colour may require compensation.

ABOVE A planned informal garden
RIGHT A herb garden.
BELOW A wall garden.

Informal gardens

Informal gardens do not have to be untidy to merit their title, and are in fact very difficult to design to look natural and continue to look good. In natural or wild gardens plants are allowed to grow almost at will without close mowing, clipping and severe pruning. It follows that the original choice of plants must be expert if they are not to swamp each other.

Wall gardens

Walls are particularly important in confined spaces and provide a great opportunity to display plants to good effect. They must be well maintained and preferably light, south-facing and not too draughty.

Low retaining walls with holes or pockets left in them can house plants such as aubrieta, alyssum and arabis. Walls of 3m (10ft) high can have wires or trellis fixed for training climbing roses, clematis, pyracantha or jasmine. High walls can be topped with troughs or boxes of plants which trail and hang down, such as eccremocarpus or ivy, to meet the climbing plants as they ascend. They will need regular watering.

Water gardens

The formal use of water

In formal settings, water is usually used in pools of regular shape, and each pool is usually surrounded with a paved or flagged area.

Waterlilies and fountains can be seen to best effect in sunlight, so avoid dull or heavily shaded spots.

Fountains can be free-standing or of the wall type. Pumps, pipes and services are best installed before the pools are made or any paving or surround is completed.

Pumps, pools and pipes are vulnerable to the action of severe, prolonged frost in winter. Bury water pipes at least 45cm (16in) deep in the ground.

The colour of the pool is important; blues and greens tend to be more subdued than white, which is also difficult to keep clean.

Water in natural surroundings

If there is a natural pool in your garden, check the continuity of the water supply, especially during the summer months, before you think about incorporating it in a planting scheme. Water always finds its way to the lowest point and the presence or absence of changes in level will, to a large extent, determine the character of the site.

In nature, there are four groups of plants which are found in or near water. First there are the submerged plants such as pond weed, which oxygenate the water and enable fish to thrive. The next category includes plants with floating leaves such as water lilies. The third group consists of plants which grow in shallow water, but hold their leaves and flowers above water. Sedges, yellow flag, bur-reed and water forget-me-not fall into this group. The last class consists of the marginal plants which like moist soil, but are not happy actually growing in water. Examples of this group include primulas, forget-me-not, mimulus, marsh marigolds and other waterside plants.

Plants for the water garden: Bog plants: Andromeda; Astilbe; Caltha; Carex; Funkia; Hemerocallis; Iris; Kniphofia; Mimulus; Myosotis; Myrica; Primula; Ranunculus; Spiraea; Trollius. Water plants: Aponogeton; Juncus; Nymphaea; Osmunda; Sagittaria.

ABOVE A formal water garden.
BELOW A natural garden pond.

129

Container gardening

Two functions are served by container gardening. Containers are invaluable in built up areas where there is no conventional garden space, while in all areas (including large gardens), tubs and troughs provide a movable feature, greatly easing the gardener's task of giving year-round interest to his garden.

Containers should be strong, durable, and deep and wide enough to hold sufficient compost to support and nourish plants. Other points include good drainage, attractive appearance, lightness in handling, and ease of cleaning.

Teak and oak are the most durable timbers for containers but require treating with wood preservative. Stone, earthenware and plastic receptacles are non-rotting; frost can break clayware holders.

Use loam-based mixtures such as John Innes potting compost, provided these have sand or aggregate included, for plants remaining more than a year in containers.

Trough gardening

Stone or earthenware containers of sufficient depth, can be planted with various small plants to create a novel miniature landscape, or used for standard bedding plants. For alpine plants, put a 6mm ($\frac{1}{4}$in) layer of clean granite chippings on the surface and around the plants, to prevent undue capping of the compost from rain or watering. Use peat for bedding plants. Where particularly choice small plants are being grown, raise the trough on to a firm secure platform before filling and planting for easy viewing.

Balcony planting

This is usually confined to covering vertical surfaces and window sills. Window boxes come into their own in this situation, and both small tubs and hanging baskets should be used where space and watering allow. Attractive window boxes are not always easy to obtain, but can be made by a handyman. Two useful sizes are 60cm (2ft) and 90cm (3ft) long by 15cm (6in) wide and deep (these are internal measurements). Make containers with 12mm ($\frac{1}{2}$in) thick wood suitably treated with preservative, and drilled with 3mm ($\frac{1}{8}$in) holes for drainage. When planting up the boxes firm the compost well and leave a 12mm ($\frac{1}{2}$in) space at the top for watering. Bracket window boxes to a wall if placed above ground level, or place in a bracketed metal cradle.

Hanging baskets

These are a useful means of softening hard walls and providing colour at a height. To obtain the best effects line the bottom with living green moss so that a 10cm (4in) layer of compost can be added. Next work in three or four plants, such as lobelia, so that the shoots jut out beyond the wire frame, with the roots planted in the compost. Place more moss inside the frame, and spread another layer of compost and repeat the planting process if the basket is big enough. Plant the top of the basket as for tubs and other containers, and cover the compost with a final layer of moss. The moss improves the appearance, hides the wire frame, and reduces the loss of moisture.

Plants for containers, balcony and troughs include Ageratum; Alyssum; Arabis; Aubrieta; Begonia; Polyanthus; Salvia; Tagetes; Tulip; Verbena; Wallflower.

Rooftop gardens

Wind is one of the major problems with these sites, and they need a low wall surround. Place containers of plants at the base of the perimeter wall. Additional protection can be provided by securing a trellis to increase the height of the screen. If there are high walls, grow climbers in containers, securing the plants to trellis or wire supports.

Spring and summer bedding plants including bulbs, wallflowers, and forget-me-nots, and summer-flowering pelargoniums, begonias and marigolds, will brighten the surroundings.

Nearby chimneys can be shut out by plants and trellis screening. Weight should be considered where a considerable amount of planting is being carried out, also provision for watering and the disposal of surplus water.

Safety rails should be placed round the edge and if there is seating it should be fixed so that children cannot drag the benches to look over the safety rails.

Plants for roof gardens include those given for container gardens with the following additions: Anthemis; Armeria; Artemisia; Campanula; Cotoneaster; Dianthus; Erigeron; Galega; Hedera; Iberis; Nepeta; Polygonum; Potentilla; Prunus; Rosa; Rosmarinus; Sambucus; Santolina; Statice; Thymus; Veronica.

BELOW Container planting is ideal for brightening up dingy basement entrances, and trailing plants such as ivy help to hide the angularity of the bricks and concrete.

Rock gardens

In the rock garden, copy conditions which prevail in the wild state (see Foliage gardens p. 134) for best effects. Select local stone, and layer pieces of rock as nearly as possible in the way they occur naturally. A few large stones are preferable to many small pieces. Rocks associate well with water or a heath type setting and are a useful means of changing level, but can also be used flat.

Limestone is one of the most favoured materials. Sandstone is also popular, although less durable, and will serve the purpose. A sunny site is preferable, although many plants will grow well in most situations. When constructing a rock garden, avoid sudden changes of materials; do not, for example, mix bricks with stone, or granite with limestone. Secure the stones and ram potting compost or similar soil between rocks as a rooting medium.

When selecting plants, include one or two dwarf conifers to ensure a more balanced type of vegetation rather than concentrating entirely on flowering varieties. Avoid planting acid-loving plants such as lithospermum among limestone rocks. Heathers of the *Erica carnea* type, which flower during autumn, winter and spring, grow and flower well in neutral soil in limestone districts.

ABOVE LEFT A glass roof for a south-facing balcony enables houseplants and a vine to grow satisfactorily outdoors.
LEFT Window boxes and hanging baskets full of colourful bedding plants brighten up city streets.
ABOVE A small rock garden (foreground) can be successfully inset on a wide concrete path.

BELOW LEFT A garden for children needs careful planning from both the safety and interest points of view. Hard paths are necessary for cycle riding, but play areas, particularly where there are climbing frames, should be soft – lawns are ideal. A small flower bed can be instructive and amusing – suitable plants range from small pansies to giant sunflowers.

BELOW CENTRE The garden for the disabled should be carefully planned with the particular handicap in mind. Raised flower beds enable many gardening tasks to be carried out from a wheelchair, and hard wide pathways allow easy access.

BELOW RIGHT The scented garden is best kept small for maximum effect. If planted close to the house, the fragrance can be allowed to penetrate through open doors and windows in summer.

Children's corner

This part of the garden is not always easy to blend in with flowers but it is nonetheless an important feature. It is important that you should be able to reach children easily if necessary, and keep them constantly in sight from the house. It must be a safe place with surfaces suitable for play.

Access to and from the play space, especially for the very young, requires careful attention. Provide protection from busy roads and parking areas. Spring-loaded gates with an automatic catch and a good secure boundary fence or hedge are of considerable assistance.

Watch for danger points such as steps, water and machinery. Close off steps and stairs with gates. Water features should be inaccessible, and machinery, tools and all chemicals kept out of reach. Unsafe trees and structures need prompt attention. Always watch for uneven surfaces, nails sticking out from walls or timber, and deal with them without delay. Paved areas, although hard, cause fewer cuts than gravel paths.

Children's play includes imitation and learning. If a small plot of soil is set aside where seeds can be sown or plants grown, a lifelong interest in plants and living things may be kindled. Simple plants are bulbs and bellis, chives, potatoes, shallots and radish. A bird table, bath and nesting boxes can provide hours of pleasure.

Gardening for the disabled

Plants can be of immense value in rehabilitating physically or mentally disabled people. Gardens which find favour with the blind consist largely of small and medium-sized scented plants and those with variously textured leaves. A useful setting for these plants is on a level where they can be handled from a standing or sitting position.

People who are unable to stoop or bend prefer troughs or trays of plants at waist height.

Particular points to watch in gardens for the disabled are that paths are of sufficient width, level and firm. Use ramps in preference to steps, and supply hand rails.

Tool handles may need modifying to enable them to be gripped for use.

132

Watering sometimes presents problems. Taps that work with a push action instead of twist or thread may be easier. Small light-weight watering cans which can be used single handed are often needed. It is important to find ways and means of enabling disabled people to get to the plants, by extending tools or bringing plants up to within their reach. Another aspect is shelter and warmth. Disabled people are often unable to keep themselves warm so a sunny sheltered spot, out of the wind, is best.

Holding and handling plant pots can present problems: an upturned tray like a tomato box with holes of different sizes can make a useful holder. In these instances time is of less consequence than the ability to carry out various jobs.

Scented gardens

The fragrance of flowers adds much to the enjoyment of most gardens but for some, scent is considered sufficiently important to be classified in categories such as jonquil, violet or roses. Perfume is also found in leaves and other parts of the plants.

With sufficient space it is possible to have twelve months of fragrance in all but the coldest climates, by careful selection of plants. Lavender and rosemary make useful scented hedges for year-round interest. Various herbs like balm, sage, mint and thyme will scent the air, particularly if their leaves are bruised. Bulbs such as hyacinths, daffodils, jonquils and various lilies are strongly perfumed. Roses, stocks, lily-of-the-valley and sweet peas can be included in any planting of this nature.

There are many fragrant shrubs and climbers which add height and colour. A few of the old favourites include honeysuckle, daphne, jasmine, hamamelis, and various viburnums. Among the border plants, no planting would be complete without carnations, pinks, phlox, monarda and violets.

Scent in plants can be unpredictable: it may be particularly noticeable at certain times and less so at others. Very often the fragrance seems stronger in the cooler part of the day, early in the morning or evening for example. To judge from experience the best scents appear to be obtained from plants growing in well-drained soils and warm sunny situations. There is much to be said for having the scented garden close to the house, to let scent and perfume waft in through the open windows.

Scented plants: Flowering shrubs and climbers: Buddleia; Daphne; Hamamelis; Jasminum; Lavandula; Lonicera; Osmanthus; Rosa; Rosmarinus; Syringa; Viburnum; Wisteria. Flowering bedding and border plants: Alyssum; Centaurea; Cheiranthus; Convallaria; Dianthus; Heliotropium; Hyacinthus; Iris; Lathyrus; Matthiola; Narcissus; Nicotiana; Nymphaea; Oenothera; Primula; Tulipa; Verbena; Viola. Scented foliage: Aloysia; Lavandula; Melissa; Mentha; Monarda; Rosmarinus; Santolina; Thymus.

Foliage gardens

Foliage gardens may be laid out formally or in the informal style using a more random arrangement of plants.

In foliage gardens the leaves of plants are exploited to provide an infinite variety of colour, texture, shape and size. With careful choice, year round interest can be maintained. The colour range too is surprisingly wide, ranging through white, grey, blue, gold, copper, scarlet, purple, variegated, brown, pink, near black, and various autumn tints. Leaf textures vary from smooth to hairy and differ greatly in size. The large-leaved *Fatsia* (aralia) when well grown can create the impression of tropical plants.

Foliage is also often used to create a formal setting. Large and small-scale topiary – the art of cutting and trimming trees, plants and shrubs into various shapes – has been used to make gardens of distinction. Archways, hedge-walls, chess figures, peacocks and mazes can be seen in some of the older gardens. The use of clipped box and other evergreens in combination with well-chosen pieces of statuary can give dignity and character. Foliage plants used formally need less space than where the aim is to imitate nature. Colour and texture can be obtained from ground cover plants, such as thymes, ivies, and variously tinted heathers. Hosta, acanthus and fatsia will have a bolder effect. Bamboos, grasses and ferns provide a shapely contrast. Hedges composed of plants of contrasting leaf colour, like green and purple beech, can be very effective but care is needed to avoid a fussy appearance. Red, gold and cream or blue variegated plants, whether of the small-leaved type like dwarf conifers, or broad-leaved plants such as maples, and hollies or climbers are still more variations.

Foliage plants: Evergreen: Aucuba; Buxus; Calluna; Chamaecyparis; Elaeagnus; Erica; Euonymus; Hedera; Ilex; Juniperus; Lavandula; Osmanthus; Pieris; Rosmarinus; Santolina; Sedum; Sempervivum; Skimmia; Stachys; Viburnum; Yucca. Deciduous: Acer; Cornus; Corylus; Diervilla; Hibiscus; Hosta; Pyrus; Rhus; Ribes; Sambucus.

Seaside gardens

The climate and other conditions close to the sea make life difficult for many plants. The chief limiting factors are high winds or lack of shelter, sandy porous soils, salt in the soil, sea spray, and strong sun.

One of the first priorities is effective wind protection. This can be provided by banked earth, walls, screens, fencing and hedging. Light sandy soils are improved by the addition of organic materials such as manure and peat. Good cultivation of plants which tolerate these conditions is the best way of overcoming these limitations.

One problem which is common to gardens in exposed positions is that the erection or growing of screens may shut out some impressive views. The solution may be to leave an opening and settle for low ground-hugging plants at the strategic point.

Some pines and maples withstand coastal conditions as do a number of plants from the southern hemisphere, such as New Zealand Daisy Bush and various close relatives of the olearia family. Various veronicas or hebes, fuchsia, escallonia, and tamarisk are all useful seaside subjects. Hydrangeas, lupins and valerian are well known for their good performance and so are various grey-leaved plants like sea buckthorn, lavender, sea holly and echinops. Brooms, gorse and genista are other colourful plants which seem to flourish near the shore.

Plants for seaside gardens: Small trees: Arbutus; Chamaecyparis; Crataegus; Cupressus; Ilex; Juniperus; Laurus; Pinus; Sorbus. Shrubs; Cassinia; Cotoneaster; Cytisus; Erica; Escallonia; Fuchsia; Griselinia; Hebe; Helianthemum; Hippophae; Hydrangea; Ilex; Lavandula; Olearia; Rosa; Rosmarinus; Santolina; Spartium; Spiraea; Tamarix.

Winter garden

The attainment of colour and interest during the dark and dismal months of the years presents a challenge, but it is not as difficult as it may first appear.

Evergreens provide considerable variety in shape, colour and texture. Hollies, ivies and periwinkle provide greens, golds and whitish shades on leaves. Dwarf and other conifers add blues, greys, olive greens and rusty shades, and mahonia produces holly-like reddish leaves.

Between bouts of frost, the winter-flowering cherry puts on a brave show of delicate pink, as does *Viburnum fragrans*. The bright-yellow winter-flowering jasmine will usually manage a show of colour intermittently throughout the winter against a wall. Among the shrubs, pink or white *Daphne mezereum*, yellow wintersweet, and witch hazel combine to produce colour and scent. Red and pink forms of flowering quince on leafless branches look attractive against a wall. Heathers can provide flower and foliage colour and interest and suit most situations. Winter aconite, the dwarf yellow *Hacquetia* flowering among snowdrops, squills and scillas or the white cups of the Christmas rose all help to cheer up the dull days of winter. Bright red berries of holly, cotoneaster and rose hips provide splashes of colour, and contrast well with white stems and trunks of silver birch.

In mild districts in the South and South West the winter-flowering honeysuckles are well worth planting. The two better known species are *Lonicera fragrantissima* and *L. standishii*.

Winter-flowering plants thrive in sunny sheltered positions, protected from north and east winds.

Plants for the winter season: Trees: Betula; Prunus. Shrubs: Arbutus; Arctostaphylos; Chaenomeles; Chimonanthus; Cornus; Corylus; Corylopsis; Daphne; Elaeagnus; Erica; Garrya; Hamamelis; Jasminum; Kerria; Lonicera; Stachyurus; Viburnum. Flowering bulbous plants: Crocus; Cyclamen; Eranthis; Galanthus; Hacquetia; Helleborus; Iris; Petasites; Shizostylis; Sternbergia. Berry bearing: Aucuba; Arbutus; Berberis; Cotoneaster; Crataegus; Euonymus; Hippophae; Ilex; Mahonia; Pernettya; Pyracantha; Pyrus; Rosa; Skimmia.

BELOW A garden in winter need not lack colour and interest. Planted here from left to right are cornus, viburnum, heathers, daphne, ivy, winter jasmine, holly, cotoneaster, winter aconite, Christmas rose and flowering quince.

Pests and diseases

Wherever plants grow pests, diseases and weeds will be waiting and ready to attack crops – usually when they are least able to resist. In order to combat them, it is necessary to have a basic understanding of the causes of trouble, and how they can be checked.

Pests
It is easy to think only of insects and similar small creatures as damaging plants, but birds, rodents and other animals including pets can be equally destructive.

Blackfly on broad bean plant.

There are two types of insect pests: those which chew like caterpillars, and sap-sucking types like aphids. Damage by chewing creatures is more readily noticed. Birds and larger animals cause physical damage and have to be discouraged with netting or repellent sprays.

Diseases
Diseases infect and spread to other plants. Fungus diseases, such as moulds and mildews, are more easily controlled than those caused by bacteria, which often cause wilt or slime in plants. Virus diseases, like yellow edge of strawberries, mosaic of cucumbers, or distortion in chrysanthemums, are virtually incurable and the only remedy is to remove and burn infected plants.

Disorders
Various ailments closely resemble diseases in appearance, and are caused not by infection, but by some deficiency, excess, or some cultural faults. Rhododendrons growing on chalk land turn yellow and look sickly due to excess chalk in the soil, but small specimens carefully moved and planted into acid soil often recover to normal health.

Weeds
These reduce crops not only by the competition for food and water, but harbour many pests and diseases, including aphids, mildews and mosaic virus. As with cultivated plants, there are annual, biennial and perennial weeds. Some members of this last group, such as nettles and thistles, can prove extremely difficult to eliminate.

The case for chemicals
Without the use of approved materials which have been carefully tested in the field and laboratory, it is extremely doubtful if many crops could be successfully grown at all. Total reliance on natural means of control would probably lead to generally unacceptable end results.

Approved chemicals have been tested and passed as safe, when used according to the maker's instructions, under the Agricultural Chemicals Approved Scheme. These can usually be identified by the letter A topped by a crown stamped on the outside of the containers.

Preventive methods
Prevention is always better than cure and can be achieved by good cultivation, hygiene and the removal of possible sources of troubles. The surfaces of garden crops or plants should be covered with a protective coating of chemical spray or dust, renewed when necessary, or the plant sap impregnated with protecting material. Chemicals which can be carried in plant sap are referred to as systemics.

Keeping an outbreak in check
Where preventive measures have been unsuccessful, swift remedial measures are needed. Identify the cause and, in the case of pests or diseases, cover the affected area with an appropriate chemical. Remove weeds among crops by hand; many can also be controlled by spraying. Remove any dead or diseased portions of plants. Maintain good growing conditions to help plants to grow and overcome any problems.

Application of chemicals
Chemical substances are directed at the offending pest, disease or weed in one of several forms. The aim is always to cover plants thoroughly with a fine coating of protective material as a preventive measure and also to deposit an active chemical where the affliction is present.

Granule applicators are a kind of giant pepper pot, generally used to scatter granules of weedkiller on paths or flower beds. These are cheap, simple and effective.

Dusting appliances are sold in a plastic puffer pack, which is squeezed to force out a cloud of dust, or a simple bellows which carries fine dust in a current of air.

Smoke generators consist of a slow-burning material in a cartridge of active ingredient which is released as a smoke. Smokes are often used in greenhouses or in enclosed structures.

Pressurized canisters with fingertip release are very useful for spot treatment of troubles. The active material is released in minute droplets of mist.

Spraying is the most widely used means of applying chemicals, and is suitable for greenhouse and outdoor use. The appliances range from simple

Widely available spraying equipment.

syringes, hand models and double action sprayers to knapsack versions. The compression type are particularly easy to use, as spraying can be carried out with one hand left free to guide the lances and nozzles. Sprayers consist basically of a reservoir for liquid, a pump and outlet nozzle.

Drenches A coarse nozzle spray, or watering can with rose, can be used to apply weedkiller or systemic pesticides to plant roots.

Before mixing sprays or drenches, read all labels carefully. Avoid inhaling or spilling concentrated spray. If spills do occur, wash off immediately. Mix materials thoroughly. Use only freshly made sprays and do not leave chemicals lying around. Make sure chemical containers are sealed and labelled before storing. Wash spray equipment thoroughly before putting away.

Garden pests

Aphid or greenfly attack a wide range of fruits, flowers and vegetables

Aphids on a rose stem.

throughout the year and are usually seen in colonies of greenish, pinkish, bluish or black colour, located in or near growing points of flowers and leaf undersides. Symptoms are stunted and distorted growing points, sticky with honeydew.

Control: spray with malathion, dimethoate or derris. A winter wash of fruit trees with tar oil sprays will kill many overwintering eggs of aphids.

Birds devour buds of many kinds of fruit trees and bushes in winter including plums, redcurrants and gooseberries and flowering cherries. Telltale signs are remains of buds and bud scales on the ground, as well as the presence of the birds, such as bullfinches and sparrows, who eat all ripening fruits. Apples, plums and strawberries will be pitted with fresh holes. Pock-marked and pitted seed beds and chewed up seedlings are further danger signs.

Control: Black cotton thread woven over seed beds, pea guards to keep pigeons off; fine mesh nettings over currants, strawberries and wall fruits will reduce damage.

Big bud or blackcurrant gall mite shows as enlarged buds, very noticeable on leafless bushes in winter; and buds failing to open in spring. Affected bushes become increasingly less productive, often having nettle shaped leaves.

Control: for a light attack, pick off affected buds and spray the bushes with lime sulphur, once just as the first flowers are opening and again as the last ones open.

Bushes severely infected with big bud mite and showing nettleleaf signs, are best dug up and burnt.

Cabbage rootfly attacks cabbages, cauliflowers and Brussels sprouts, causing them to become severely stunted and die. The roots of affected plants are swollen, some of them hollow or harbouring dirty whitish or greyish grubs.

Control: dust round plant stems immediately after planting with HCH insecticidal dust or granules.

Capsid threatens apples, currants, strawberries, chrysanthemums and dahlias, resulting in reddish brown spotting and distortion of young leaves, and badly shaped fruits. The common green capsid is an agile, bright green insect, not easy to spot among the foliage.

A common green capsid.

Control: tar oil winter spraying of fruit trees and bushes can kill the overwintering eggs. Routine applications of HCH or fenitrothion during the growing season will keep this pest in check.

Carrot fly causes widespread damage to the roots as its larvae tunnel through. Other crops occasionally affected are parsnips and celery.

Carrot fly larvae in a turnip.

Control: not easy, but seeds dressed with HCH before sowing, crop rotation and burning of thinnings will lessen the chances of a ruined crop.

Caterpillars cause considerable damage as they chew their way through leaves and stems, leaving them full of holes. Most tree, flower, fruit and vegetable crops can be attacked.

Control: spray caterpillars on sight with derris or fenitrothion. Tar oil winter spraying of fruit trees and bushes and the removal of all rubbish and litter will do much to reduce their numbers.

Codling Moth is responsible for dirty whitish grubs found in the centres of apples. They are usually accompanied by holes in fruits containing *frass* (chewed up apple and larval excreta), rendering them useless.

Control: spray fruit trees about four weeks after flowering with fenitrothion and again 14 to 21 days later. Bands of corrugated paper, tied round trunks of fruit trees in July, will trap many grubs. Remove and burn the bands at fruit picking time.

Apple, rotted by codling moth.

137

Cutworms are dull-green caterpillar-like pests that eat tender stems at ground level or just below. Seedlings with leaves severed from their roots and which fall over are a fairly certain sign of this pest.

A cutworm.

Control: dust round the stems of lettuce or cabbage plants with HCH immediately after planting.

Earwigs are night-feeding creatures that mainly attack flowers and flower buds. Dahlias and chrysanthemums are often particularly badly damaged, resulting in holed petals or loss of whole flower segments. The earwig is a shiny brown creature with a pincer-like appendage at the tail end.

Control: dust round the base of plants with HCH. One old-fashioned, but effective, method is trapping. Invert a 7.5cm (3in) pot, half-filled with hay, pressed in. Place the pot over a cane or support among the flowers. Inspect the pot regularly, and kill any pests found inside.

Leaf hoppers and cuckoo spit are at work when, in growing points and young leaves, greenish bugs surrounded by froth can be seen. Plants

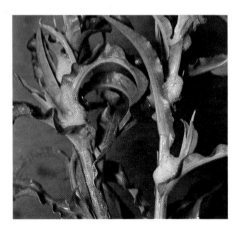
Cuckoo spit.

138

can be considerably weakened by their feeding activities. Flowers, vegetables and weeds are host plants.

Control: Spray with malathion.

Leather jackets are more common to turf. Weak patchy areas of grass, often accompanied by considerable bird activity, and the presence of dark coloured leathery grubs at or near the surface are indicative of this trouble.

Leather jacket.

Control: water turf with chlordane worm killer at the first sign of trouble and again about September.

Millipedes are slow-moving soil-inhabiting creatures which can be black, brownish, or grey with spots and have four legs to each segment of the body. Millipedes feed mainly on the lower stems and underground parts of peas, beans and rootcrops.

Common millipede.

Control: rake HCH dust into the top 10cm (4in) of soil. Do *not* use this material before planting potatoes. Potatoes must not be grown on treated land for a minimum of 18 months after this treatment.

Onion fly cause weak, dead and dying bulbs with small grubs inside.

Control: crop rotation; clear away thinnings; treat seeds and soil with HCH dust before sowing outdoors.

Red spider mite. Although there are several different kinds of red spider which can attack a wide range of crops, their appearances are very similar. The adult mites are very small, reddish and are usually found on leaf undersides. The foliage becomes pale yellow, speckled or bronzed in severe attacks. Dry warm weather favours the development of red spider mite.

Control: Tar oil winter spraying of fruit trees and bushes can kill over-wintering eggs. Spray fruit bushes, strawberries and roses with dimethoate or malathion during spring and summer. Crop rotation is also important.

Root aphid attacks lettuce in late summer, causing a stunted and yellowing plant. When pulled out of the ground the roots will be seen to harbour bluish aphid-like insects. The early crops are not usually affected.

Control: when planting or thinning summer lettuce, give each plant a watering with malathion solution.

Slugs and snails will attack almost any plant, at soil level as well as above and below ground, leaving their telltale trails of slime.

Black slug.

Control: leave slug bait near all newly planted or succulent young crops, especially lettuce plants. Wet weather favours these creatures, and bait covered with a piece of wood or slate, propped up on one side with a stone or similar, usually works well.

Wasps are often particularly troublesome when fruits are ripening.

Control: find and destroy wasp nests. This should be carried out by the local authority.

Weevils and flea beetles leave circular or semi-circular holes in young foliage or seed leaves.

Control: dust seed beds of cabbage, cauliflower, Brussels sprouts, and other brassicas with derris or HCH

Rhododendron leaves damaged by weevils.

dusts. Other types of weevil attack apple crops and can also be checked with HCH dusts.

Whitefly are more common on indoor plants than outside. They appear as small, active, white flies, and can be controlled by malathion sprays applied to the leaves.

Wireworms are tough, shiny yellowish worms that attack many root crops, usually being most troublesome for the first two or three years after grass areas have been dug up.

Control: mix HCH dust into the top 10cm (4in) of soil; *do not* grow potatoes on treated land for 18 months because

Wireworm.

of possible taint. Grow resistant crops like peas and beans, or brassicas, and onions, which are less likely to be attacked than potatoes and carrots.

Woolly aphid can be detected by the cottonwool-like tufts which surround them in cracks and crevices of bark on apple trees.

Control: Tar oil winter washes and summer sprays of dimethoate or malathion, combined with pruning and burning the affected pieces, will do much to eliminate this pest.

Worms Coils of soft mud on leaves, particularly during autumn and spring.

Control: as for leather jacket. Apply chlordane when worm casts are fresh and again in autumn or spring.

Diseases

Botrytis (grey mould) occurs on many crops, on strawberries, fruits, on lettuce leaves and on rose blooms, appearing as grey mould, which gives it its common name.

Strawberries affected by botrytis.

Control: remove affected parts, and dust or spray plants with benomyl or thiram.

Black spot appears as unsightly dark spots on rose leaves which will cover most of any infected leaf surface if left unchecked.

Control: spray with captan if outbreaks occur in early summer and repeat this once or twice at 14-day intervals. Rake up and burn diseased leaves in autumn.

Black spot on rose leaves.

Blight often attacks potatoes and tomatoes. The affected foliage turns black: potato tubers and tomato plants rot and wither with an unpleasant smell.

Control: Spray potato and tomato plants with copper fungicide in late June. Keep potatoes well earthed up and lift crops early. Resting the ground from potatoes will reduce the chances of remaining disease-infected tubers affecting a new crop.

Cane spot on raspberry, blackberry and loganberry stems or canes will weaken plants.

Control: spray infected canes with benomyl or copper sprays. Cut out and burn old rods or canes after fruiting. Keep new rods separate and above old canes to prevent spore-carrying rain drops infecting new growth.

Celery spot shows as characteristic black leaf spots. In wet seasons, leaves and plants rot and collapse unless checked.

Control: use clean seed, or obtain healthy plants. Spray plants in the early stages with benomyl or copper fungicide, and repeat twice at 21-day intervals.

Club root causes swollen, evil-smelling roots, stunted growth and malaise, particularly to members of the cabbage family.

Broccoli affected by club root.

Control: set out only healthy plants; drain and lime land before planting; and use crop rotation. Dip the roots of seedlings into a slurry of calomel paste and water before planting out. Calomel is poisonous and it must be handled with care.

Damping off (wirestem) is a condition which frequently occurs in seedlings and is caused by a number of disease organisms. Affected young plants have brown shrunken stems at ground level and either topple over or remain dwarfed with hard wiry stems.

Control: work proprietary seed dressings, thiram or quintozene dust into outdoor seed beds before sowing; or dip seedlings into captan solution when pricking out.

Fire often damages tulips which will have a burnt or scorched look.

Control: do not grow tulips on the same ground for at least two years; rake quintozene or suitable proprietary fungicide into the top 10cm (4in) of soil at planting time.

Grey mould See botrytis.

Leaf spot can be found on currants, carnation and Sweet Williams as well as many other plants. Unless checked, plants can be seriously weakened.

Control: spray infected plants with copper fungicide, taking care to avoid open flowers.

Mildew affects many garden plants, of which the more notable are roses, chrysanthemums, apples and currants.

Mildew on rose buds.

The leaves of infected crops have a downy or powdery whitish covering. Flower buds and stems can also be damaged.

Control: sprays of benomyl or dinocap, repeated if necessary, will keep mildew in check.

Peach leaf curl.

Peach leaf curl causes the leaf of peach, almond and close relatives to become curiously distorted and highly coloured.

Control: apply lime sulphur, copper or captan sprays before the buds swell in spring and again in autumn as the leaves fall.

Rust is more frequently seen on flower crops than vegetables and fruit. Various disease organisms are involved and the general effect, as the name suggests, is of rusty browns and oranges. Sensitive subjects include antirrhinum, carnation, chrysanthemum, roses and Sweet William.

Control: Use copper or thiram sprays at the first sign of trouble and again in 14 days, repeated if necessary.

Rust on sempervivum.

Scab, caused by different species, results in roughly similar effects on such unrelated plants as potato and apple. Both crops have dark spots and marks on tubers and fruit respectively.

Control: successive captan sprays from the green bud stage with apples and pears can give a good degree of

Black scab on apples.

protection. With potatoes, avoid heavily-limed land and give generous dressings of manure before planting.

Virus diseases Most garden crops are susceptible to infection by members of this group. Unlike many fungus diseases there is no cure which the amateur can achieve. The only control is to dig up and burn infected plants. Raspberries, blackberries, blackcurrants and strawberries are notoriously susceptible fruits. Buy healthy, Ministry-certified virus-free stock plants, including potatoes, when planting afresh. Aphids and insects are the main natural means of spread, but infected sap carried on knives or hands can transmit the disease from infected to healthy plants.

Control: lift and burn diseased plants, control aphids by spraying. Do not touch healthy plants after handling diseased specimens without washing hands and knives first.

Disorders

Frost injury to fruit trees and bushes and strawberry plants causes blackened leaves, flowers or eyes. Autumn crops like lettuce and self-blanching celery become slimy after a keen frost, dahlia foliage turns black and withers. Bedding plants in spring, after a touch of frost, may be blackened or have scorched dry patches between leaf veins.

Frost damage on blossom.

Wind damage from drying winds or gales can cause bronzing of foliage on one or more sides of plants or trees, as well as scorching the leaf margins. Severe gales can, of course, cause physical injury. Freezing winds or salt spray result in more pronounced scorching, to the point of defoliating plants in severe cases.

Drought, especially when combined with intense sunlight, can cause scorching. Seedlings dry out and become bleached, bigger plants are scorched and discoloured. Lawns turn brown. Tender plants like lettuce, even if dried out only for a short spell, can suffer from tip-burn – the leaf margins turn brown, and dry. Apples and tomatoes can suffer from scalding of the fruits.

When rain follows drought various troubles are encountered, such as splitting of apples, plums, currants, tomatoes and other fruit. Root crops like carrots and parsnips split, and potatoes put on bumps and knobs due to secondary growth.

Nutritional imbalance between the major plant elements such as nitrogen, phosphate and potash, induces symptoms of deficiencies or excess. Apples and gooseberries, for example, develop reddish brown discoloration of the leaf margins when potash is in short supply. The non-setting of fruit on tomatoes can be due to excess nitrogen, as well as other causes – poor light for example.

Overcrowding is a common failing, especially with young seedlings, when for one reason or another these have not been transplanted quickly enough.

Plants become tall and spindly. Similar effects can be seen in shrubs, borders and beds, when plants have been put too close together.

Waterlogging occurs when plants are flooded and left standing in stagnant water and this kills the roots.

Weed control

There are weed killers for most purposes in and around the garden, but they should be used with caution. The basic situations for the use of these materials are the control of weeds in drives and paths, and the elimination of unwanted plants in lawns, and hedge bottoms, shrubbery and flower borders, and among food crops.

Weed killers are either total or selective. Total herbicides kill or harm any vegetation they touch and are used mainly on paths, drives and hard surfaces. Sodium chlorate is an example of this type. Selective weed killers, when used as directed, kill or injure certain plants only and leave others unharmed. The best-known example among gardeners, is the use of weed killers such as those based on 2, 4-D on lawns – a hormone type weed killer.

Application of weed killers

Timing the use of these materials is important for best results. Certain weed killers, such as those based on paraquat, are effective only if the weeds are in leaf as they have little or no effect on the seeds. Other weedkilling materials, based on simazine or similar-acting chemicals, kill germinating weed seeds, but have less effect on weeds in full leaf.

Drives and paths need to be cleared of existing weeds, and further weed growth prevented. Remove the existing top growth by hand if possible. Annual weeds can be killed off in 24 hours by using paraquat-based herbicides, and do not leave long-lasting harmful residues. Persistent perennial weeds require spot treatment or spraying with a hormone-type weed killer. This must be used with great care to avoid possible damage to cultivated plants from spray drift. Once the existing weeds have been removed, the area can be kept weed-free by using residual weedkillers based on simazine.

Lawns and hedge bottoms are best dealt with by selective weed-killers to remove unwanted plants without

harming the lawn or hedge. Two weed killers of this type are available, one for broad-leaved weeds like daisies and dandelions, and another for more difficult weeds like clover, yarrow and veronica or speedwell. Hedge bottoms can be cleaned up with a paraquat-type weed killer where annual grasses exist, but nettles and thistles present problems. Repeated cutting down of the difficult weeds and treating new growth with a hormone-type weed killer, taking care not to spray the hedge, will eventually clean up the area.

Shrubberies and flower borders. With the use of chemicals to control weeds before and after planting, there is always the danger of giving an overdose to new or even established plants. It is important to start off with weed-free beds, to remove any harmful residues of chemicals before planting, and to use weed killers suited to your plants and needs. Mixed herbaceous borders are best weeded by hand, but shrub and rose beds can be kept weed-free by the use of residual herbicides to stop the weed seedlings from developing.

Vegetables and fruit. There are many chemicals which, with certain provisions, have been officially ap-

Applying weed killer.

proved for use among food crops, but they should be used as little as possible. One of the safest methods at present is the use of a paraquat-based weedkiller for annual weeds, just before planting, to give crops a clean start. Similar weed killers are effective around currants, gooseberries and raspberries in the pathways. Control by chemicals results in less material for the compost heap as you should never put chemically treated matter on a compost heap.

One very important point is that cans and buckets used for weedkiller should *NOT* be used for watering or spraying seedlings, even if washed thoroughly.

141

General information

Suppliers

Home gardeners are supplied by stores and shops, garden centres, nurseries, mail order firms, garden societies, friends and neighbours. Branded hardware of the same quality is not always the same price everywhere. Plants really have to be seen before purchase and, generally, the shorter the distance from nursery to garden the better.

It can pay to buy in advance and take advantage of special or out-of-season discounts, although this is not always true of clearance offers at the end of the season. The cheapest buy is not necessarily the best, and free gifts of diseased or rampant weed-like plants can prove expensive to grow.

Societies

Horticultural organizations provide a valuable link between suppliers of goods and services and gardeners. Advice and information on varieties, local shows and events and the chance to meet people of similar interests, are some of the benefits offered by local clubs. Your local library or information office can usually give you the name and address of the nearest society. Garden and allotment trading societies often buy seeds, peat and fertilizers in bulk and offer them for sale to the gardener more cheaply than most retail outlets.

The really keen enthusiast who wants to know much more about gardening should consider joining the Royal Horticultural Society, Vincent Square, Westminster, London, SW1 2PE, or one of the specialist societies. Details of these can be obtained through the gardening press, newspapers or from your local society.

Qualified advice on gardening subjects by experts is available to members of the Royal Horticultural Society.

Exhibitions and shows

These are well worth visiting and are often a source of much useful information. Intending exhibitors can discover the best show varieties to grow, and new plants, tools and equipment, or floral arrangements are on display.

There are national shows such as the Chelsea Flower Show, which is internationally renowned and attracts overseas exhibitors and visitors. Regional shows like those at Southport, Shrewsbury and Manchester draw exhibitors from all over the country. Local shows are a good source of friendly rivalry. The Royal Horticultural Society offers a programme of shows throughout the year for the serious gardener. Advance notice of shows in your area or nationally can usually be obtained through gardening publications, the press or direct from the organizers. Exhibitors are advised to study carefully all show dates and schedules. The rules governing exhibiting and judging need to be understood, and any changes or special points should be noted. A useful guide to the intending exhibitor is the *Horticultural Show Handbook,* published by the Royal Horticultural Society.

Gardens open to the public

There are many outstanding public and private gardens which can be viewed at certain times of the year, as well as some fine botanic gardens.

In England and Scotland there are four schemes or organizations which publicize the most noteworthy of these gardens. The National Trust is responsible for numerous properties, of which more than a hundred have fine gardens worth visiting. Further information is available from the National Trust, 43 St Anne's Gate, London, SW1H 9AS. Under the National Gardens Scheme, over 1,250 interesting private gardens are voluntarily opened to the public. The proceeds from any charges are given to the National Trust and to benefit district nurses in need. Details can be found in *Gardens of England and Wales open to the Public,* obtainable from The National Gardens Scheme, 57 Lower Belgrave Street, London, SW1W 0LR. The National Trust for Scotland is responsible for some of the most outstanding gardens in Scotland which are open to the public. Full details are available from The National Trust for Scotland, Publicity Department, 5 Charlotte Square,

ABOVE The Corana, Athelhampton, Dorset.

Edinburgh. Under 'Scotland's Garden Scheme' many of the most interesting privately-owned gardens in Scotland can be viewed by the public. Details can be obtained from Scotland's Garden Scheme, 26 Castle Terrace, Edinburgh.

A short list of some outstanding gardens open to the public includes:
Bodnant, Gwynedd, North Wales
Chatsworth, Derbyshire
Edinburgh Botanic Gardens, Midlothian, Scotland
Glasnevin Botanic Gardens, Dublin
Hidcote Manor, Gloucestershire
Inverewe Gardens, Ross and Cromarty
Kew Gardens, Surrey
Mount Stewart, County Down, Northern Ireland
Nymans, Sussex
Royal Horticultural Society Gardens, Wisley, Surrey
Sandringham, Norfolk
Sheffield Park, Sussex
Tatton Park, Cheshire
Tresco Abbey, Isles of Scilly
Wakehurst Place, Sussex
Wallington, Northumberland

RIGHT The lake at Savill Gardens.
BELOW The pond garden at Hampton Court.

Law and the gardener

Most gardeners are law-abiding citizens, but there are occasions when patience and tempers are sorely tried. Some of the more common causes for differences over gardening matters are goods and services failing to reach expectations; boundaries; damage to people or property from trees or plants of your land; landscaping requirements; Tree Preservation Orders; Notifiable Weed Orders; and Notifiable Disease Orders. Information about your legal responsibilities can be obtained from your local authority. There are various by-laws governing bonfires in smokeless zones; water abstraction; planting by water courses such as rivers and canals; and Town and Country Planning Acts and Regulations.

Trades descriptions act

Customers are protected under this act, in the case of newly-purchased plants, tools or services.

Boundaries

If in any doubt over boundaries, refer to property deeds: however, any legal battle is usually costly, always time-consuming, rarely satisfactory and sours relations. Disputes are always best resolved by discussion, if possible. Your local authority or Citizen's Advice Bureau will advise you on any need for a solicitor. In the case of any dispute be sure of your facts and have supporting documentary evidence.

Safety in the Garden

This important aspect is often only fully appreciated after an accident, but it is better to anticipate the more obvious dangers. Children, pets and elderly people are particularly vulnerable to slippery or uneven surfaces, rickety railings and loose steps. Gates and fences or hedges should be erected to prevent very young children and pets from wandering on to busy roads. Unsafe trees, buildings or play equipment should be put right immediately.

Some of the more serious accidents in gardens happen to young children, and many are avoidable. Tools left lying around, motorized equipment and poisonous chemicals within reach, are a few hazards. Correctly label and lock up chemicals. Electrical appliances, especially where the cables are worn or not properly insulated, could be lethal in wet conditions. Inflammable liquids like petrol or paraffin invite trouble, and bonfires should definitely NOT be livened up by pouring these liquids over them. It is unwise to have water gardens where there are young children. Steps and ladders should be tested and used only if they are firm and on level ground. Mix chemical sprays in the open air if possible, and avoid spillage. Spray on calm days wherever possible, to prevent spray from drifting around to harm people, pets and ponds. Garden seats and furniture should be sturdy and well-maintained.

LEFT Many fine private gardens are opened to the public for a few days each year. These are well worth visiting, particularly in your neighbourhood as they are likely to offer similar planting prospects as far as soil and climate are concerned.
RIGHT The 'White Garden' at Sissinghurst, Sussex.

Gardener's Calendar

January

During frosty spells when the ground is hard, barrow manure or compost, gather up and burn or dispose of tree trimmings, complete the pruning of apples and pears, and cut back any newly planted summer raspberries. Check any tree stakes, supporting framework and ties, correcting these if necessary. Protect currants and gooseberries from bird damage by covering the bushes with fine mesh netting.

On recently dug land carry out liming if needed.

Prune any late flowering shrubs such as *Buddleia davidii*, *Hydrangea paniculata* and climbing or shrub roses.

Place potatoes in boxes to chit (form firm shoots) in a light, airy, frost-free place.

When trees and bushes are dry and the weather calm and mild, give apples, pears, currants and gooseberries a tar oil winter spray to control pests and diseases.

Peach or almond trees should be sprayed now, to control peach leaf curl disease.

Prepare frames for the earliest seed sowings, and place cloches over dug ground to take advantage of any sun to warm the soil.

February

Sow early cabbage, Brussels sprouts, cauliflower and cabbage lettuce in frames, for planting outside later.

Mulch and feed currants and gooseberries, pruning any newly planted blackcurrants as well as established gooseberries and redcurrants. Cover strawberries with cloches for early crops.

Prepare the ground and plant shallots. On well-worked soil, sow in the open broad beans, early peas such as Feltham First, and round-seeded spinach. Sow quick-maturing cabbage under frames or cloches.

Give peaches and almonds a second spray of fungicide against peach leaf curl.

Feed fruit trees with a balanced fertilizer dressing.

Cut back Autumn-fruiting raspberries to ground level, and shorten the tips of summer fruiting varieties to 1.5m (5ft) to divert plant energy into fruit production.

Complete any outstanding digging in readiness for the rush of spring seed-sowing and planting. Strawberries can still be planted, but should be de-blossomed (have the flowers removed) the first spring.

March

Sow quick-maturing cauliflowers early in the month, and plant early potatoes in sheltered situations. Sow early carrots in warm borders. Plant broad beans and peas started under cover last month. Lift, divide and replant herbs such as thyme. On well-prepared beds, plant onion sets, carefully trimming the tops. Plant out autumn-sown cauliflowers that have been properly hardened off, if soil and weather conditions allow. Make the first sowing of beetroot, 'Boltardy', preferably under cloches in warm districts.

Sow cos lettuce in frames or cloches and make successive sowings of cabbage, carrots and cauliflowers until May and June according to district.

The main planting of early potatoes can be made towards the end of the month.

Finish the pruning of all tree and bush fruits, and complete all outstanding planting. All spring-planted fruits (or any other) will need watching for dryness, and water as needed.

Complete the planting of all ornamental trees and border plants. There is still time to set out container-grown subjects.

Prune hybrid tea and floribunda roses.

Bulbs of gladioli and montbretia can be planted in batches between now and May to provide a succession of colour.

Plant out well hardened-off sweet peas and border carnations, Brompton stocks and violas which have been over-wintered in frames.

Complete preparations for new lawns and sow grass seed, keeping off birds by using treated seed and other means.

April

Prepare for and plant out cabbages, cauliflowers and onions. In cold districts, make the first sowing of beetroot in warmer spots. On well-prepared seed beds outside in sunny sheltered spots, sow cauliflowers for autumn use, and cabbages and savoys for autumn and winter cutting. Plant maincrop potatoes on well worked ground. Continue to make succession sowings of carrots, cauliflowers and spinach beet. Cut winter greens, clear and prepare the land in readiness for leeks. Sow sweet corn and dwarf French beans under cover. Other sowings which should be made at this time include seakale beet, round and long varieties of beetroot, and savoys for the latest crops. Plant out cabbage seedlings raised in nursery beds. In mild districts, stop the earliest broad beans when they are in full flower to discourage blackfly.

Weed and hoe strawberry beds, spraying the plants against aphid and mildew if necessary before strawing. Deblossom spring-planted strawberries. Hoe raspberry beds, thinning out the canes of autumn-fruiting varieties, if necessary, to about 10cm (4in) apart.

Move or transplant evergreen trees, shrubs and bamboos.

Water the plants thoroughly and apply a mulch to retain moisture.

In exposed sites, protect newly planted evergreens for a few weeks with hessian on timber supports, placed on the windward side.

Sow delphiniums and lupins in frames or under cloches.

Prepare seedbeds and sow biennials for next year's spring bedding, for subjects like bellis, forget-me-not, Sweet William and wallflowers.

Prune spring-flowering shrubs such as forsythia.

Examine rose bushes for aphids and spray if necessary.

Harden off indoor-raised, half-hardy bedding plants in readiness for planting outside next month.

May

Plant out cauliflowers and maincrop Brussels sprouts. Sow carrots for storing, runner beans and sweet corn. The last two require warm, sheltered situations.

Marrows can be sown under frames or cloches now. Harden off tomatoes and marrows which can be planted out from the end of the month. Plant out celery into well-manured and prepared ground. In cold districts sow turnips for storing.

Place straw round the remaining strawberry plants to keep the fruit clean.

Spray fruit trees and bushes as soon as aphids or caterpillars appear.

Plant out early-flowering chrysanthemums and dahlia tubers. Harden off dahlia cuttings for planting out next month.

Remove old flower heads of azaleas, lilacs and rhododendrons.

Prune or lightly trim specimen evergreens into shape as necessary.

Check from now on for aphids on any crops, moulds, mildews, and black spot on roses. Spray plants thoroughly at the first sign of trouble.

Hoe weeds whenever possible.

June

In mild districts or sheltered spots, sow runner beans, sweet corn and marrows outside.

Plant marrows and tomatoes under frames and cloches in northern areas early in the month. Sow quick-maturing varieties of beetroot and carrots on land cleared of broad beans or peas. Plant cauliflower for late summer, cabbage for autumn and winter and Brussels sprouts for the latest crop. Sow swedes and turnips for winter storing. Plant leeks and maincrop savoys. Celery will require copious watering for best results.

Plant kale for winter and early spring use. Make the last sowing of stump-rooted carrots. Use the hoe to control weeds.

Give apples and pears a first thinning before the June drop (or natural shedding) of fruits.

Peg down runners from healthy strawberry plants into prepared soil or potting compost, keeping them watered in dry weather.

Spray any fruiting plants that have aphids, pests or diseases. Spray raspberries 10 days after flowering to check raspberry beetle.

Stop early flowering chrysanthemums by mid-month. Lift, divide and replant flag iris.

Transplant seedling biennials and perennials and take cuttings of pinks, helianthemums and santolinas.

Raise the cutting height of lawn mowers in hot dry weather to avoid cutting the grass too short.

July

Cut and dry herbs such as sage. Sow spinach beet and plant late savoys after clearing old strawberry beds. Feed tomatoes, cucumbers and marrows, stop and remove side shoots.

Sow spring cabbage and salad onions in cold districts. Sow turnips for storing, and spinach for autumn and winter. In the second half of the month sow onions to overwinter, and turnips to provide tops in spring.

Spray potatoes and tomatoes against blight. Summer-prune cordon or intensive forms of apples, pears, red currants and gooseberries. Protect fruits from birds with netting or scaring devices.

Prune summer-fruiting raspberries after cropping.

Prop up heavily laden branches of apples, plums and pears and give final thinning of fruits.

Plant strawberry runners when rooted.

Prune philadelphus, weigela and similar shrubs after flowering.

Layer border carnations, watering as required.

Trim beech, holly, hornbeam and yew hedges.

Take softwood cuttings of shrubs, rooting these under frames.

August

Sow spring cabbage and winter spinach in southern districts. Sow lettuce for overwintering to be transplanted in October.

Remove the suckers or growths from around trench celery plants, carefully earthing up this crop afterwards.

Sow lettuce for winter use, and Japanese F1 hybrid onions for harvesting next summer.

Lift and dry off onions, storing them in an airy dry place.

Continue to plant out rooted strawberry runners. Fruit stores will need cleaning and making ready for the new crop.

Tie in autumn-fruiting raspberry canes, so that high winds cannot cause undue damage.

Take cuttings of pelargoniums, and of various shrubs, such as forsythia, philadelphus and lavender.

Take cuttings of penstemons and shrubby calceolarias to over-winter in frames. Sow hardy annuals for early flowering next spring. This is not too early to prepare ground for making lawns this autumn, by draining, digging and weedkilling.

September

Pick green fruits from outdoor tomato plants before the arrival of frost.

Start autumn digging in earnest for all crops, manuring and attending to drainage as necessary.

Begin lifting carrots and beet for storing. Lift maincrop potatoes as the foliage dies down.

Cover lettuce with frames and cloches, and sow lettuce in frames for overwintering.

Prune stone fruits, but only as little as necessary, also currants.

Where gooseberries have been attacked by American gooseberry mildew, remove diseased branch tips, and carry out normal pruning early. Cut out infected wood and burn affected pruning.

Complete strawberry planting as soon as possible.

Order trees, shrubs and plants, including fruit, in good time for autumn planting.

Clear summer bedding plants, and take fuchsias, heliotropes and pelargoniums indoors.

Plant crocus, daffodils, Regal lilies and tulips, and spring bedding plants like wallflowers.

Renovate existing lawns by scarifying, spiking and top dressing. New lawns can be finally prepared and sown.

Lift tuberous begonias and dry the tops off before storing.

October

Earth up trench celery as necessary. Continue autumn digging and manuring, and double dig for peas, beans and onions. Plant out spring cabbage, and transplant or thin lettuce sown last month. Lift remaining beetroot, carrots and potatoes, putting these into a frostproof store or clamp.

Make a compost heap with healthy vegetable and plant remains.

Pick any remaining apples and pears when dry and put these into store. Start pruning apples, pears and black-currants. Take cuttings of all currants and gooseberries from healthy plants.

Buy Ministry-certified stock currants, raspberries and strawberries for planting now.

Plant evergreens and conifers.

Lift, split and replant herbaceous perennials or defer until March or April on heavy soils.

Plant deciduous trees, shrubs and roses from the end of the month in suitable soil and weather conditions.

Lift bulbs such as gladioli and montbretias, hanging them up to dry before storing in a frost- and vermin-free place.

Lift dahlias as soon as the foliage is blackened by frost.

Dig and box up or pot early-flowering chrysanthemums.

November

Prepare the land for, and sow broad beans and round headed peas either in the open or under cloches. Protect celery, potatoes in clamps and roots in store from severe frost by a covering of straw. During cold weather cover garden frames at night with hessian or other mats to give extra protection. Remove dead and yellowing leaves from winter greens.

Make sure that all water taps and pipes are covered with sacking or lagging to prevent them bursting after frost.

Inspect all fruits in store, removing any that are rotten or decaying. During any mild spell when fruit trees and bushes are reasonably dry, give a tar oil winter spray, and start with plums, bush and cane fruits. Prune apples and pears.

Cover the more tender rock plants with sheets of glass. Christmas roses can be much improved by covering the plants with a frame or cloche now. Protect the crowns of herbaceous plants such as delphiniums, lupins and pyrethrums from being eaten by slugs, by covering them with washed and weathered cinders. Put down slug pellets nearby to give added protection.

Clean out hedge bottoms, which are ideal hiding places for pests and diseases.

December

Continue to dig vacant ground when conditions permit, barrowing out manure and compost in hard weather. Lime the ground where necessary for brassicas or other crops. In cold districts where the ground is likely to be frozen for long spells, lift and store garden swedes.

Roots of celery, leeks and parsnips are more conveniently lifted before prolonged frost and snow.

Complete the planting of fruit and other trees and bushes by the end of the month where possible.

Protect red currants and gooseberries with netting against birds, and defer pruning until spring.

If any parts of the garden seem to be very wet, check any ditches or drains for obstructions.

Root-prune trees which are too vigorous and unproductive.

Finish off the tar oil winter-spraying of plums, which start into growth before apples and pears. The last two can be left for another three or four weeks.

Order seeds and sundries for the new season.

Examine all roots and fruits in store for rot or vermin, which should be dealt with promptly.

Hardy climbers on walls and pergolas should be pruned if not already attended to.

149

Glossary

Acid soils contain little lime

Alkaline soils are rich in lime

Annual plants are sown, grow, set seed and die within a year

Bedding plants are set out in flower beds to give colour and are lifted within a year

Biennial plants require two years from sowing to seeding and death

Blanching consists of excluding light from plant stems/leaves to make them pale and improve the flavour, as with leeks

Bulbs are flowering plants with swollen underground stems, for example, tulips

Chlorosis occurs when plant leaves turn yellow due to excess lime at the roots

Compost; garden compost is a type of manure; potting compost is a complete rooting medium

Conifers are cone-bearing trees, usually evergreen, for example pine

Cordons are tree forms restricted to a single main stem

Crocks are broken pieces of plant pot placed inside a pot for drainage

Crown is a term used to denote the branch network of trees, also a root clump

Cuttings are portions of plants detached without roots

Dead-heading consists of the removal of old flower heads

Deciduous trees lose their leaves in winter

Dibbers are generally pieces of wood used to make holes to insert small plants in soil

Dormant describes an inactive plant, for example, seed is dormant in winter

Earthing up consists of moulding soil or earth round plant stems

Evergreens are plants which retain their leaves all year round

F1 Hybrid describes the first generation arising from crossing two plants

Fertilizers are concentrated plant foods

Friable soils are crumbly and fine grained, not lumpy

Fungicides are any substances used to control fungus diseases

Germination is the first stage of a plant between seed and setting

Half-hardy plants are unable to survive winter without shelter

Half-standard trees have clear stems of 75 to 120cm (2ft 6in to 4ft)

Hardening-off consists of conditioning indoor plants to the outside climate

Heel cuttings have a piece of node at the point of severance

Hybrids are new species resulting from cross-breeding between parents

Inorganic materials contain no carbon, for example, superphosphate

Intercrop describes the growing of two crops together, for example, radish between lettuce

Internodes are the section of stems between leaf joints, or nodes

Larva is the name given to an immature form of insect, for example, caterpillar

Laterals are secondary shoots arising from a stem or branch

Lime consists of various forms of calcium compounds

Loam is a friable soil mixture with neither too much clay nor excess sand

Manure is usually a mixture of vegetable and animal waste

Marginal plants grow round the edges of ponds or water

Mulches are thin layers of materials such as peat, placed on the soil surface around plants to conserve moisture

Neutral soils have a pH of 7 and are neither acid nor alkaline

Node is the swelling on the plant stems at the junction with leaf stalks

Organic substances contain carbon

Peat consists of partly decomposed mosses and sedges built up over a prolonged period

Perennial plants are those which flower or live for more than two years

pH is a scale used to indicate acidity or alkalinity especially of soils. 7 is neutral, 6.5 and below acid, above 7 is alkaline (see page 17)

Pinching out consists of removing the growing points of plants

Plunge describes the process of sinking plant pots up to the rim in soil or peat, or buying bulbs in pots in peat or cinders.

Potting consists of placing plants in pots containing soil or loamless composts

Pricking off consists of giving seedlings their first move, usually into boxes

Propagation is the term used to denote the process of increasing plants

Pruning consists of removing shoots or roots to regulate plant development

Resting periods in plants are phases, during winter, for example, when active growth ceases

Rootstocks are the lower parts of grafted plants

Runners consist of small plants produced at the ends of shoots, as in strawberry

Scions are the upper part of grafted plants and are different from their root stocks

Seedlings are young plants which develop after seeds have germinated

Shrubs are plants consisting of many woody stems arising from ground level

Specimen plant describes an individual plant such as a shrub rose, grown for its beauty

Spit consists of a spade depth of soil, 25 to 30cm (10 to 12in)

Staking consists of supporting plants with bamboo canes or pieces of wood

Standard trees have a minimum length of clear stem of 1.5m (5ft) from soil to lowest branch

Tender plants require warmer conditions than an outdoor climate provides

Terminal shoots are the leading growths of plants

Tilth describes the physical condition of the top 5cm (2in) of soil

Top dressing consists of applying fertilizer or soil mixture to the soil surface around plants

Transplanting consists of lifting plants and replanting them elsewhere

Tubers are swollen pieces of stem used by plants for food storage, for example, potato or dahlia

Index

152

153

156

Acknowledgments

The publishers would like to thank the following organisations and individuals for their kind permission to reproduce the photographs in this book:

A-Z Botanical Collection Limited Front and Back endpapers, 6 below (55), 73, 79, 80 centre, 95 centre, 128 centre and below, 129 below, 146; Bernard Alfieri 21, 23, 41 above left, 84 above, 89, 96 right, 100, 108 right, 115, 123 below right, 139 below centre; Barnaby's Picture Library 13 below, 17 below right, 98 right, 120-121; Pat Brindley 26 below, 41 below, 81, 88, 96 centre, 97 left, 102, 103, 117, 128 above left, 129 above, 131 below right; Dr C. P. Burnham 15 above left, centre and right, below left and right; Camera Press Limited 145 below; Steve Campbell 31, 85; C. M. Dixon 144; Derek Fell (Horticultural Picture Library) 11; Ron and Christine Foord 138 above left; Brian Furner 84 above and below left, 95 left, 96 left, 97 centre, 98 left, 99 left and centre, 108 left, 118 below, 139 above centre and right; George Hyde 84 below right, 137 above right and below left, 138 below left, above centre and below centre, 139 above and below left, 140 left and above centre; Leslie John's & Associates 6 above (13 above), 8-9, 28 below, 72, 102 left; Bill McLaughlin 71 above, 130, 131 above; Ray Proctor 104; John Rigby 136 below; Donald Smith 118 right, 120; Harry Smith Horticultural Photographic Collection 10, 22, 27 above and below, 28 above, 29 above and below, 40, 41 above right, 66 below, 68 above and below, 71 below, 80 above, 84 centre, 94 left, centre and right, 95 right, 97 right, 98 centre, 99 right, 105, 114, 116 above and below, 118 above left, 119, 121, 123 above right, 124 above and below, 125 above and below, 126, 127 above and below, 131 below left, 134, 136 left, 137 above left, and below right, 140 right and below centre, 145 above; Spectrum Colour Library 12, 26 above, 66 above, 122-123, 138 right, 141 below, 147; Peter Stiles 16; John Topham Picture Library 109, 113, 122 above left, 141 above;

Illustrators
Rosemary Chanter: 72, 80, 81
Sheila Fisher: 60-62, 106-107
Will Giles: 52-53, 66, 69, 82-83, 135
Roger Gorringe (R. P. Gossop): contents spread top centre, 14 below, 16, 17, 20, 23, 24, 56-57, 63, 90, 91, 94, 104
Jim Marks: 10, 11, 12, 14 above, 25, 44, 45, 47, 54
Prue Theobalds (B. L. Kearley): contents spread centre, 74-75
Craig Warwick (Linden Artists): contents below right, 18-19, 30-39, 50-51, 58-59, 64-65, 76-77, 86-87, 92-93, 110-111
Ann Winterbotham: title spread, contents below left, 42-43, 46, 48-49, 70, 73, 78, 79, 132-133, 146-149

Gardener's Diary Notes

January

February

March

April

Gardener's Diary Notes

May

June

July

August

Gardener's Diary Notes

September

October

November

December